Praise for *Leading in Analytics*

"Advanced analytics helps turn data into intelligent insights for better decision-making. Reading the hype may convince you that you need it, but does not help you to realize it. To move from concepts to real-world implementations, start by studying *Leading in Analytics*. Then build your team and have them study *Leading in Analytics*."

—**Karl Kempf, PhD**, senior fellow and director of
Decision Engineering, Intel Corporation

"In an era when analytics is creating more value for companies than ever before, Cazier creates a blueprint for a successful analytics career. A must-read book for anybody working with analytics to drive company value."

—**Patrick Getzen**, retired chief data and analytics officer, BCBS of NC

"*Leading in Analytics* is a must-read for business executives who are ready to move toward successful analytic projects. This easy-to-follow guide is devoted to sharing practical information that will help you construct a road map to success for your analytic projects. These concepts are further illustrated through interesting real-life examples from a long list of executives with an impressive track record. Increase the likelihood of success for your next project by following these same methods as described in *Leading in Analytics*!"

—**Paige Valentine**, senior director, SAS

"This knowledge is exactly what I have needed for a long time in regards to running Liferithms. The information has already added priceless value to my approach to running my companies and showed me how to prioritize analytics. It is easy to get lost in the possibilities of what can be done with data; now I have a clearer picture of what should be done and a head start on how to get it done."

—**Olu Ogunlela**, founder and CEO, Liferithms

"As an executive with just enough knowledge of analytics to be dangerous, I wish I had this book 20 years ago. Seeing, and acting on, the big picture as outlined in *Leading in Analytics* would have taken us to levels of success we did not know were possible."

—**D. Terry Rawls**, former university president, entrepreneur

"I have been coding analytics for over a decade and have now reached a point in my life when I want to shift from an analytics coder to an analytics leader, and I found this book a very practical guide for this purpose."

—**Olim Atabayev**, data engineer, Allstate Insurance

"As a young analytics professional, this book was a very eye-opening experience for me. In the past, my understanding of analytics was focused on low-level concepts such as probability distribution, p-values, and Python. However, this book has provided me with a fresh and insightful perspective on analytics, focusing on people, leadership, and impact."

—**Ting Jennings**, data analyst at PwC

"Cazier takes the reader on a journey far beyond the theories of analytics. he breaks down every aspect of application of methods, techniques, behaviors, historical background, and even the subject of ethics through responsibility. Through his step-by-step approach he calls tasks, he sets the stage with Task 0, where he explains the sense of urgency in the professions who uses analytics, failure rates across industries, and the roots of failure, all while citing some of the most distinguished people in the field. This book is a useful guide for me personally, and will be for thousands of others for years to come."

—**Darren Long**, USAF (ret.) and advisory consultant at MSS BTA.

"Through this book, you not only learn the end-to-end analytics process but can also discover how to optimize your efforts to bring about value-driven changes."

—**Jabari Myles**, senior data scientist, MetLife

"In a perpetual asymmetric battlefield of analytics, Professor Cazier delivers *The Art of War* for the digital generals of the tomorrow."

—**Sai Pranav Kollaparthi**, MS-ISM student, Arizona State University

"I am absolutely thrilled to witness the long-awaited publication of *Leading in Analytics*, masterfully crafted by Professor Cazier. Taking the readers on a captivating journey through the intricacies of success, this remarkable guide serves as a treasure trove for those eager to harness the potential of data analytics and emerge as leaders in the field. With a wealth of practical knowledge and methodologies curated from the invaluable experiences of industry pioneers, this book illuminates the path to embrace a data-driven future and equips readers with the essential tools to excel in the ever-evolving realm of data analytics."

—**Keerthana Bandlamudi**, MS-ISM student, Arizona State University

Leading in Analytics

Wiley and SAS Business Series

The Wiley and SAS Business Series presents books that help senior level managers with their critical management decisions.

Titles in the Wiley and SAS Business Series include:

For more information on any of the above titles, please visit www.wiley.com.

Leading in Analytics

The Seven Critical Tasks for Executives to Master in the Age of Big Data

By Joseph A. Cazier, PhD, CAP

WILEY

Library of Congress Cataloging-in-Publication Data Is Available:

ISBN 9781119800415 (Cloth)
ISBN 9781119801009 (ePDF)
ISBN 9781119800996 (ePub)

Cover Design: Wiley
Cover Image: © Weiquan Lin/Moment/Getty Images
Author Photo: © Shelley Valdez

SKY10055392_091523

To my wife and children in the hope that better, and more responsible, analytics will help build a better world for us all.

Contents

Foreword

Another book on analytics. Do we need one? Well, there is no doubt that every organization in every industry today is on a journey to increase their knowledge, skills, and abilities to leverage data for higher value. Some are early on in their analytics journey, trying to achieve higher value by leveraging data with descriptive and diagnostic analytics to increase their hindsight of what has happened so that they can better make sense of current situations for decision-making. Others have been on the journey for a while now and are leveraging data with predictive and prescriptive analytics to forecast what may happen and how they can best position their products and services for the future—and maybe even create the future, to some extent.

Where are you, your team, and your organization on this journey? Are you early on in the journey, perhaps serving as the only person in the data analytics and business intelligence unit of your company—the person hired to manage Big Data and find yourself on a daily basis helping the leaders of your organization understand the difference between their elbows and eigenvalues and explaining the critical, often time-consuming, nature of data cleansing as you dredge the organization's data lakes and data puddles and data streams for helpful insights into customer behaviors and untapped market possibilities?

Or are you part of a slightly larger team debating the nuanced advancements of the latest software and tools that help manage data variety, velocity, veracity, and volume so that you can help the business achieve real value? Regardless of your current location on the journey, no doubt you are looking to get better and better and better. The companies you and I work for, and all other companies for that matter, share that common goal. We are each on a journey looking to help our organization mature its data analytics capability.

Whether you are a business analyst, data engineer, chief data officer, business intelligence manager, data analytics translator, statistician, Big Data dude, giga data gal, numbers nerd, or go by some other title, you are leading your organization in analytics and this book is for you. Dr. Joseph Cazier has given us all a gift with *Leading in Analytics*. This is not just another book about probability distributions, *p*-value calculations, or R versus Python. This is a leadership book that doubles as a compass to navigate our journey in data management, science, and analytics.

As you dive into the content, you will immediately recognize Cazier is an optimist. He is focused as much on helping data scientists better understand the art of leadership as he is on helping business leaders better understand the science of data analytics. His work here has a 10-to-1 ratio equivalent to business-leader-to-data-scientist, which is representative of the work carried out in any organization. He knows that for every one data scientist in an organization there are (at least) 10 business leaders all of whom need to increase their individual and collective capacity to convert data into value.

The urgency of this need is easily found in any rudimentary search on the success rates of data analytics projects. Your search findings, as well as your own experience, and mine, too, will spotlight a need for improvement. Indeed, most data analytics projects fail or struggle to yield intended value, with sources citing a failure rate reaching almost 90%. Want to be part of the minority—the 10%—success rate with your analytics projects? Read this book and apply the recommendations from Cazier.

Our data analytics work is hard, and it is getting harder, which makes this book as informative as it is timely. Our project failure rates are clear. We can do better. Cazier helps us recognize critical points of failure and how to mitigate them so that we are on the minority side (the winning side) of the success/failure equation. The concepts he outlines are clear, logical, and immediately actionable to navigate the challenges and issues that the teams in my organization and all others I have worked alongside have been wrestling to resolve. They are the same challenges and issues you are wrestling to resolve, too.

Cazier balances content that is well researched with his own firsthand experience as a data scientist. And, it is not just his research and experience. More than three dozen experts materially contributed their time, wisdom, and the best practices that have helped them succeed to the contents of this book. These experts come from all levels and types in organizations who are engaged with furthering analytics success. From seasoned c-suite executives to rising analytics professionals, you will hear perspectives and advice from the technical, analytics, business, and management sides of the organization along with accomplished consultants.

So, beyond Cazier's insights and experiences, you will learn from dozens of experts, each of whom helped to change my thinking and my approach to data analytics—in all the right ways; so much so, I built the Leading in Analytics academy on the foundation of their wisdom. I have seen firsthand the growth and positive reactions from leaders everywhere as they heard from many of these experts, in their own words, how best to lead in analytics. Now, it is all here, distilled in one place, so that you can reference it clearly and easily from anywhere, while diving deeper into the content with richer detail and tools to help you along the way.

I have known Joseph for years. We are colleagues, collaborators, business partners, and friends. He is passionate about leveraging data for good—helping people learn in the classroom and in the boardroom so that they, in turn, can help provide better products and services to their customers and for the benefit of the communities in which we live. As noted, this book is a gift. The task Cazier has carried out so diligently—researching and writing this book—has not been easy. As digital transformation continues to cascade across all aspects of our work (and lives), data becomes increasingly important; it is the new oil, and to mine it appropriately requires the science of great analytics and the art of great leadership. This is not an academic tome, but rather a compass to help us navigate the complexity of our journey.

Another book on analytics. Do we need one? Yes, this one!

Tim Rahschulte, PhD
Chief executive officer
Professional Development Academy

Acknowledgments

First, thanks to my wife and family for supporting me on this three-year-plus journey to research and write this book, with getting up before the sunrise and staying up well after sunset to research, write, and analyze the wisdom shared by our expert contributors. I could not have done it without you and your support, advice, and nurturing along the way. Mom, dad, sister, brothers, kids all also played an important role and I will always be grateful.

Second, thank you, Dr. Karl Kempf, for being the inspiration for this book and graciously sharing your knowledge and wisdom with me, making this journey possible. To learn more about Kempf's inspirational legacy, please visit the Afterword at the end of this book.

Third, thank you to my cousin, brother, and friend, Wayne Thorsen, for involving me in his internet start-up 25 years ago and inspiring me to dig deeper into the technology sector and all it has to offer. It has been an exciting journey. Thank you, Wayne, for that first push that got this journey started.

Fourth, thank you to the more than three dozen experts who willingly and thoughtfully gave their time and wisdom to share their best practices, and especially to Dr. Terry Rawls and Dr. Tim Rahschulte, who were both there every step of the way as we interviewed, digested, and documented their wisdom, which makes this book, and the companion Leading in Analytics course offered by Rahschulte at PDA, so rich and valuable.

Fifth, thank you to the many mentors I have had along the way. There are too many to list all of them, but Ms. Artaburn, Ms. Bendixon, Dr. Mel Cambell, Uncle Andy Cazier, Uncle Ben Cazier, Mr. Jim Chesterfield, Mr. Noel Commeree, Dr. Doug Dean, Dr. Bill Dean, Dr. Steve Eskelson, Mr. Fletcher, Dr. Paul Godfrey, Jeff Mason, Ms. Meek, Mr. Jim McLean, Mr. Morash, Mr. Ogden, Dr. Benjamin Shao, Dr. Scott Smith, Dr. Robert St. Louis, Aunt Susan Thorsen, Mr. Wishkoski, Dr. Martin Wistensen, Dr. Warner Woodruff, and many others all played leading roles in guiding my education in important ways.

Finally, thank you to the many reviewers and helpers in writing and reviewing this book, including Olim Atabayev, Keerthana Bandlamudi, Dr. Carrie Beam, Shaun Doheney, LeAnne Hill, Ting Jennings, Sai Kollaparthi, Preston MacDonald, Jabari Myles, Rocco Pagano, Dr. Tim Rahschulte, Dr. Terry Rawls, Richard Rogers, Sam Volstad, Dr. Wendy Winn, Paige Wright, and others. Included in this list are several former students who were willing to listen to their professor, and fix his mistakes, one last time.

To all of you here, and dozens of others not mentioned by name, you are here in the knowledge and help you shared along the way. THANK YOU ALL!!!

Introduction: The Last Analytics Mile

THE LAST MILE TO ANALYTICS SUCCESS

Analytics became widely known and accepted as a competitive imperative in 2006 when Thomas Davenport published his landmark article, "Competing on Analytics," which soon became one of the top-10 must-read articles in the history of *Harvard Business Review*.[1] Analytics had always been helpful, but as long as your competitors were not using it, you had a chance to survive without it, too.

Now that analytics has become affordable and practical to do at scale, *everyone* is doing it, and so must you if you wish to survive in the new age of Big Data, and the intense competitive pressure brought on by those who know how to "compete on analytics" well. Ahmer Inam, chief data and AI officer at Relanto, painted a stark picture of the competitive landscape when he said businesses in today's world must "do analytics or die."[2]

Most businesses know the importance of using analytics, prompting them to invest more than $100 billion by 2018,[3] which shows what was collectively spent by organizations to take advantage of the power of analytics. Unfortunately, close to $90 billion of those funds missed the mark by *failing* to generate the expected return on investment (ROI). That is right: nearly 90% of all analytics projects failed to generate "significant financial benefit," according to a report that MIT released in 2020.[4] No matter how good we analytics professionals are at building models, if they are not adopted and integrated into the organization in a way that creates value, they will be perceived to be failures.

In some ways this failure rate is to be expected, because all young disciplines fail in the beginning as they learn to walk. Analytics is, in fact, still a very young discipline, and one that is changing more rapidly than nearly any other, so it is understandable that the failure rate is so high. Understandable, yes, but it is still unacceptable, and is a tragic waste of resources that could be used much more effectively if analysts and business leaders were able to more effectively work together to manage and avoid the preventable, the manageable, causes of analytics failure.

Yes, some projects will always fail, just like some planes still crash and some bridges will still collapse. However, these rates are much less than they were in the beginning. The failure rates in other professions have been dramatically reduced as they have matured and developed a set of professional best practices that taught them and their sponsors how to work together to succeed. This can be true of analytics as well.

Indeed, this must be true for analytics. We must make it true. Analytics is not just about making more money, or even about firm survival in a competitive landscape, as important as those things are. It is also about doing things better, doing them more efficiently, sustainably, and intelligently. It is about, or can be about, with the right moral and ethical practices, building a better society that uses analytics to compete, but also uses it to make our world a better place to live and work.

We know that this concept can be true because a handful of companies such as Capital One, Amazon, and Intel have shown that it can be done well. Even so, in that same MIT report showing only an 11% average success rate of adding significant value, they also reported that some firms had achieved as much as a 73% success rate. That is nearly a *sevenfold* increase in success and something to which all of us can aspire. Even more, I believe the value created by these successes is far greater than the cost of all of the failures put together, as shown in Figure 0.1.

The firms that have succeeded in achieving these astonishing levels of success with analytics had a few things in common. The most important of which is that they achieved a high level of organizational learning for, with, and on behalf of AI and analytics. They learned from analytics how to change because of it, and they were willing, even eager, to change. Not just among the analytics professionals, but across the entire organization, along with their partners who were able to learn, adapt, and grow to apply and support analytics and did so at an industrial scale across the organization.[5]

What is the secret to this level of organizational learning about analytics? Certainly investment in people, tools, and technologies. Certainly commitment to do it. Certainly competitive pressure pushing for it. But none of these reasons are enough on their own. It also takes many more analytics supporters and enablers than analytics doers, maybe on the order of 10 to 1, for the organization to learn, grow, and succeed at this much higher level.

To be the type of organization that truly takes advantage of the potential of analytics, one that succeeds much more often than not, the organizational leadership as

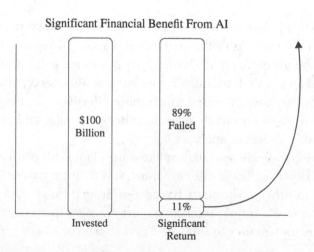

Figure 0.1 Many Failures, Some Astonishing Successes

a whole, not just the analytics professionals, need to know their role in adopting and supporting analytics. They need to develop the skills to work together with the analytics team, and vice versa, to understand the business value of analytics and the critical nontechnical role they have to play in analytics success. They need to become an adaptable learning organization that uses, and is continuously and skillfully driven by, analytics to compete, grow, and improve in their efforts.

Nontechnical employees need something more than data literacy, but less than coding, to succeed in analytics. They must become fluent in the best practices of analytics, at least the ones that interact with their role and function in and around the organization. Yes, analytics professionals need to also learn to better interact with the business, as has been identified many times in many places, but it will *never* be enough. Analytics professionals are not capable of doing it on their own. They must be guided and supported by at least an order-of-magnitude times as many skillful analytics supporters and enablers to succeed.

This organizational learning should not be confined to the analytics team, though that is part of it, too. Indeed, it cannot be confined to the analytics team if we want analytics to move from the lab into production. There are three core groups of people in the organization who must work together skillfully for analytics success. This is what Dr. Rudi Pleines, head of business transformation at ABB Robotics, calls the *minimal viable team* needed for analytics to succeed.

This minimal team includes (1) an executive champion to sponsor the project, (2) a business process owner who is able to integrate a tool and the related analytics into the processes of an organization to ensure they are used and the generated value is maximized, and (3) the technical analytics person or team to do the analysis. Notice the technical and analytics teams are necessary, but they cannot succeed on their own. Even working together, it still takes skillful collaboration aimed at overcoming common causes of failure to succeed.

Most of the causes of analytics failure are manageable, wrote Dr. Karl Kempf,[6] head of analytics at Intel, whose team is responsible for documented savings exceeding $55 billion from analytics. Manageable means preventable, if you are smart and skilled enough to manage the causes of failure correctly. The analyst has direct control over only one of the five manageable tasks Kempf identified as necessary for analytics success.

This means that the entire organization, including many more non-analytics professionals than analytics professionals, need to learn how to engage with and support analytics effectively for long-term analytics growth and success. This community effort is how analytics becomes a profession: by growing beyond a few innovative pioneers into a standard, repeatable, organization-wide process that can consistently add value.

This is the last mile of analytics: learning to work together to get more projects into production successfully. We, as analytics professionals, cannot walk that last mile alone. It takes all of us, working together, skillfully, to dramatically increase the success rate of analytics and provide value to the organizations we work for and with.

This book is about how you, whoever you are and whatever your function, can more effectively lead, guide, support, and integrate with analytics to build the kind of mature analytics organization that succeeds, not just on a few projects, but on most of them. It is a collection of best practices addressing each of the manageable tasks in analytics, the preventable causes of failure that destroy projects, and how you can use them to compete on analytics as Thomas Davenport advised in his 2006 *Harvard Business Review* article. It is about how you can help analytics cross that last mile to analytics success and maturity as a profession into a practice of success.

EXPERT CONTRIBUTORS

The knowledge and experience of more than three dozen highly successful experts is condensed and shared as best practices in this book, along with their many stories, illustrating what analytics can do and how to use it. I am grateful they agreed to share some of their time and wisdom in an effort to help build analytics as a practice and profession and increase the analytics success rate.

These experts were all handpicked for this book because they have something unique to offer through their wisdom, insights, and experience at all levels of the analytics process. Some are practicing data scientists, some analytics executives or educators, and still others come from the business side. Some are young and fresh in their careers and others have decades of experience. Some work in deep complex analytics, others more with business intelligence and/or visualizations. Some have backgrounds in technology firms, others in retail, logistics, engineering, or manufacturing. The depth and breadth of their collective knowledge comes together here with the one goal of helping you learn how to lead your analytics efforts successfully. These are the geniuses who made this book possible. See Table 0.1 for a list and description of these contributors.

Table 0.1 List of Expert Contributors

Experts	Background
	Hina Arora, PhD, is a clinical associate professor who teaches analytics at Arizona State University. Previously, Arora was a senior data scientist lead and analytics manager at Microsoft and a software engineer at IBM.
	Josh Belliveau is a principal solution engineer and data science product specialist for Tableau at Salesforce. In this role, Belliveau helps enterprises across a variety of industries find increased business value through their effective use of the analytics ecosystem. Belliveau previously worked for a variety of other technology companies, including Sight Machine, Lavastorm, and Appalachian State University as an analytics program manager.
	Anthony Berghammer is a research data scientist at RTI International. Berghammer previously worked as a senior decision data analyst at USAA and Data Scientist Ernst & Young.

Table 0.1 *(Continued)*

Experts	Background
	Antonio Rafael Braga, PhD, is an accomplished data scientist and professor at the Universidade Federal do Ceará in Brazil. Previously, Braga was a doctoral fellow in the Center for Analytics Research and Education at Appalachian State University.
	Joseph Byrum, PhD, is CTO at Consilience AI and is a leader known for delivering results through knowledge-based solutions. Byrum has demonstrated expertise across traditional domain boundaries to bring new capabilities to Fortune 500-level companies. Byrum is a frequent thought leadership contributor to a number of publications from *Forbes, Fortune, Fast Company,* and *TechCrunch,* to *Analytics Magazine* and *ISE Magazine.* Byrum received honors from the Aspen Business & Society Long Term Strategy Group and earned the INFORMS Edelman Prize, DAS Practice Award, ANA Genius Award, and Drexel Lebow Analytics Top 50 MSU CANRAA Outstanding Alumnus Award.
	Joseph Cazier, PhD and CAP, is a clinical professor and associate director of the Center for AI and Data Analytics at Arizona State University. Previously, Cazier served as the executive director of the Center for Analytics Research and Education and as associate dean at Appalachian State University. Cazier also served as chief analytics officer for HiveTracks and as a faculty fellow for the UNC System, leading projects in innovation and analytics.
	Joshua Cazier is the global head of solution and demo engineering at Qualtrics and is one of the founding team members and the fourth active tenured employee. As an analytics executive, Joshua Cazier leads teams and companies to make better decisions with data. Joshua Cazier is also the author's smarter, and better looking, little brother.
	Libor Cech is the former CEO of Chemoprojekt and current board member of Bochemie. Over a long career, Libor Cech has led many analytics and automation projects at companies such as Global Process Automation, Hi-Grade International Engineering, and GE Infrastructure.
	Thomas Cech is a senior data scientist at National Council for Community and Education Partnerships (NCCEP) and focuses on improving educational outcomes and graduation rates. Thomas is also Libor's son.
	Dan Cohen-Vogel, PhD, is the principal at DataWorks Partners. Previously, Cohen-Vogel served as vice president for data and analytics for the University of North Carolina System and assistant vice chancellor for the State University System of Florida.
	Bill Disch, PhD, is an analytics educator for DataRobot. Disch served as chief analytics officer for a variety of firms and teaches statistics at Central Connecticut State University.
	Shaun Doheney, PMP and CAP, is a research scientist in Operations Research and analytics manager at Amazon Web Services (AWS). Previously, Doheney was the chief analytics officer for an Inc. 5000 small business. Doheney leverages experiences from a career as a Marine Corps officer and operations researcher to actively give back to the larger analytics communities.
	Grant Fleming is a senior data scientist at Elder Research. Fleming is also the lead author of *Responsible Data Science* (Wiley, 2021), a guide for data science practitioners and managers on the ethical implications of developing and deploying AI models, and has delivered several talks on the subject.

(Continued)

Table 0.1 *(Continued)*

Experts	Background
	Bill Franks is the director of the Center for Data Science and Analytics within the School of Data Science and Analytics at Kennesaw State University. In this role, Franks helps companies and governmental agencies pair with faculty and student resources to further research in the area of analytics and data science. Franks is also chief analytics officer for the International Institute for Analytics (IIA) and serves on the advisory boards of ActiveGraf, Aspirent, DataPrime, DataSeers, Kavi Global, and Quaeris.
	Patrick Getzen recently retired as the founding chief data and analytics officer for Blue Cross Blue Shield of North Carolina, and served in a variety of roles, including chief actuary. Getzen currently serves on several advisory boards, helping companies with business and analytic strategies as well as organizational management.
	Sherrill Hayes, PhD, is the director of the School of Data Science and Analytics and professor of conflict management at Kennesaw State University. Hayes has more than 20 years of experience in program development and evaluation, working with families, organizations, court systems, and higher education.
	LeAnne Hill is a manager at the accounting and advisory firm FORVIS LLP in the enterprise risk and quantitative advisory practice area. Hill previously led efforts in fraud analytics at American Credit Acceptance and LPL Financial and as a senior associate at Grant Thorton LLP.
	David Houser is the chief revenue officer for ReverseLogix and was previously the EVP and head of the Global Account Program at Koerber AG. From earlier days at Oracle using current BI analytics tools to Houser's current position using BI everywhere tools, Houser has become an industry expert and daily user of advanced analytics to promote more efficient business solutions within the supply chain and now in reverse supply chains.
	Ahmer Inam is currently chief data and artificial intelligence officer at Relanto and has previously served as the head of analytics for Centific, Cambia Health Solutions, Nike, PwC, and Sonic Automotive. Inam's breadth and depth of analytics experience includes contributing to the XPRIZE, World Economic Forum, the Forbes Technology Council, and the International Institute for Analytics.
	Piyanka Jain is the founder and CEO of the data analytics firm Aryng, and the author of the best-selling data analytics book, *Behind Every Good Decision*. Jain is a well-known keynote speaker and analytics advisor to several firms and was previously head of analytics at PayPal and analytics manager at Adobe.
	Cecil John is an enterprise architect with 25+ years of experience. John works with the largest organizations in the world to migrate and build secure regulatory-compliant Azure cloud infrastructures and platforms.
	Karl Kempf, PhD, is the head of analytics at Intel where Kempf's team recently won the Franz Edelman Prize for Impactful Analytics with documented savings for Intel of over $55 billion under Kempf's leadership. Kempf studied math and artificial intelligence before it was cool and used these skills to help Christopher Reeve fly in the 1980s Superman movies, among other notable adventures noted in this book's Afterword. Kempf is also the originator of the five manageable tasks that inspired this book.
	Stephen Kimel is a senior data scientist at Red Hat and former data scientist for NetApp.

Table 0.1 *(Continued)*

Experts	Background
	Alexandra Koszegi is a technical sales engineer at D-Wave Systems Inc. and helps organizations harness the power of quantum computing solutions.
	Diego Lopez-Yse leads digital projects for Moody's in Latin America. Lopez-Yse held similar roles at Bayer, PwC, and SAP and is a recognized speaker, writer, and thought leader for data science in Latin America.
	Preston MacDonald is a marketing data scientist at Red Hat and was formerly a senior data analyst for the Wounded Warrior Project.
	Lindsay Marshall is a data scientist and director of data and analytics at Gilbane Building Company. Marshall held similar data science roles at Cisco, SAS, MetLife, and ECRS.
	Polly Mitchell-Guthrie is the VP of industry outreach and thought leadership at Kinaxis, a supply chain management and analytics software company. Previously, Mitchell-Guthrie was director of analytical consulting services at the University of North Carolina Health Care System and also worked in various roles at SAS. Mitchell-Guthrie has an MBA from the Kenan-Flagler Business School of the University of North Carolina at Chapel Hill and also received a BA in political science. Mitchell-Guthrie is a member of the Foresight Advisory Board for the International Institute of Forecasters, has been very active in INFORMS (the leading professional society for operations research and analytics), and cofounded the third chapter of Women in Machine Learning and Data Science (there are now more than 100 chapters worldwide).
	Jabari Myles is a senior data scientist at MetLife. Previously, Myles held similar roles at Red Hat and SAS. A few years ago, Myles started giving back by teaching analytics concepts to young college students. After finding tremendous enjoyment from teaching, Myles is shifting careers to earn a PhD to teach, research, and mentor full time.
	Olu Ogunlela is the cofounder and CEO of Liferithms, a tech start-up using lifestyle data analytics to help people reach their productivity, wellness, relationship, and life goals. Liferithms is advancing humanity's state of wholeness by improving an individual's chances of achieving one goal without compromising their ability to attain all others. The company is accomplishing this objective by aggregating activity and biometric data from users' wearable and connected devices alongside its weekly activity wholeness index, known as Life Score, while users also work with a team of dedicated coaches.
	Albert Owusu is a graduate of the Federal Chief Information Officers' Competencies Program. Owusu has more than 20 years of experience in engineering and information technology with more than 12 years of experience in developing solutions for enterprise management systems and enterprise database management, including extensive experience in IT high availability architecture solutions using Oracle RAC, Data Guard, Streams, and GoldenGate. Owusu has excellent analytical, research, communications, and leadership skills and is customer-focused and highly motivated.
	Chris Pitts is lead information security engineer with experience leading security teams for TIAA and Duke Energy. Pitts is a certified information systems security professional and certified blockchain expert.

(Continued)

Table 0.1 *(Continued)*

Experts	Background
	Ruediger (Rudi) Pleines, PhD, is head of business transformation at ABB Robotics, a leading global technology company with more than 100,000 employees that operates in more than 100 countries. Previously, Pleines worked for more than 15 years at the global management consulting company Kearney, where he helped clients make data-informed decisions to improve their businesses.
	Tim Rahschulte, PhD, is cofounder and CEO of the Professional Development Academy, former chief learning officer for Evanta, a Gartner Company, and former analytics leader for the state of Oregon.
	D. Terry Rawls, EdD, is a retired university president, administrator, and entrepreneur who practiced data-driven cultural change everywhere he served. Today, Rawls focuses on bringing new ideas to institutions and organizations worldwide.
	Skylar Ritchie is a data scientist with experience at Boeing, Prestige Financial, and Natural Partners.
	Max Rünzel is cofounder and CEO of HiveTracks, Inc., which is on a mission to build a platform for community-based and verified sourcing of environmental data. Using analytics, HiveTracks Inc. unlocks the value of a vast, untapped reservoir of environmental data by building a digital, scalable solution that incentivizes local biodiversity monitoring for beekeepers and their bees to improve planetary health.
	Steve Stone has led the transformation of Lowes into a data-driven firm with rapidly accelerating growth as their CIO. Stone then moved to similar roles with Microstrategy and L Brands as a c-suite executive focused on delivering bottom-line results.
	Wayne Thompson, PhD, is the retired chief data science officer for SAS who pioneered many analytics products and projects there. After a short retirement, Thompson jumped back into the action as executive director at JP Morgan Chase, building and managing a team focused on data verification services.
	Johann Vaz has decades of experience as a CIO/CTO for a variety of multimillion-dollar organizations in the technology, pharmaceutical, and finance industries. Vaz also shares wisdom and experience in the university classroom helping a new generation learn how to effectively use technology.
	Sam Volstad is a data analytics service manager at the national accounting and advisory firm GHJ, with prior analytics experience at Grant Thorton.
	Beverly Wright, PhD and CAP, is head of data science at Burtch Works. Wright brings more than 30 years of experience leading and delivering data science and analytics solutions through corporate, consulting, nonprofit, and academic experiences.

Figure 0.2 Sample Logos From Experts' Organizations

Figure 0.2 provides a graphic representing a few of the organizations these experts have worked for. We thank them for allowing their wisdom to be shared.

NOTES

1. https://www.tomdavenport.com/published-articles/
2. Private interview for this book.
3. M. Colas, I. Finck, J. Buvat, R. Nambiar, and R. R. Singh, "Cracking the Data Conundrum: How Successful Companies Make Big Data Operational," Hg. v. Capgemini Consulting (2014). https://www.tandfonline.com/doi/full/10.1080/10580530.2021.1894515
4. Sam Ransbotham, Shervin Khodabandeh, David Kiron, François Candelon, Michael Chu, and Burt LaFountain, "Expanding AI's Impact with Organizational Learning," *MIT Sloan Management Review* (October 2020): 1.
5. See Task 6: Analytics Maturity for more information about industrial scale analytics.
6. INFORMS, *Analytics Body of Knowledge* (ABOK) (Wiley, 2018), Chapter 2.

TASK **0**

Analytics Leadership

KNOWLEDGE BEGINS IN FAILURE

The first time we try to do something new, we often fail. Through those failures, we learn what not to do, and through that pain of failure, we feel the desire to do better. Eventually we, or others we know, do something right and succeed. With enough successes, general principles emerge and best practices are developed. When that knowledge is practiced and shared, it grows into a profession with a set of best practices, enabling us to learn to succeed much more often than we fail.

Analytics is a young profession with a very high failure rate. Statistics often cite a rate in the range of 80% to 90% for failure to deliver meaningful value or achieve an expected ROI. Note, this is not necessarily a failure to generate a great insight or to build a model that could be incredibly useful. True, it is sometimes that. However, if that incredibly useful model is not successfully deployed and used to create value for the organization that funded it, it will be regarded as a failure. Indeed, it *is* a failure, despite all the efforts and insights generated, if it has failed its core mission, the reason for investment: to create value.

It does not need to be this way. As with any profession, the more we learn from our failures and share the wisdom of our successes, the faster the analytics profession grows and matures as it puts the lessons learned into a body of knowledge that can guide us to many more successes than failures.

From building bridges to flying airplanes, most of the professions we know went through a similar arc of high failure when they were new to the development of a set of general principles and best practices that guide a mature profession to a high success rate. Analytics, as a profession, is also on that path. By learning from the pains of failure and applying lessons of success, we too can succeed in analytics.

But we cannot do it alone. Just as every other profession, from engineering to aviation, works with others to guide, scope, and support their projects to realize value, analytics must grow this way as well. Most of the critical causes of failure, and the best practices needed for success, are outside the direct control of the analytics professionals. It takes all of us—analytics professionals and supporters—learning what it takes for analytics to succeed and skillfully working together for that success at scale.

In particular, it takes a minimum of three different groups intently and skillfully working together to achieve analytics success in a business context. This is what Dr. Rudi Pleines, head of business transformation at ABB Robotics, calls the *minimal viable team*, which we introduced in the Preface. Sure, sometimes more engagement is needed and is generally helpful from others, but without the full support and knowledge to manage and implement analytics of at least this group, projects will not generate the expected value for a business.

The groups, as identified by Dr. Pleines, include these roles:

- **Executive champion.** Executives have the power to execute on projects or kill them. That makes their role crucial in driving change. Executives must use their power and position to drive adoption of the tools in a lead-by-example manner by demonstrating they use these tools and insisting others also make decisions with them. Their primary role is to push the organization over initial barriers and resistance toward new approaches by providing resources, removing roadblocks, communicating the importance of adoption, and then demanding adoption. This strong leadership is necessary to overcome the initial resistance phase that causes many projects to fail.

- **Business process owner.** Business process owners control how the business operates, carrying out the critical day-to-day tasks the business needs to run effectively, and usually supervising many staff members who need to become analytics adopters. Their main role is to help integrate tools and analytics into the processes of an organization so they become part of the daily business and are not introduced as stand-alone tools with the hope people will use it. They guide the technical team to meaningful data cleaning, sense check and interpret results, developing useful training materials using their unique vocabulary. By doing so, they give analytics a clear purpose and help the entire organization to change and improve. Without their skillful support, most projects will fail.

- **Technical team.** This is the analytics and IT teams, often working together, who discover, build, and support the actual project. They work with executives to identify high-value project areas and then hand-in-hand with the business process owners to ensure that tools work error-free, are easy to use, and of the right scope to support the processes in the most effective ways. Hard-to-use projects and those with technical errors are like poison to adoption efforts. This makes it critical to work closely with these groups to design an efficient error-free solution, provide technical support, and provide realistic views on project feasibility, impact, needs, costs, and risks.

Members from each of these groups, and sometimes from others, need to learn to work together toward a common purpose and avoid the most common causes of failure to increase the odds of analytics success. If you are missing participation from *any* one of these three groups, here is what happens:

- **Missing technical team.** Project will be desired but remain only a dream without the technical and analytics team to build it.

- **Missing business process owner.** Risk developing a costly and technically advanced visually appealing stand-alone system that does not integrate into existing processes and will never get adopted in a way that adds real value.

- **Missing executive champion.** Risk of failing because of limited funding or stalled implementation due to insufficient implementation authority.

This book contains a collection of best practices, based on failures, including my own, as well as successes from some of the smartest people I know. It contains a set of best practices focused on preventing the seven most common manageable causes of failure, those that can be avoided or prevented with skillful leadership inside and outside the analytics team who are focused on the task of best managing the primary causes of failure. No, it does not contain all of the best practices—no book can, and many are yet to be developed. But I am convinced what this book does contain is valuable and useful and will help our profession grow.

This book will show the executive champions how they can succeed in analytics through leadership by bringing the Pleines's minimal viable team together skillfully and managing failure. It will illustrate the role of business process owners in collaborating with and supporting technical analytics teams and guiding them to what will work. It will show the technical analytics teams how to more effectively work with these groups so more of their projects make it out of the analytics lab and into successful production.

There is no math in this book, no coding or deep technical discussions, just practical advice, stories, and best practices from those who know how to succeed to show how we can all work together toward success. Success means that the potential value from the insights and models built in the analytics process is realized in the firm. It means that what is built is put into practice and that it has the desired measurable impact. It means that value is created and the business earns the ROI they expected. It means that action was taken, goals were met, and the world is better because of your analytics efforts, not just that insights are generated.

This is a book designed to help executives understand the key causes of analytics failure, the best practices they need to employ to overcome those key causes of failure, and how to build an analytics culture that learns and grows at scale in and fueled by analytics. It is a book that can help everyone in the organization, including business process owners and analytics professionals, work together more effectively to become an adaptable learning organization eager to engage with analytics and experienced in achieving success from it.

Above all, this is a book about leadership—analytics leadership—and how to effectively lead analytics initiatives in a way that creates and realizes value for the organizations investing in those initiatives. It is a book that includes the collective wisdom of dozens of highly successful professionals who lead and work with analytics. Some are senior, some junior, some technical, some on the business side, all of whom learned how to more effectively lead and work with analytics, who learned how to succeed and compete with analytics.

But first is the story of how this book began, born in failure but with an aspiration to learn and share what it takes to succeed in analytics.

My Analytics Failure

This book is a result of failure. *My failure*. Trying to learn from and make sense of that failure created a passion in me to help others succeed. You see, after many years with a long stream of successes, my team and I started a project that was to be our crowning achievement. This project was a notable public good with great potential to help society and had international partners supporting it. It was written about in newspapers globally and a colleague and I even gave a keynote presentation introducing the project, and the good it would do, at a prestigious United Nations event. We were incredibly excited about this project and how it could have worldwide impact!

Then it all came crashing down. Not for any technical reasons: the math, data, impact, and project were solid. It was a brilliant idea with tremendous support here and abroad. However, it failed due to other factors, factors that at the time I did not fully understand or manage well. It was a failure of *organizational culture*, which means there was a lack of desire to support analytics, a deficit on the needed knowledge to support analytics sufficiently by non-analytics professionals, and resistance to change that doomed my project. It was also my failure to effectively build that culture of analytics success, to form the proper partnerships across the organization. (Curious? See the write-up of its failure in Task 2: Teams or its origin story in Task 7: Responsible Analytics for more details.)

I had a very hard time reconciling with the failure of this high-profile project. For a time, this failure led me to question everything I thought I knew about analytics, who I was, and what I wanted to do with the rest of my career. It hurts to have a prominent project fail, especially one that was the culmination of years of work and the fruit of many successes. I did not want that to happen again to me or to anyone else.

Therefore, I stepped down from directing the analytics research center I founded and refocused my efforts on researching analytics successes and failures. I dove into the literature and conducted detailed, structured interviews with many experts, many of whom you will hear from in this book. This book is a summary and introduction to some of the most important principles I learned on my journey and a guide that I hope can lead you to fewer failures and more successes.

Analytics High Failure Rate

The reality is that *most projects fail*. That is right, more than four out of five analytics projects fail to lead to sufficiently beneficial actions to be considered a success. Consider these statistics:

- 85% of Big Data projects fail.[1]
- 87% of data science projects never make it to production.[2]
- Only 11% of executives describe analytics as a "significant financial benefit."[3]

Notably, these numbers represent projects in which a trained data scientist and an executive had reason to *believe* there was enough relevant data and benefit that the project was worth the effort! In many cases, they would have developed a potentially valuable model that would have benefited the business, but it was never deployed or adopted.

Yes, *all* professions develop from a mix of failures and successes, learning what to avoid and building on shared principles. However, there are a few features that make it even more challenging to succeed in analytics than in many other professions as seen in this list.

- **Youth.** Analytics, as a profession, is relatively young. Though seeds of analytics have been around for a while, we are still developing and sharing the best practices needed to succeed.

- **Change.** There are few professions changing as quickly as analytics and the technology that supports it. These changes provide new opportunities for where, when, and how to use analytics, but they also make it even harder to keep up and manage projects effectively.

- **Complexity.** The field of analytics and its supporting math and technology are very complex, making it hard for people to follow, understand, and know where to jump in and help.

- **Invisible.** Analytics is not visible or tangible like a bridge or building. Most of analytics is invisible, which is even more true today as much of it is in the "cloud." This key difference makes it harder for people to understand analytics, slowing adoption and increasing failure.

- **Fear.** My friend Richard Rogers pointed out another reason to me while reviewing this book, one I had missed as an analytics professional who loves data and analytics, and one that I expect many of my colleagues would miss, too: fear. For an important segment of the population, new technologies, especially ones they do not understand, generate intense fear that stands in the way of engaging effectively and sometimes leads to direct sabotage. (Curious? See the discussion of Luddites in Task 6: Analytics Maturity.)

- **Discovery.** Unlike sister professions such as software development, analytics is more about discovery than production. Although the two have a lot in common, the fact that analytics rests on discovering something useful rather than producing something designed to be useful makes the outcome much less certain.

Taken together, these characteristics make the integration of analytics, between those who do it and those who enable and support it, much more complex and challenging. Analytics professionals *must* work with and be supported by others in the organization and the broader ecosystem to have an impact. But it is harder for non-analytics professionals and the analysts to know how to do that effectively with the attributes of the analytics profession described here.

These added challenges make analytics seem more like magic than science, and as Polly Mitchell-Guthrie, VP of industry outreach and thought leadership at Kinaxis, said in her interview, "If you think it is magic, you are not ready." An understanding of what analytics can do and how to support it, by those doing and enabling analytics, is critical.

FROM FAILURE TO SUCCESS

Through my research, I discovered the work of others and tried to build on and expand their insights. Some identified the roots of failure and others identified best practices and paths that, more often than not, led to success.

Roots of Failure

Dr. Karl Kempf, head of analytics for Intel, and one of my all-time analytics heroes, wrote about the causes of failure in the Institute for Operations Research and Management Science (INFORMS), *Analytics Body of Knowledge* (*ABOK*). INFORMS is one of the oldest and most well-developed professional associations focused on helping all of us make better decisions with data. The *ABOK* is a collection of knowledge-based best practices for analytics professionals, which is exactly what a young profession needs to mature, and is a great complement to this book for those wanting to take a deeper and more technical dive into analytics from the perspective of the analyst.

In the *ABOK*[4] Kempf identified the five most common roots of analytics project failure.

- **The problem.** A failure in the selection, definition, and focus of the business problem
- **The team.** A failure in the building and managing of the team, broadly defined
- **The data.** A failure in data quality, relevance, quantity, or availability
- **The tools.** A failure in the design, use, application, adoption, or development of analytics tools
- **Execution.** A failure to execute effectively in a way that creates value

This list does not cover every cause, but they are the biggest five reasons for project failure, and a failure in even one of these five virtually guarantees the entire project will fail. When I asked where these roots of failure came from, Kempf cited personal failures that were all from painful lessons. Kempf's statement about learning from personal failures really affected me. Of course, we do learn from failure, as Kempf did, and as I was attempting to do. However, what surprised me was that this was my analytics hero, talking about personal failures.

You see, these failures initially surprised me because Kempf was known for a good share of amazing successes; Kempf and his analytics team were one of only two teams in the history of analytics to win all three of the top, most coveted prizes in the whole analytics profession, including the INFORMS Prize, the Daniel H. Wagner Prize, and the Franz Edelman Award[5] in Analytics.

Kempf is also no less famous, from my perspective, for helping build computerized models to help my favorite superhero actor, Christopher Reeve, fly in the 1980s Superman movies, working with Formula 1 racing, and automating aerospace manufacturing, among many other achievements. (Curious? Check out the Afterword at the end of this book for more details, including pictures.)

Kempf also pointed to studies, such as the one by the consulting firm Capgemini, referenced in the *ABOK*, that verify these lessons. The experts I interviewed for this book universally agreed that these lessons were the major causes of failure they had seen and experienced, further supporting this list.

Yet, most importantly, Kempf discovered that these roots of analytics failure could be managed, as Kempf learned to do, leading up to those incredible successes. Sure, there are some impossible ideas that cannot (at least not yet) be done, but these can be managed, even if it is to identify them beforehand and to focus on those that can be managed. Hence, the name Kempf gave them—the *five manageable tasks*—meaning leaders have the potential to manage each of the tasks effectively to succeed in analytics.

Most Project Failures Are Outside Analytics Team's Control

Four of the five tasks are outside of the analytics team's direct control. The team can largely control how they use the tools of analytics to practice their craft. But the key to managing most of the critical tasks is left to others, mostly from the executive champion and business process owner ranks, to ensure a successful outcome.

The analytics team has a role, to be sure, in the other manageable tasks, but all they can really do is advise and influence, not directly manage. Even there, managing the business is not their specialty, and sometimes they lack the deep business knowledge and credibility to be able to manage those other tasks effectively, even if they try. The implication is that analytics teams left to go it alone will fail. Yes, let me emphasize: *loners almost always fail*.

10-to-1 Ratio for Success

The Global Consulting firm McKinsey was on to something in their influential 2016 analytics report[6] when they identified an approximate 250,000 shortage of deep data scientists needed for the current data revolution. But it was not the shortage of data scientists that should have gotten all the attention. The bigger insight was that they identified an even bigger shortage of business leaders who might not code but do understand how to incorporate and guide analytics into their business in a way that adds value. That shortage is more than 10 times greater than the shortage of data scientists—between 2 and 4 million leaders.

I believe it takes a ratio on the order of 10 smart, savvy business leaders and supporters to every 1 analytics professional to secure long-term success. I am not saying this is exactly what McKinsey had in mind, or that it is exactly 10 to 1. Yet I do believe, and my research supports, that it takes many more analytics enablers and supporters than it does analytics professionals to succeed over the long term, and that this difference is at least an order of magnitude more supporters than doers.

Nearly every analytics executive I interviewed, including Ahmer Inam, Polly Mitchell-Guthrie, Piynanka Jain, Lindsay Marshall, Dr. Dan Cohen-Vogel, Dr. Sherrill Hayes, Dr. Rudi Pleines, Patrick Getzen, and Dr. Karl Kempf, strongly emphasized the sentiment that "loners fail." Analytics professionals cannot do it alone; it takes strategic partnerships and alliances to succeed.

It is not just that analysts who do not work with other analytics team members fail, though this is often also true. It is that even when analytics teams work together flawlessly, they will still fail if they do not engage well with business process owners, executive champions, and others inside and outside the organization who are relevant to success. For many analytics professionals, this engagement does not come naturally. Nevertheless, it must be learned if they are to help lead successful analytics projects.

Organizational Learning

A 2020 study conducted jointly by MIT and the Boston Consulting Group (BCG)[7] gives further evidence of the need for a broad ecosystem for analytics to succeed over time in organizations. The researchers also found that only 11% of companies achieve significant financial benefit from AI and analytics initiatives. Notably, this study did not just look at the failure rate. It looked at what those who consistently succeeded did differently.

The key difference between those who mostly succeeded and those who mostly failed is organizational learning. As the report highlights, it is not just machine learning that creates value, but also the organizational learning companies put in place that takes advantage of it. Indeed, the number one finding of the report was that "Only when organizations add the ability to learn with AI do significant benefits become likely."

Organizations must be willing to learn and adapt based on what they learn from their AI and analytics efforts. It is only when they are willing to learn and change that action can take root and deliver sustainable value, and potentially a sustainable competitive advantage. This result is only possible with clear, focused, and skillful analytics leadership.

The payoff for doing it right is incredible. Researchers found those firms that successfully built an ecosystem focused on organizational learning, one that knew how to support analytics, were eager to do so, and that those who were willing to change and adapt based on what they learned had a 73% success rate. That is a sevenfold increase in success and value, and a signal to all of us that we can succeed if we focus on building the right analytics culture and the skills needed to support it.

Action-Centric Analytics Drives Organizational Learning

As we just saw in the last section, organizations that achieve organizational learning jointly with analytics have the highest success rate in analytics and realize the most value and competitive advantage. To date, most of this organizational learning has come from leadership, with executives and others learning to lead their organization in supporting and adapting to analytics in a skillful way, something we also share in this book.

Yet, most of the analytics we see in traditional firms today are decision centric. Decision-centric analytics focuses on a particular decision to be made with the goal of making a better decision. This is the most well-known and practiced approach to analytics, especially by non-digital-native organizations. It is also the best place for most organizations to start their analytics journey. We have seen many successes and astonishing value created from this approach, but it is not the only approach to analytics and no organization should stop there.

Many digital-native companies have shown that incredible value can be created from another approach called *data-centric analytics*. Rather than starting with the decision, this approach starts with the data and then looks at what value can be added to the organization based on that information. This approach can lead to many novel insights and pathways to harness the value of data. In fact, *Forbes* recently reported that some firms' data is actually worth more than the entire company,[8] in part because of the value that can be harnessed through data-centric analytics.

Data-centric analytics can guide and provide insights and value that are generally missed by the traditional decision-centric approach. It is part of what makes this approach so valuable because it enables organizations to surprise their competition and can lead to a competitive advantage or new ways of doing things that most would not have considered on their own.

Decision-centric analytics is guided by people to address the needs they have. This approach is important and, of course, should always be done. But to have a true learning organization, you need the back-and-forth with people and analytics machines learning from each other, as found by the MIT and BCG study just referenced. Data-centric analytics can magnify the learning between people and analytics, carrying the learning both ways and magnifying the impact and integration of analytics for a deeper and richer learning organization that, in turn, will have much greater success.

Importantly, the next step is using action-centric analytics to accelerate and scale organizational learning from both decision-centric and data-centric analytics, leading to faster, fuller adoption and better monitoring of the impact. Action-centric analytics focuses on facilitating the action that needs to be taken by using analytics as a tool to drive that action.

Leadership will always be critical to organizational learning and analytics success, but leaders who use analytics to drive that learning, along with all of their other leadership skills, can accomplish more, more quickly, and more thoroughly than the other two techniques alone.

All three of these approaches—decision-centric, data-centric, and action-centric analytics—should work together synergistically to direct, explore, and guide organizational learning to achieve success. The firms that use analytics to make decisions find new opportunities and use analytics to monitor, drive, and guide action to ensure and accelerate change and at a greater scale than those firms that use only one or two approaches alone.

Together, these approaches make up the DAD (decision-centric, action-centric, and data-centric) analytics framework, which drives analytics maturity and is introduced and expanded on at the start of Task 1: The Problem.

Beyond the Project

The five manageable tasks framework Dr. Karl Kempf wrote about caught my attention and became the framework and basis for this book. Even so, through the course of my research, I came to understand that although these tasks were critical to project level success, there were more tasks that needed to be managed beyond the project in order to ensure durable and repeatable success. These tasks include building a mature analytics culture and practicing responsible analytics by building ethical processes into your culture at the organizational level.

Analytics Maturity

The sixth task for executives to master is to build a culture of analytics maturity, one that embraces analytics, incorporates the skills to support it effectively, practices organizational learning, and uses all the tools of the DAD framework to do so. Organizations need a mature analytics culture with the technology and skills to support it effectively. They need to build analytics maturity into their organization so they can fulfill the role of the ecosystem, and leverage its scale, to optimize the value from analytics.

Responsible Analytics

The seventh task, perhaps even the most important for all of us, is to embrace responsible analytics, including practicing ethical analytics and using analytics to do good. Analytics is a powerful tool that can do great good, but it can also do, has done, and is doing great harm. We see examples of analytics for both good and bad nearly every day: from concerns about bias and ethical issues in data to questionable persuasive practices, abuse of privacy, and other harms done to society and the world we live in.

Although there may be some short-term gain for firms engaging in unethical practices, they hurt us all and also threaten the advancement and acceptance of the analytics profession. If we do not first make sure we do no harm, there will be a price to pay, and, I predict, quite a terrible one.

However, we also see stories of analytics being used for incredible good. Max Rünzel, CEO of HiveTracks, and Olu Ogunlela, CEO of Liferithms, both interviewed for this book, are trying to do incredibly beneficial things for society with the analytics their firms are using. Libor Cech, former CEO of Chemoprojekt and current board member of Bochemie, who was also interviewed, has spent decades pioneering ways to use analytics to improve sustainability in lumber production.

Libor Cech's son, Thomas Cech, has dedicated his career to using analytics to improve quality education. Dr. Beverly Wright, head of data science for Burtch Works, is leading analytics for good groups helping nonprofits across Georgia. Dr. Julie Swann, INFORMS president-elect and endowed professor at North Carolina State University, has led many analytics for good initiatives to improve global health outcomes. Jabari Myles, now a senior data scientist at Metlife, spent earlier career time using analytics to reduce traffic accidents using an innovative data-centric approach, helping us travel more safely.

There is so much potential with analytics to help improve and better society and so many perils that can damage it that, for me, and for all of us, the seventh task must focus on practicing responsible analytics, including having the wisdom to avoid perils from security and privacy breaches to avoiding societal backlash or harm from self-serving analytics.

THE SEVEN TASKS FOR ANALYTICS SUCCESS

Now you know the names of the seven tasks, and you also know that it takes an eco-system, guided by skillful executives and business process owners with the support and engagement of other professionals across the organization, for analytics to succeed over the short and the long term. It takes leadership from each member of Pleines's minimal viable team to effect organizational change and turn analytics into a successful and sustainable competitive advantage.

Analytics Leadership

Executive champions need to bring the analytics team and business process owners together effectively to understand what can be done and what will be adopted. They need to lead and guide the analytics and changes in a way that benefits the organizations they lead. They need to understand analytics well enough to know what it can do, what it cannot do, and how to avoid the manageable causes of failure. Most important, they need to stay laser-focused on ensuring that action is taken to realize value or the project will still fail.

Business process owners need to be willing to change to adopt a better way. They need to communicate their needs clearly in a way that analysts will model. They need to understand analytics well enough to overcome fear and engage where appropriate. They need to help identify areas to improve to find value. Most of all, they need to be willing to learn, grow, and change to be committed to continual improvement and success. They need to actively look for and lead the change they desire to succeed.

Members of the technical and analytics teams need to listen. They need to understand the current processes and objectives of the firm. They need to build domain knowledge and see how to build on current processes. They need to learn how to communicate effectively in business terms on important business impacts, not just present statistical findings. They need to prioritize and engage to be of service while leading with vision. For this reason, Task 0 is titled Analytics Leadership, that is, leadership by executive champions, leadership by business process owners, leadership by the technical and analytics teams, and support from everyone else.

This book contains the collective wisdom of those who know how to succeed and have succeeded. In addition to this book, you can also take the accompanying course from the Professional Development Academy, an organization created in collaboration with the late General Colin Powell to teach leadership. In their remote hybrid course led by a competent coach, participants in their Leading in Analytics course will hear directly from many of the experts interviewed for this book and share insights with peers for four to five total hours a week over an eight-week period. Please see www.leadinginanalytics.com or https://pdaleadership.com/ for up-to-date information on these and other opportunities that may arise.

Preview of the Seven Tasks

The main focus of this book is to illuminate what the seven critical tasks for executives to master in the age of Big Data are and to share best practices for managing these seven manageable tasks well. Analytics is a dynamic and fast-changing field, as is the world we live in, so although the tasks are intended to be useful and helpful, they cannot be exhaustive.

Here is what you will learn in the rest of this book.

- **Task 0: Analytics leadership.** It takes a commitment to leadership in analytics from executive champions, business process owners, and the technical analytics team to succeed, as well as the study and application of the following seven key tasks, to do it well
- **Task 1: The problem.** How to find, evaluate, and prioritize valuable and achievable analytics problems that lead to value and can drive organizational learning using the DAD framework
- **Task 2: The team.** How to effectively build and manage your analytics team and those in the ecosystem working with them
- **Task 3: The data.** How to manage your data for quality and relevance, and how to design your data collection for value
- **Task 4: The tools.** How to understand the tools of analytics, what they can do, what they cannot do, and how you and your business's ecosystem can help
- **Task 5: Execution.** How to proactively execute well with analytics and what traps to avoid and how to avoid them
- **Task 6: Analytics maturity.** What a mature analytics organization and ecosystem looks like and how to build one
- **Task 7: Responsible analytics.** How to build an analytics organization that can last for the ages, that practices responsible and ethical analytics, and uses analytics for good

These tasks are presented more or less in the order they naturally occur on a project or in an organization. I sincerely believe these seven tasks are the most important ones when it comes to surviving and thriving in the age of Big Data. I also firmly believe it takes an ecosystem for organizations to change, and that without that organizational change supported by the 10-to-1 analytics ecosystem, little value will be created or sustained.

My goal has been to consolidate the collective knowledge and experience of the dozens of analytics experts interviewed in-depth for this work, supplementing with other valuable resources where needed. I have tried to synthesize their wisdom and share their stories to the best of my ability. Please credit any wisdom you find in this book to the supportive experts, many of them bona fide geniuses. If you find any errors or deficiencies, please blame them on me, the author, alone.

CHAPTER SUMMARY AND EXERCISES

Task 0: Summary

Most analytics projects fail and most of the root causes of failure are outside the direct control of the analytics professional. This truism means analytics professionals can do everything absolutely right and still fail. However, the primary causes of failure are known and manageable. When executive champions, business process owners, and analytics professionals proactively exercise leadership by skillfully working together, most failures can be avoided and many more successes will be achieved. Loners, however, almost always fail.

Task 0: Exercises

1. Consider the rate of analytics failures presented in this book and chapter, and the astounding amount of money invested in analytics.
   a. Take a few moments to reflect on these numbers and do some of your own research to verify or refute them. Write down your thoughts and a few key observations.
   b. Choose three numeric metrics of analytics project success or failure from this chapter. One should be a failure rate, one should be a monetary investment, and one is your choice.
   c. Next, do your own research and verify or refute each number in your presentation.
   d. Make an oral presentation providing a 60-second overview of analytics projects failures to a CEO-level audience who is unfamiliar with the material. Include the three numeric metrics, the research cited here, and your own research, and highlight where your research agrees with or disagrees with the numbers presented here.
   e. End with two sentences about how this will affect your career and the careers of other analysts working for this CEO.
2. We hear a lot about analytics successes, especially the very valuable ones. Of course, most organizations prefer not to share or talk about their analytics failures, or they spin them in a way that makes them look successful in some way. Nonetheless, only a few have, to date, proven truly valuable.

   a. Take some time to do your own research. Identify some high-profile analytics projects or initiatives that have succeeded, and have done so spectacularly well. Try to diversify your research to look at a range of industries and analytics applications. List and describe your top five analytics successes. Be sure to include the organization's name and description, the goal of the project, how it worked, and its impact on the business and/or other stakeholders. When possible, include metrics of success.

   b. Now, continue your research into failures. They will be a little harder to find as most organizations prefer to forget them. However, if you look, you should be able to find some projects that may at first appeared to succeed, and got some press for it, but in the end turned out to be more harmful than successful to the organization. Similar to the previous exercise, list and describe two or three failures, what they were, and what their impact was. This time, it is okay to leave the name of the organization out. But try to at least include a description of the type of business it is and as much of the information from the first exercise as is practicable.

   c. Compare and contrast the successes and failures. What do they have in common? What is different? What can we learn from this comparison? Share your thoughts and views from this analysis.

3. We listed and briefly described seven critical tasks for executives to master, which will be the main contents of the rest of this book.

   a. Please list and describe each of them and reflect on your own experience with many of those concepts.

   b. Write a one-paragraph summary under each description that describes what you expect you will learn from each of these tasks throughout the book.

   c. Skim through the table of contents and flip or scroll through the rest of the book quickly, noticing anything that jumps out at you or looks interesting. Ask yourself how well the content does, or does not, line up with your original expectations and share a final reflective paragraph of your observations.

4. Imagine yourself now, or in the near future, as an analytics leader, business process owner, or executive champion. Identify your preferred role and write down a few thoughts to share concerning what you might actually do to more effectively work together with the other groups and perhaps what you might do differently yourself.

5. Consider the observation that "loners fail" highlighted in this chapter. Reflect on your own experience with observing loners on a team or in an organizational environment. Have you also found it to be the case that most loners fail? If so, why do you believe this is the case? If not, why not? Write down a few thoughts to share on your observations and the reasons for them.

NOTES

1. https://designingforanalytics.com/resources/failure-rates-for-analytics-bi-iot-and-big-data-projects-85-yikes/

2. https://venturebeat.com/ai/why-do-87-of-data-science-projects-never-make-it-into-production/

3. Sam Ransbotham, Shervin Khodabandeh, David Kiron, François Candelon, Michael Chu, and Burt LaFountain, "Expanding AI's Impact with Organizational Learning," *MIT Sloan Management Review* (October 2020).

4. INFORMS, *Analytics Body of Knowledge* (Catonsville, Maryland), pp. 31–42.

5. https://www.informs.org/Recognizing-Excellence/Award-Recipients/INTEL-Corporation

6. McKinsey Global Institute, "The Age of Analytics: Competing in a Data-Driven World" (December 2016). https://www.mckinsey.com/capabilities/quantumblack/our-insights/the-age-of-analytics-competing-in-a-data-driven-world

7. Sam Ransbotham, Shervin Khodabandeh, David Kiron, François Candelon, Michael Chu, and Burt LaFountain, "Expanding AI's Impact with Organizational Learning," *MIT Sloan Management Review* (October 2020).

8. Douglas B. Laney, "Your Company's Data May Be Worth More Than Your Company," *Forbes* (July 22, 2020).

TASK **1**

The Problem

SOLVE THE RIGHT PROBLEM

My friend Polly Mitchell-Guthrie, an analytics thought leader and senior executive at Kinaxis, likes to say, "Whatever else you do, don't solve the wrong problem." She is absolutely right! This is actually what scientists call a *type III error*,[1] finding the right answer to the wrong question (curious about type I and type II errors? See Task: 5 Execution for more). Finding and solving a valuable, worthwhile, and impactful problem in which you can actually succeed is the critical first task, maybe even the most important one, and not as easy as many think.

You can succeed in many low-value analytics projects and still fail in your business. Not every problem that can be solved is worth solving, nor is every problem worth solving amenable to an analytics solution. There are many high-value analytics problem areas out there and too little time, talent, and resources to address the important ones, let alone the low-value ones.

Successfully making a difference with analytics means focusing on finding, screening, prioritizing, and solving the most important and achievable analytics problems for your organization. Our experts agreed that Pareto's 80/20 rule applies here: 20% of solvable problems that come your way will yield about 80% of the value, and the rest should be deprioritized. The unsolvable problems should be handed off to be managed another way.

Knowing where to find the right analytics opportunities for your organization, at the right time, making sure they are solvable, and then prioritizing which to do when and which not to do is absolutely key to analytics success. There are many factors to consider in this process. Perhaps the first should be identifying what approach to analytics is right for you, your project, and your organization at this time.

That thought process begins with a discussion of the DAD (decision-centric, action-centric, and data-centric) analytics framework, which is designed to help executives, business process owners, and other leaders understand the approaches they can take to analytics, to know how these approaches interact with each other, and, importantly, to stay focused on action, which is needed to realize value. Next, we look at best practices for each approach and their synergies. Then, we learn how to screen potential projects for viability by ascertaining if a project is amenable to an analytics solution, that is, if analytics is likely to be able to help solve that problem. Finally, we learn best practices in prioritizing viable projects.

THE DAD FRAMEWORK FOR ANALYTICS ACTION

I believe the *a* in analytics should stand for action. Value is realized only when actions are taken, and it is well understood that analytics can help determine the best actions to take. But what is less understood is that analytics can, and should, also be used to ensure that those actions are taken and to then monitor their impact. Identifying how and where to take those actions is only half the value; executing on them and learning from them is also essential.

The DAD framework was developed to help guide that process, to remind us that it is not just about making better decisions but taking action on them, and analytics can assist there, too. This framework reminds us we can use action-centric analytics to ensure action is taken and to change the culture through organizational learning, which is the key to sustainable analytics success.

Which of these three broad approaches to analytics—decision centric, data centric, and action centric—is determined by the specific situation. In the DAD framework, decision-centric and data-centric analytics both point to action-centric analytics as the primary goal; hence, action is in the center of this framework, as shown in Figure 1.1.

There are valuable problems best solved with each type or approach. Executives must learn to recognize which approach is best for each time and place in their organization. Although each approach has value on its own, when they are used together they create synergies that can drive organizational learning. However, leaders must recognize that action-centric analytics is an important tool for accelerating organizational learning at scale and is especially effective when coupled with leadership.

Approach Interactions and Examples

Because we briefly introduced each approach to analytics with Task 0: Analytics Leadership, we start with a highly simplified example of each approach from when I was chief analytics officer for HiveTracks. At HiveTracks, we aimed to use all three approaches to analytics and benefited from them interacting synergistically as we moved between approaches, applying what we learned from each one. Afterwards, we will provide more context, theoretical support, and examples for each to fill out the details so you can see them in action.

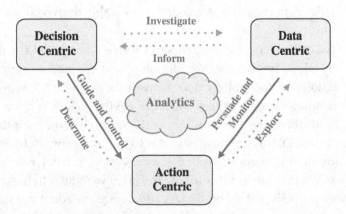

Figure 1.1 The DAD Framework for Analytics Action

Data-Centric Example: HiveTracks

One of our first tasks was to look at the data we had and search for value. After testing several ideas to add value with the data, we identified community intelligence as an important approach that aligned with our strategy and values. Under this model, we realized that data from other beekeepers, the actions they were taking, and the ecosystems they were observing, such as flowering blooms and native pollinators, would be very useful. The data could be processed, digested, and visualized for beekeepers and organizations to improve bee health and monitor environmental health and biodiversity impact. It could prove to be particularly useful across the Global South, as Max Rünzel posted in a blog about using AI-driven climate-smart beekeeping to support rural women in Ethiopia and Uzbekistan.[2]

We had some of this data already, enough to prove the concept and its value. However, to really scale, we needed more reliable and consistent data and more expansion of what we were collecting. We knew that community intelligence has the potential to demonstrate the value in data beyond the individual, starting a virtuous circle that allows for crowdsourcing environmental data to monitor biodiversity. In addition, beekeepers have been relying on local groups, mentors, and associations to compare and learn from their practices. Digitally supporting these relationships was a recurring need expressed by many beekeepers, particularly vis-à-vis an overall deterioration in bee health and more extreme climatic events. We turned to action-centric analytics to encourage participation and enhance relevant data collection for community intelligence and use of it.

Action-Centric Example: HiveTracks

The data-centric approach validated the value of some of the data we had to others outside the company and pointed to additional data that would expand and enrich the value. The next step was to collect and improve it. Some data were relatively easy to add, such as weather data. Others required much more customer support and engagement. We needed to identify what we could do to encourage, nudge, or drive our users to share high-quality data regularly to maximize the value derived from it for the local beekeeper community.

We first looked at existing academic theories to see what drives the desired action. In this case it was adoption and use. We identified and adapted a theory as a starting point to drive action the technology acceptance model,[3] which has been validated, with various permutations, many times since the 1990s, including a few times by me!

The theory holds there are two core factors that influence the adoption of technology. These (simplified) factors are how easy it is to use and how useful it is. Other factors, such as enjoyment (technically called *hedonic factors*), privacy risk, and others can also matter. We knew that our environment, an apiary with bees flying around, as well as sticky honey or propolis getting on fingers and devices, made it hazardous for using a smartphone to input images taken and data gathered from hive inspections. So we adapted and tested the theory, using actual data use from the application.

As a result, we were able to identify key factors that were and were not being used on the web and in the application and how they related to actual use. Oh, and yes, being in a hazardous environment also played a role. We even published a peer-reviewed journal article[4] about the findings, going full circle and extending the theory for others to build on it. We wanted to give back and imagined that firefighters, soldiers, and others might have similar hazardous places where this construct was important and we wanted to share it with the world.

Using these and related insights, a complete redesign of the application was done, with leadership from CEO Max Rünzel, cofounder Dr. James Wilkes, and others. Preliminary feedback has been excellent.

Decision-Centric Example: HiveTracks

First, we explored our data, looking for what could be done with it to create value (data centric). Then we focused on actions to increase and leverage that value (action centric). The next step involved using decision-centric analytics because our goal was to decide what practices to recommend to our users. The following is one small example of many we took that worked together to encourage action.

We partnered with some contacts, now friends, affiliated with the United Nations Food and Agriculture Organization (UN FAO), headquartered in Rome. They had a set of best practices in beekeeping in which their expert network had already identified recommendations. Our task was to validate, and then hopefully adopt, these practices. Because most of these practices were based on either local experiments or theory, field testing them, at scale, was critical.

Fortunately, because we already had data from users around the world, we were in a position to do some of this testing. We selected the United States as our site because it was a large country with diverse climates, and we had enough data that we could use five-plus years of historical data for a broad analysis, smoothing out seasonal variations. We were able to validate best practices for hive inspections with a few interesting and surprising results that will likely lead to updates in theory. Another peer-reviewed article has been accepted for publication, enabling us to give knowledge back to the community, and should be in print about the same time as this book.

The point is that we used all three approaches to analytics at HiveTracks, and we received significant value from the synergies among them. There was no particular reason that data-centric analytics needed to be first. We could have also started with another analytics-centric approach to create value. Ideally there will be a place for all three, but even two is better than just one approach. The important point is to fit these approaches to your organizational needs.

For example:

- **Decision to data centric.** If you have a decision, you can use a data-centric approach to investigate creative, out-of-the-box solutions, beyond what has been tried before, to find a possible answer.

- **Data to decision centric.** If you find something interesting in the data, or have an idea for what could be done with the data you have, it can inform possible decisions, suggesting other approaches.
- **Decision to action centric.** If you have a decision to make, this approach can guide or even control the appropriate action. This line in Figure 1.1 has a solid arrow because it is a more common, stronger, and more intuitive approach than approaches with the dotted arrows.
- **Action to decision centric.** If there is an action you need to encourage or enforce, you might use decision-centric analytics to determine if it is having the desired effect or which approaches or practices may perform better.
- **Data to action centric.** If you find something interesting, you can use analytics to help persuade people to take action and monitor the impact of those actions to sustain engagement and adjust as needed. This line also appears as a solid arrow in Figure 1.1 because this is a more common, stronger, and more intuitive approach.
- **Action to data centric.** If you have an action that needs to be taken, you may use a data-centric approach to explore various possibilities and suggest the best ways to guide it.

All of these approaches work together, but the primary focus should always be on action. Solving a problem might be fun, but unless action is taken it will have little impact. The DAD framework is designed to help you think about the various approaches to analytics, identify possible problems in your organization that each approach could address, and help you plan how they can all work together to drive action on valuable problems.

Now that we have seen each approach in action, let us go into a little more detail.

Decision-Centric Analytics

Decision-centric analytics is centered on the decision. The focus is on taking a known problem or decision important to the organization and improving that decision with analytics. You might think of this as a problem looking for data to solve it. It is the classic and most well-known approach to analytics.

My team and I used another decision-centric approach when working on projects for the power industry. The goal was to predict when energy consumption would peak or reach its highest point. This energy was (1) the most expensive the utility could purchase because of high demand charges, making it as much as 2000% more per KWh during that time, and (2) the least sustainable energy as all types of energy generations were mostly used to meet demand, even the most environmentally damaging.

The demand forecast was highly dependent on weather, among other factors. We built a decision-tree-based algorithm that predicted when peak demand would be, more than 24 hours in advance, with more than 90% accuracy. This approach enabled the utility time to shift demand, saving dollars and reducing the environmental impact, while improving the load management decisions they needed to make every day.

For most business leaders, decision-centric analytics is the first, maybe the only, type of analytics they think about. When they have a problem, they want someone to help them solve it, whatever the problem is, and analytics professionals are the ones they call. This approach has the advantage of a clear ROI because it is focused on a known problem with identified value to the organization. It generally follows a formal methodology or process for solving problems through a logical, repeatable process. Organizations can get quite good at following this process and, with the focus on known problems, the odds of success are quite high.

Its downside is that it has a short-term focus on current problems that can be solved quickly, which means it often misses new, out-of-the-box or game-changing opportunities to do something differently.

Analytics professionals with a business orientation, discussed in Task 2: Teams, tend to do particularly well with the approach.

Data-Centric Analytics

Data-centric analytics is centered on the data. The focus is on taking known data and looking for an interesting problem it might be able to solve. You might think of it as data looking for a problem, when someone has an idea and validates it for doing something interesting you were not necessarily looking for, but provides a lot of potential value.

For example, my friend, Libor Cech, former CEO of Chemoprojekt, with decades of experience applying analytics and automation in natural resource industries in Europe and the United States, used this approach in the lumber industry.[5] Cech saw that daily lumber price data was becoming available for different dimensions and grades of lumber and that data from new scanning technology, similar to an x-ray or magnetic resonance imaging for logs harvested, could be used to increase lumber yield from each log, and therefore profitability and sustainability of lumber. Figure 1.2 shows an image of Libor Cech with a log ready to be analyzed.

Knowing that lumber could never be uncut, it was important to maximize the value of that first cut. Also, a very high percentage of lumber was wasted because each log was unique in shape, and premium properties in different spots could be cut with different value propositions. Cech was able to analyze the shape of log from the images and data generated by the scan to increase the yield by an average of 16% to 26%, reducing waste while simultaneously increasing profit with more volume to sell. Moreover, by seeing the data from the scan, and using automated saws and algorithms linked to the spot market, Cech was able to evaluate every possible cut of each unique log and simultaneously maximize the value by ensuring higher value premium cuts. This consideration led to much higher prices for each cut, that when coupled with machine learning algorithms and automation to execute, Libor's company was able to increase the total market value realized per log by an average of 27%.

Figure 1.2 Libor Cech Explaining Lumber Analytics
Source: Image Courtesy of Libor Cech.

This data-centric approach has the advantage of being able to use moonshot out-of-the-box approaches that might become an innovative step forward and lead to a sustainable, competitive advantage. However, the downside is that this approach is also quite risky, because it is focused on discovery, which is trying to find new and interesting uses for your data to add value and solving problems you may not know you have. When you find something, it might be incredibly valuable or only nominally so. Consequently, the results are harder to predict and more challenging to justify investment from a short-term ROI focus.

Executives should encourage their data scientists to develop broad business knowledge, in their industry and also in other related and some non-related ones. Many of the best ideas come from seeing how others are achieving success and getting an inspiring idea or test that might work out. Going to conferences, trade shows, and other venues can offer good ideas to explore. The goal is much more about the right mix of breadth for ideas and depth for execution and evaluation. Another best practice is making sure the analysts who are working for you share ideas and successes, noting and sharing important variables and concepts that worked or did not work in the past.

It should be recognized that this approach to analytics has a higher failure rate than decision-centric analytics. However, many would argue if you have no failures, you are not taking enough chances. For all analytics approaches, especially this one, there needs to be room to explore and try new ideas. By allowing analysts room to explore, and setting things up so that if they fail they fail fast, they capture what they learn and move on. This rapid cycling is essential for innovation and long-term success. It is often true that failed ideas lead to other ideas that might work.

However, there is some risk that goes with the prospect of a high reward from data-centric analytics. Most organizations find it useful to start with a decision-centric approach and gradually expand into a data-centric approach as trust is built in the data and systems. Even if analysts come up with a brilliant idea, the organization is generally less ready to adopt it than they are with decision-centric analytics. Executives less involved in the process are less likely to understand it and therefore less likely to embrace it.

Moreover, to win with data-centric analytics, you must be willing to change at a fundamental level. Few organizations are. With decision-centric analytics, you are doing something you are already doing, just better, making it easier to change. With data-centric analytics, it is likely something you have not done before, and thus it is much more difficult for it to take root in many traditional, non-digital-native organizations.

Analytics professionals with a seeker orientation, discussed in Task 2: The Team, tend to do particularly well with this approach.

Action-Centric Analytics

Both decision-centric and data-centric analytics should be chosen and refined with action in mind, but it is not the same as action-centric analytics. Action-centric analytics assumes that the decision has already been made, through any means, including non-analytical means. The task of action-centric analytics is to help carry out that action and monitor its impact. You might say this is analytics-driven action from a solved problem, an insight, or a desire.

If the action was based on a decision-centric process, the action might be focused on providing guidance with advice and gentle nudging and suggestions. Or, more authoritatively, it may be used for control with rewards and/or consequences for compliance/noncompliance. This approach is more commonly used for employees or gig workers, or sometimes for policing citizens of an authoritarian state. Those with low levels of autonomy are common targets for control, those with higher levels of autonomy are more likely to be offered guidance. However, guidance and control do not have to be for a person; they can also be used for a device, robot, or animal.

If the action was inspired by a data-centric approach, you are more likely to focus on persuasion and impact monitoring to encourage action. The goal here is to persuade decision-makers with a very high degree of autonomy that it is the right or best course to take and to provide feedback and rewards through monitoring to verify or adjust as needed. However, although these methods are most commonly associated with the source of the desire to have an action done, the desire can come from anywhere and any of these mechanisms could be used to encourage or enforce those actions.

Real examples clarify how each approach can ensure actions, because ensuring action is needed for value creation, regardless of how that action was decided. This condition makes it important for leaders to consider how action will be communicated and carried out when identifying and prioritizing potential problems for analytics to address. If there is no real path to action, the value will be limited. The following examples show how actions can be used synergistically to complement and support each other for cascading value creation.

Guidance

Analytics is put in place to guide workers and some decision-makers to the best decisions and actions for the task they are attempting to do, helping them do it better. This action is usually based on results of earlier decision-centric or data-centric approaches, but sometimes from non-analytics-driven decisions. It is not just reporting, as helpful as that is, but guiding, mostly workers, to take given actions based on a set of inputs.

Joshua Cazier, an executive at Qualtrics, shared how his organization worked with clients to guide action in customer interactions by monitoring not only the customers' transactional data but also by having an AI system listen to and analyze the customers' tone of voice, in real time, to help guide how the customer service or sales agent should best react to get the desired outcome with that customer.

Good customer service agents have always done this back-and-forth intuitively, if not consistently. But now emotional intelligence and appropriate response can be scaled and implemented consistently to get the desired interaction once the best approach has been modeled with a mix of historical and real-time data. It is not about controlling their actions, which is the focus of the next section, but about helping customer service agents do better at what they already want to do.

Control

Whereas guidance is about helping customers or workers do their jobs or tasks better, control is about controlling their behaviors and enforcing rules or policies. Put another way, guidance makes your customers or employees smarter or better at a task that they are already doing, or want to do, whereas control is about making sure they do the tasks that you want them to do when and how you want that task to be done.

It is more common for guidance to be used for those with more education, expertise, and autonomy, historically white-collar workers, and for controls to be used for those with less education and autonomy, such as those focused more on efficiency than creative problem-solving. The blue-collar worker is often in this group as well as others in the gig economy, such as Uber or Lyft drivers and other low-skill workers.

Rather than guide these workers to do what they already want to do better, these analytics are used to control their behavior to meet the organization's goals, usually for efficiency, rather than growth and creativity, as is the goal for guidance. It has its roots in various systems and controls that have been around since the industrial age, but is more automated and intelligent than before, allowing for more adaptability by the firm to adjust in real time, based on feedback and situational awareness of the outside environment. Managers have been using these types of control mechanisms, with less data, automation, and intelligence, for as long as there have been large organizations.

The difference is in scale, enforcement, and optimized guidance, allowing managers much more effective control than in the past.

Michael Wooldridge argues in his book, *A Brief History of Artificial Intelligence*,[6] that it is exactly this type of action analytics and these control systems that have enabled the rise of the gig economy. It also allows for other large organizations that have instant micro-level control of their workers. Never before have organizations had quite the ability to control such a distributed flock of workers, serving their goals at such a large scale efficiently and instantly based on near real-time analytical data and analysis made possible by action-centric analytics.

A beneficial use might be a shipping or logistics company that uses analytics to monitor the driving habits of its employees. Managers might place various sensors on the vehicles that can tell them how fast the drivers are going, where they are, how hard they are braking, how fast they are accelerating, and how many times they hit a curb or other undesirable activity. It could also monitor whether maintenance is done correctly and any number of other tasks. Managers can then analyze all of the data that comes in, maybe even in near real time, to give a driving safety score and take interventions when needed to meet their compliance goals for the safety of all involved.

Analytics professionals with a native orientation, discussed in Task 2: The Team, tend to do particularly well with this approach, once the actions and enforcement mechanisms have been well designed. However, there are also many real and potential uses of control analytics that most people would consider unethical and demeaning. These uses are discussed in more detail with Task 7: Responsible Analytics, which focuses on ethical analytics and a few other relevant topics. Executives should carefully weigh the pros, cons, and ethical aspects before using control analytics.

Now we look at the persuade and monitor arrow from data-centric to action-centric analytics.

Persuade

Analytics has an incredible ability to persuade, at least for those focused on improving results. This is true of both decision-centric and data-centric analytics. However, for data-centric analytics, this feature is even more important because you are trying to fundamentally change the organization to do things they have never done before, rather than making incremental improvements to existing processes. Because it is a harder task, effective persuasion is even more important to encourage adoption and use.

Therefore, the analytics must convincingly show not only how they will be used but also how those uses will add value in a clear and sustainable way. This value needs to be presented in a way that matters to the people hearing it and in their language, which often has a monetary or time-saving angle.

Dr. Rudi Pleines, mentioned previously, talked about how the ability to persuade people to action with facts and numbers was one of the most important attributes of analytics, and he has used it effectively in many engagements.

Figure 1.3 HiveTracks Application for Community Intelligence
Source: Image courtesy of HiveTracks CEO Max Rünzel.

Max Rünzel uses analytics to incentivize and empower current and new beekeepers to make better decisions with data-driven advice from their beekeeper platform. HiveTracks communicates through a mix of methods. First, they demonstrate the value to individual beekeepers by showing how many other beekeepers in their region are being supported by the app, for example, "400 beekeepers in your region have performed an inspection" (see Figure 1.3).

Second, the HiveTracks app ensures when beekeepers do in fact enter quality, relevant, and standardizable data into the system that can be analyzed by their software, in real time, and shared with the community as actionable recommendations, beekeepers can use the information to keep their hives alive and healthy. This community intelligence is a vital part of the HiveTracks' strategy to encourage accurate data collection for hive inspections, flower blooms, and diseases to monitor environmental health and improve biodiversity locally and globally.

It also encourages beekeepers to share their data, because they are empowered by the direct benefit they receive from the community, alerting them to early opportunities to feed or prevent swarming, and helping them monitor and respond to risks, including diseases or weather-related events. The key is the synergistic benefit communicated clearly and acted on wisely. HiveTracks is also working on a gamified incentive mechanism that pays beekeepers for the ecosystem services their bees contribute to for the health of local ecosystems and biodiversity.

Monitor

As you deploy analytics and make decisions based on the data, it is important to monitor the impact and usefulness of your models so you can learn from them, change them when they are wrong or become outdated, and spread the story of your success. All of these components are important to building a culture of analytics, especially when you have many business leaders who may be hesitant to change.

Patrick Getzen, former chief data and analytics officer for Blue Cross Blue Shield of North Carolina, shared that their executives were worried about how the pending legislation that came to be known as Obamacare might affect their business model. The big unknown was the relative health of the currently uninsured population that was going to be covered as insured. Getzen met with many political leaders at the state and national levels and personally dug deep into the numbers to provide guidance to those leaders, while estimating the impact on quality health care and costs for his organization.

When the law was enacted, Getzen's team put procedures in place to monitor the impact and assess how the models they prepared performed. Getzen soon learned that the team was wrong about the level of health of the uninsured, but less wrong than everyone else who did not use a data-driven approach or one that was less in-depth. Because they had identified the most important variables, and what to look for in their earlier analysis, they knew how to monitor it. Hence, they saw where they were right and wrong very early and had more time than most to adjust and benefit from their analysis. Monitoring their models and the impact this massive change had on their business goals was their key to success in this uncertain environment.

Analytics professionals with a business orientation, discussed in Task 2: The Team, tend to do particularly well with this approach, once the actions and enforcement mechanisms have been well designed.

FINDING VALUABLE PROBLEMS TO SOLVE

This section is centered on finding valuable problems to solve. In the early stages of analytics maturity, it is important to focus on servicing and supporting known business needs with established processes. This focus offers the best potential for a clear ROI and project acceptance and starts to build an analytics culture. It is decision-centric analytics at its best.

Although analytics should continue to address known business needs forever, as the organization matures and accepts analytics into their standard operating process, people within the organization will slowly become more open to using analytics to address other unknown business needs, taking advantage of new and emerging opportunities and becoming more adaptable and analytically driven. This progression makes room for both data-centric and action-centric analytics to take hold and grow in the organization.

There are a few general principles that apply to all three approaches to analytics, but there are additional things to consider for each type. We include these principles in the decision-centric section, then highlight a few differences in the data-centric and action-centric sections that follow.

Decision-Centric Analytics

The following principles can guide you in your search for the best decision-centric analytics projects. They are written primarily for analytics professionals looking for valuable projects, but the principles apply to all leaders guiding analytics in the organization.

Strong Business Impact and Interest

Look for an area with the potential to have a strong business impact and one that is of current interest to the organization. Your early projects should be small enough to be achievable but big enough to be noticed and make a difference. Even at stages of advanced analytics maturity, this principle is still a good one to follow.

Although it is always important to make sure that any potential project has the likelihood of a meaningful business impact, this goal is not enough. It must also be an active area of interest for decision-makers and line up with their short-term and long-term goals, especially the short-term ones receiving a lot of attention, where analytics is likely to help.

At any given moment, a large organization will face many competing pressures and opportunities. There are often a seemingly infinite number of opportunities that could have a business impact. Although a good ROI is important, it is not enough. It has to fit into the current thinking, strategic direction, and, yes, the politics of the organization if it is to succeed.

If you are an analytics professional, do not try to steer the ship in the early phases of analytics. Rather, observe where the ship is going and try to help it sail more smoothly and efficiently on its chosen course. When your analytics is new and unproven, focus on understanding where the organization is going and finding the persistent pain points standing in the way. Listen to what people complain about, where there is a flurry of activity, and where there are opportunities for analytics to help.

Yes, look at established key performance indicators (KPIs) and pay attention to which ones are doing well and which ones are struggling. That said, it is also important to look at durability. Assess if it is a long-term strategic goal of the organization or a fad that may pass. It should be core to the organization for the foreseeable future if you want leadership support to be with you to the end. Otherwise it will be abandoned, even if it has support in the beginning, as the winds change or other core areas emerge and take precedence.

If it is an important enough problem, the executives will be with you to the end, notes Piyanka Jain, CEO of Aryng, as long as you show progress that leads to tangible benefits. Analytics projects that have strong, meaningful alignment with established business goals result in leadership support now and in the future, which is critical to ensuring action is taken from your analytics projects. This is the definition of successful analytics.

By knowing what analytics can do and being aware of what people are trying to do, opportunities will start to present themselves. But it is not enough. These opportunities still need to be achievable, actionable, and have a desired noticeable impact on the speed, efficiency, and direction of the leaders steering the ship. Again, business impact alone is not enough. If it is not helpful in getting the company to where it is interested in going, it is likely to be rejected and fail.

Collaborative Leaders

After you have identified a few areas with strong business impact on the path the organization is interested in going, the next step is finding a collaborative business leader who can help you get there. Keep in mind, not all business leaders are equally interested in analytics. Some may be unwilling or unable to champion projects for any number of reasons. This may include a distrust of technology, a preoccupation with day-to-day tasks, the high analytics failure rate, fear of disrupting a smooth process, or political considerations.

It is important to factor in someone who has both an eagerness (not just willingness) to work with you on implementing analytics solutions and the ability to champion your project effectively to see it through final implementation and adoption. As you prioritize projects, leadership support is critical to success.

More than title consideration, it will take time, resources, and political skill to persuade, lobby, champion, fund, and support someone for any analytics project. Choosing the right leader for collaboration is almost as important as choosing the right project. Careful thought should be taken in finding the leader and ensuring their commitment and ability to support the project. You want this person to be not only supportive of this project but also able to help build your analytics reputation across the organization to help future projects succeed as well.

In addition to being able to support and champion the project politically, the leader needs to be in a position to either take action based on what you build or discover, or ensure others do. If they cannot ensure action on the analytics, little will be accomplished and the project will be perceived as a failure.

Build on an Existing Decision Process

Every organization follows processes for making decisions. They may or may not be very sophisticated processes, but they work because decisions get made. A great starting place with analytics project selection is understanding the existing processes and then looking for opportunities to improve on them with analytics.

Steve Stone, retired CIO for Lowes, L-Brand, and other companies, talks about finding success by building on where the organization gets its answers now. In discovering where the organization gets its answers now, you learn a great deal about how decisions are made, the extent to which data drives the decision process, and how formalized the process is. All of these considerations can give you valuable clues about what you can do to improve the process.

It is quite difficult to get people to change how they do things. If you come up with a good solution that does not integrate well into employees' existing workflow and their approach to problems, there is a high risk of adoption failure. You need to take steps to mitigate the risk and help them get used to using and benefiting from analytics.

The best approach is to integrate analytics into employees' current workflow and make it easier to use and better in some impactful way. Thirty years of research into technology adoption supports the idea that these are two of the most important factors in adoption (ease of use and usefulness) and a key part of the technology acceptance model.[7] Building on their current process will make it easier to use and more likely to be perceived as useful because the leader will be familiar with it and understand how the process works. This is true even when the new solution may, in fact, be more useful, because adoption is driven by perceptions, not necessarily facts.

But note that just one of those factors is not enough. The solution must achieve both to have lasting impact and staying power, which is only possible by understanding and building on the employees' current process. From there you can later add some additional improvements, such as making it faster, prettier, or other new features, but it has to be adopted and accepted first. Take it a step at a time while you are still building your analytics culture.

Focus on Action

Insight is interesting, but action has impact. It is easy and natural to chase insights, to seek to understand, but action is better. To effectively succeed in analytics, you must look at what actions could and would be done differently based on your analytics. If, in the end, nothing changes, you have to ask if it is really a priority or just something interesting to know.

Investigate what actions could potentially be taken and how likely they would be taken if the project bears insight. But do not stop there. It is not just that action would be taken, but that action actually needs to matter. Determine the effect of those actions on the bottom line or other strategic goals of the organization. For example, a small improvement spread over a large number of customers might be more valuable than a very large improvement for a small number of customers. Calculate or estimate the likely impact of those actions, if they were taken, and use this information to guide you to analytics gold.

Develop a Balanced Portfolio

Not all analytics projects will succeed, no matter how hard you try. Even if they do, more of the same is not always the best approach, which may be a sign you are being too timid and not taking the potentially game-changing risks you need to take to stay in the game. Therefore, in addition to the known projects with clear and tangible ROIs, a percentage of your portfolio should be devoted to three additional types of projects: those that grow talent, test game-changing technologies, and enhance your organizational infrastructure to expand its analytics capabilities.

Grow Talent and Reputation

Several years ago, a few friends and I had the privilege of working with a team in an innovative subsidiary of a well-known FANG company (originally named for Facebook, Amazon, Netflix, Google). As mentioned, the goal was to develop and launch a new technology that would help automatically collect data remotely from beehives. Using a radio-based mesh network, it would turn each hive into a transmitter that could relay data in near real time from places without service, exactly the kind of locations where beekeepers like to place their hives.

The project was risky, using a new technology in a yet-to-be-proven way. Even so, there were a number of potential benefits. One of these benefits was the chance to test and develop talent for a new technology that the firm thought could provide many additional benefits. Another benefit was that by focusing their efforts on a societal good (saving the pollinators), the FANG subsidiary saw the potential for a lot of positive PR. The societal good also served another purpose: it would give the team members an added incentive to work hard and learn, even outside their usual roles, given the potential impact.

Finally, if there was a project failure, it was unlikely to have a negative effect on the firm because it was not focused officially on a clear ROI but aimed for a societal good. Thus, it was less likely to tarnish their reputation inside or outside the firm, and quite likely have the opposite effect due to their efforts to do good. This focus greatly reduced their risk, while maximizing their talent development, which could then be used for projects with a clearer ROI after this near risk-free foray into this new space.

The firm benefited from this experiment by building their reputation internally and externally and by growing their talent in a way that enhanced their capabilities. Investing in analytics, even when there is not a clear ROI, may be perceived as a failure but it can also hold the seeds of future success if lessons are learned, skills are enhanced, and foundational technologies are developed that can lead to other projects that succeed enough to make the investment worthwhile in the long run.

My team and I had a similar experience when developing a blockchain traceability system powered by analytics that was designed to help women in rural, impoverished areas of the world climb out of poverty by giving them better access to international honey markets. Part of your analytics portfolio should be set aside, very thoughtfully, for projects that either (1) grow your talent and/or (2) enhance your reputation by giving back and/or by being perceived as an innovative leader in your field.

Test Game-Changing Technology

Once you arrive at a stable level of analytics maturity where there is sufficient support for your efforts to breathe a little, a portion of your analytics portfolio should be devoted to understanding potentially long-term, game-changing technology and understanding how it could affect and possibly improve your industry.

Although this benefit is related to growing talent and reputation, it has a different flavor in that the goal is to not be blindsided by advances in your area, but to actually preserve the possibility you could lead in this area. Patrick Getzen made this objective a priority, helping build and maintain their reputation as a leader and better preparing his teams for structural changes in health care.

Getzen shared an example of seeing a presentation from an AI company that would take all the information and data from a deceased person and attempt to create an electronic personification of that person with their data and fill missing elements in with reasonable extrapolations. This AI avatar could then be asked questions and would give reasonable answers intended to be congruent with what that person might have said or how they likely would have responded.

Getzen saw no immediate implications for health care in this scenario or a few other technologies they tested, but he thought they were interesting and, if a small part of the budget was set aside for these moonshot technologies, they could learn from them and be ready when these or similar technologies became relevant to their industry. Another benefit was improving team engagement: analysts were able to enhance their skills, learn new things, and play with new technologies, which analytics professionals generally crave. Investing at least some portion of the budget in game-changing technology, as part of a wider diversification strategy, made a difference for Getzen and his team by helping them anticipate how changes in technology would affect their business, and it could for you, too.

Expand Analytics Capabilities

Some projects may not have a short-term ROI but can have a long-term impact by enabling other projects. Steve Stone shared how investing in data quality at Lowes enabled them to build many analytics and business successes on top of that platform. It may have been hard to justify the cost on its own, but not doing it would have limited many future projects. Consider important investments in infrastructure, process improvements, and good data governance that can have downstream impacts.

Data-Centric Analytics

All of the decision-centric principles also apply to data-centric analytics, perhaps with the exception of understanding the decision process. Although it can be important to learn and understand the current decision process to see how to change and improve it, keeping your focus on data-centric analytics to find new ways to do things can be difficult if you are too entrenched in the current ways of doing things. This can bias the results toward the status quo.

The approach works best when analysts are given a clear goal and then plenty of flexibility to try new things with lots of resources and freedom to experiment and test new ideas. Along that line, it is often a best practice to insulate and sequester this group away from the traditional business operations to give them freedom to explore.

Capital One used this approach by separating a significant portion of their analysts into one location, encouraging their own culture to build on discovery and experimentation with the focus of better gauging risks in loans. The results were quite remarkable, with upwards of 80,000 experiments a year being done. It also sustained innovation in business processes that were driven by analytics and a culture of change.[8]

Action-Centric Analytics

Action-centric analytics can be very powerful in building an analytics culture. But because it involves changing people's behavior through analytics, it takes very careful management and can easily have unintended consequences, just as any effort to change behaviors can.

For example, Amazon used action-centric analytics to control their warehouse workers, using a metric called *time off task*. They would carefully measure times employees were not doing their primary jobs, such as scanning barcodes. Employees reported feeling dehumanized by being so closely monitored, which drove attrition and created ill will between Amazon and many employees. In fact, it reached the point where New York State[9] passed a law restricting the use of this flavor of action-centric analytics, what many deemed "dystopian," which added to the growing negative press about Amazon's management practices.

Executives should instead start by trying to build on current systems, improving them with analytics, and focusing on practices and expectations that are already well accepted and understood in the organization. As leaders gain more experience with their use and results, it can be easier to expand to newer areas of interest.

Many of the key concerns with action-centric analytics are ethical in nature, as shown in the Amazon warehouse worker example. They are centered on the type of society we want to be and the possible ethical backlash for employees, customers, and the broader society. As mentioned, these issues are discussed at length in Task 7: Responsible Analytics.

Five-Step Process for Finding Decision-Centric Analytics Opportunities

This section can be summarized with this five-step road map to finding the right analytics opportunities for you to consider.

1. **Identify** an area of strong business impact and interest.
2. Find a **collaborative** business leader in that area who is willing and able to help.
3. Take time to analyze and **understand** the business owners' current decision process.
4. Clearly identify what **outcomes** you and the business leader expect, including what actions can be improved as a result of an analytics project.
5. Create and manage an analytics **portfolio** to support your needs now and in the future.

These five steps can get you heading in the right direction, but there are still a few more things to do before committing to them, as we discuss in the next sections.

THE PROBLEM STATEMENT

By now you have a pretty good understanding of the business problems to address and their likely impact. It is now time to take the business problem and turn it into an analytics problem that you and your team can solve. To be clear, this is *not* just having a "general idea" of a few problem areas and diving into the data to see what fish you can find. At the early stages of analytics maturity, you need to have a crystal-clear problem statement that is achievable with your current resources and has tangible and measurable benefits.

Charles Kettering, former head of GM Research, is famous for saying, "A problem well stated is half solved."[10] It is worth the time to get this part right. It is not enough to find useful areas for analytics, even with willing partners eager to support you. There must be clear communication and goals, written down, that all parties agree would add value. During the interview for this book, Cecil John, an enterprise architect with 25+ years of experience, said, "if you can't write the problem down with clear simple goals and objectives, you *don't understand it well enough to solve it."*

This idea was confirmed in a recent *MIT Sloan Management Review*[11] article and may help explain why a good problem statement is so important. Remember, it is the first of the five manageable tasks. The article emphasizes this critical function with these words: "Too often, teams skip right to analyzing the data before agreeing on the problem to be solved. This lack of initial understanding guarantees that many projects are doomed to fail from the very beginning."

The problem statement should focus on action. All three types of analytics—decision centric, data centric, and action centric—need clear problem statements that can guide the project, document goals, ensure everyone is on the same page, and illuminate the path to value resulting from some action.

Although each approach needs a clear problem statement, the wording of each is a little different depending on the focus. Each approach should have a fundamental question guiding it for clarity. These questions begin with why for decision-centric, where for data-centric, and what for action-centric analytics.

Focus on Why for Decision-Centric Analytics

Most of the time when a business leader comes to an analytics professional with a problem, what they are really asking for help with a symptom of a problem, not the real problem. They feel some pain and describe that pain to the analyst and ask them to make it go away. Yet, the pain they describe is seldom the real problem, only one manifestation of it.

Similar to a skilled doctor, the analyst and executive should work together to identify the root cause of the symptoms so they can see clearly to address them. Similar to medicine, one problem can cause many different symptoms, and a symptom can be caused by a wide range of potential problems. Without identifying and diagnosing the real cause for medical and business pain points, the chances of solving them are slim.

My friend, Dr. Beverly Wright, head of data science for Burtch Works, calls this the *why-why*. That is, you have to understand why they are asking you to solve this problem in order to do so effectively. You have to get to the why behind the why so you can see the root cause you need to address.

One of my personal favorite ways to uncover the root cause of a problem is a concept similar to Wright's why-why. It is a technique championed by INFORMS called the five whys. The idea is to keep asking why as you dig into the problem, and seeking answers at each level, maybe even getting more data and answering the why at each stage. Usually by the time you get to the fifth why you have a good understanding of the real problem and can use that information to craft a better, more-focused problem statement.

Lindsay Marshall, director of data and analytics at Gilbane Building Company, shared how often using this technique can get to the real issue, and how it helps Marshall and the team stay focused on the root of the problem in a way that improves impact. At a previous place of employment, Marshall and the analytics team were struggling with getting the sales team to adopt any analytics model at all. So they took the time to listen, to find out why, with a technique similar to the five whys.

They found that many sales team members, with decades of experience, just trusted their gut and experience more than an analytical model they could not understand. They did not want to risk their jobs and commission on a model that did not make sense to them. Marshall and the analytics team refocused their efforts on a simple and transparent solution that they could explain in a way the sales team would understand. Once the sales team finally understood the model, they adopted it, and this small change increased sales by more than $1 million in a month. This result was achieved because Marshall's team dug deep enough, with the five whys, to understand the *real* problem so they could address it effectively.

Sam Volstad, the data analytics service manager at GHJ, shared a hypothetical example of how this might work in a case similar to Marshall's:

- "I don't want to adopt the model."
- "Why? What's the hesitancy?"
- "I don't think it's better than my own gut/experience."
- "Why? What is it that makes that difficult for you?"
- "Well, I've been doing alright on my own, and I don't want to risk my commission on this model."
- "Why? I understand your commission depends on your sales ability, but all of the models indicate an *increase* in sales if adopted."
- "Well, I just don't really understand how it will lead to an increase. How am I supposed to risk my income on trusting something that I don't understand?"

Understanding the why behind the pain of the person you are trying to help is critical to finding a solution that works, one where action can be taken. Marshall concluded with the advice that you should never do the first project you are asked to do, or accept the first rejection, but you should always dig deeper to make sure you are addressing the real issue.

Criteria for Good Decision-Centric Problem Statements

One of my favorite analytics books, *Bulletproof Problem Solving*, by Charles Conn and Robert McLean, contends that poor problem statements lead to many project failures.

They elaborate on why this is the case and give useful criteria for good problem statements. Here are a few highlights of their main ideas:

- **Inefficient.** If you use a scattergun approach to data gathering and analysis, it *always* leads to more effort than necessary.
- **Miss the mark.** If you do not take time to understand the decision-maker's values and their boundaries for what is possible, the analyst will miss the mark and the point of their analysis.
- **No action.** If the decision-maker does not feel like their question was answered, even if they may not have asked it well, they will not act.

It should come as no surprise that their criteria are made to address these problems:

- **Outcome-focused.** A clear statement of the problem to be solved is expressed in outcomes, not activities or intermediate outputs.
- **Measurable.** A clear statement of the problem is specific and measurable wherever possible.
- **Decision-maker's values.** A clear statement of the problem is designed to explicitly address the decision-maker's values and boundaries, including the level of accuracy needed, the scale of aspirations, and level of risk they are willing to tolerate.
- **Creative flexibility.** A clear statement of the problem is structured to a sufficient scope for creativity and unexpected results. Problems that are too narrowly scoped can artificially constrain solutions.
- **Organizational level.** A clear statement of the problem needs to be solved at the highest level possible. It needs to be one that works for the organization as a whole, and not just one optimized for a part of the organization at the expense of the whole.

Focus on Where for Data-Centric Analytics

The approach for data-centric problem-solving is quite different. Although domain knowledge helps, there is also a danger in being too rooted in what has been done before and having a bias toward the current process. Here you want to allow for creativity, exploration, and out-of-the-box ideas that might transform your business.

This approach requires less structure on the front end of problem-solving, the opposite of the decision-centric approach, and careful analysis of ideas after some initial exploration. Much like brainstorming, you do not want to dampen the creativity too early. Rather you need to give time to analysts to explore, experiment, validate, and prioritize.

It is helpful to have a clear focus area, like Capital One[12] did on using analytics to price risk appropriately while allowing experimentation on how to achieve it and a rigorous testing process to find out fast if it works. The problem statement should communicate a clear understanding of what needs to be achieved.

Analysts can also benefit by following good scientific principles of experimental design to justify their idea with some reason to believe it will work. Theory, as it functions in science, can help by guiding to more plausible outcomes and weeding out areas unlikely to be productive. This process also helps build confidence in the results and leads to more stable and reliable models.

For example, LeAnne Hill, now an analytics manager at FORVIS LLP, had the clearly defined goal of detecting fraud in financial transactions and preventing it before loan authorization. As the lead analyst on the project, Hill was given freedom and flexibility to try to expand and improve their early detection of fraudulent loan applications.

As Hill explored the data, it became apparent that the majority of fraud that could be detected early was in income and in payroll numbers that had been altered or completely fabricated. Hill realized if these red flags could be identified *before* the loan was authorized, they could reduce fraud. However, Hill also knew that people needed quick answers on loan decisions, or they would go elsewhere, so the process had to be somewhat automated to ensure it could flag potentially fraudulent applications in real time for deeper review.

Being a person dedicated to broad, lifelong learning, Hill came across Benford's law.[13] This is a law of numbers that predicts the distributions of random numbers, focused on key digits for different types of applications. Hill realized that when people change numbers, they are usually not random, and therefore would not be likely to follow Benford's predicted distributions.

With Benford's law as a guide, Hill began to write code that would test the idea on their historical data, and she was able to see that using this theory could significantly increase their capability to catch and prevent fraud, in near real time. Hill next began writing code to identify these transactions in real time and was able to flag many more potentially fraudulent applications than before, saving the firm from significant losses. Clear objectives, combined with the flexibility to explore and experiment, led to this valuable approach the organization gladly adopted.

In decision-centric analytics, the problem statement is agreed on and set up front, in detail, with criteria for success. With data-centric analytics, the focus is on criteria for success with freedom to explore to achieve those goals and quickly know if the approach is viable.

Focus on What for Action-Centric Analytics

For action-centric analytics, there must be a great deal of clarity for the desired actions and the appropriate agreed-on mechanism for carrying out those actions, using a clear set of rules before application. The problem statements here are more like software development designs with clear, measured steps outlined for when the model detects a behavior of interest.

For the analytics problem statement, clarity is needed on exactly what behavior is being detected or encouraged, in very specific terms that can be modeled and programmed. This specificity needs to be to the level of blueprints for a house that gives a clear plan for what needs done, rather than general criteria to aim for as with data-centric analytics.

Expanding on an previous example, a few friends and I, including Max Rünzel and Dr. James Wilkes, were asked by some partners affiliated with the UN FAO to analyze our data to test the opinions of experts regarding a few best-practice recommendations for beehive inspection. The thinking of most of these experts was that you should not inspect the beehive during the winter months because the cold air could be disruptive to the hive and lower its chances for survival.

There was some evidence to support this opinion, including from studies of opening hives in freezing temperatures that did hurt the hive. However, these studies were limited in time and geography. We were able to do a five-year historical study across the United States, with matched climate data, focused on this issue. The goal was to determine the action we wanted beekeepers to take: whether they should or should not open their hives in winter. The plan was to then nudge or incentivize beekeepers to follow whichever best practice was proven by the data, instead of opinion and trials limited in time and scope.

Our study showed that hives that were in fact inspected during the winter, contrary to expert opinion, were more likely to survive than those that were not, even when controlled for a variety of other factors. This was true in all climate regions tested, from those with mild winters to those with severe ones and across multiple years.

Using weather and climate data, we saw that, as you might guess, beekeepers who did inspect in the winter did so on comparatively warmer winter days, which was less likely to hurt the hive. We also surmised that by looking at the hives on these days, beekeepers were better able to see and address small problems before they became big ones.

Therefore, we were able to comfortably recommend the action that beekeepers should check on their hives on warm winter days and the software could even send beekeepers push notifications when weather conditions aligned, encouraging them to follow this validated best practice, determining what action should be taken and encouraging beekeepers to actually take that action when the conditions were right. If you are curious, you can read about the study in this peer-reviewed journal article.[14]

One important is note that any action, especially those involving people, should also go through an ethical review before implementation.

CHECKING FOR PROJECT VIABILITY

Analytics can be a solution to many problems, but it is not the best answer for every problem. After identifying problem areas of high potential, the next phase of your journey is to assess whether your project idea is amenable to an analytics solution. *Amenable* is a mildly technical term used by analytics professionals to signify that analytics may be a good solution to a given problem, meaning it is likely solvable using analytics.

This book takes a broad view of the term *amenable*, which includes considering the organization's cultural readiness to accept a given analytics solution, because that is the only way for your organization to receive real value from your analytics. Following are the key variables needed to determine whether a problem is likely amenable to a successful analytics solution:

■ **Data availability.** Most analytics efforts require data. If you do not have the required data available, or if the data you have is compromised or otherwise questionable or unavailable, you may need to focus first on setting up processes and procedures to collect and govern data that is most likely to be useful for your business. In some cases, it may be legally or ethically questionable to use certain datasets for a given purpose, necessitating alternatives such as synthetic data, which has similar properties and internal relationships as the real data it is synthesized from, but is anonymous. Or else you might need to consider terminating the project.

■ **Data culture.** It is important to assess whether your company is open to data-driven decision-making. Most say they are, but very few actually put it into practice. The clues are in the willingness to trust data and alter decision-making to include data. If this is not the case, your first order of business is to build a culture on data-driven decision-making. This initial step is best done with quick projects that demonstrate meaningful results.

■ **Stable environment.** Much of analytics uses data from the past to prepare for and predict the future. This approach works well in relatively stable environments when the future is likely to look a lot like the past. However, in areas of high volatility, low predictability, and a large degree of uncertainty, your future predictions are not likely to be very accurate or useful. They may even lead you astray. Ask yourself how likely the past is to represent the future before you go too deep into the analytics process.

■ **Business impact.** Analytics can be very beneficial, but not all analytics affects the business equally. You have to assess the likely impact of using analytics for your project on your business, in business terms, to make sure it is worth the cost and effort. If there is little business impact, it is not likely to be worth the time and effort to do it. For this reason, it is imperative to have both analytics and business leadership on the team from the start.

■ **Executive support.** Clear business impact is always required and a good first step, but it is not a guarantee of success. The highest level executives in your organization control the budget and so are in a position to demand that the recommended actions resulting from an analytics project are implemented. That is true success. Getting executives' buy-in during the prioritization process, and then continually updating them on progress and potential benefits of success, is an important job for the analytics and business leaders engaged in a project.

There is a simple tool that can help you discern whether your project is amenable to an analytics solution at the end of this chapter.

PRIORITIZING VIABLE PROJECTS

There will always be more "great analytics projects" in need of attention than there will be time and resources to do them. Now that you have identified promising areas for analytics and screened them for their amenability, it is time to prioritize them.

Here are a few key things to consider as you prioritize:

- **Must-do projects.** There are some projects that simply must be done. They are sometimes contractually driven, and very often they are motivated by legal or regulatory considerations. Occasionally the motivation for a project may be for competitive reasons, when the viability of the business is threatened. Other must-do projects are those that lay a foundation for future projects. Good data governance is an investment that all organizations must make when starting down the data-driven path, allowing for an increase in value down the line. Whatever the reason, start with the must-do projects.

- **Organizational vision.** As discussed previously, it is quite important to align your project with the core vision of the organization. Piyanka Jain shares that aligning the project with the organizational vision by focusing on impactful KPIs helps ensure executive support now and in the future. A high degree of alignment is a critical factor to consider during project prioritization.

- **Time to value.** Sometimes it takes a few highly visible wins, even if the impact is modest, to build support and trust in analytics. Doing so can help acquire additional support and resources, enabling bigger impacts down the road with an emerging data decision-making culture. Time to value is an important consideration for building an analytics culture and should always be factored into prioritization processes. Additionally, when volatile market conditions and technological uncertainties are present, it may be prudent to focus on a short time-to-value project due to the unknown future impact of non-foundational longer-term projects.

- **Model complexity.** Most business leaders will not adopt a model they do not understand. Complex models are harder to understand, can be more error prone, often take more overhead to run, and are difficult to integrate into existing business processes. A simpler model can increase time to value and the likelihood of adoption and impact.

- **Project complexity.** Complex projects have more risk than simple ones. Sometimes the rewards are worth it, but simple projects should be given a few bonus points for achievability and complex ones penalized for the increased failure rate.

- **Visible impact.** The ability to quantify the business impact in a way that shows the value of a project is an important consideration in prioritizing projects. This is the value side of the time to value variable. Yes, speed matters, but so does the level of impact. Keep in mind that cultural change is most effective when everyone sees the impact and trusts the results. So use metrics that are commonly accepted, used, and valued in the organization.

- **Synergy.** Dr. Bill Disch, educator at DataRobot and former chief analytics officer at another firm, shared how good prioritization often creates synergy because projects aimed at similar goals can often cluster together and multiply value. Look for possible synergies as you prioritize projects to magnify your impact and opportunity.

- **Foundational.** Consider whether the project provides a firm foundation in skills, technology, data, or other factors that can make future projects more successful or easier to complete.

- **Timing.** Another point made by David Houser and Dr. Rudi Pleines in their interviews is the importance of timing. Most project ideas have a shelf life, and their value changes depending on the internal and external environments. A highly relevant project may gain or lose its urgency based on changing markets. Firms can only effectively focus on so many things at once.

It is important to have a process in place to evaluate these and other potentially relevant variables. The tool provided in Figure 1.4 at the end of the chapter can be a useful guide. It is equally important to make the process fair and transparent so that those who need to adopt the analytics feel like they were meaningfully part of the process to create it. Including key analysts and business stakeholders in the prioritization process is generally a best practice, as long as you can minimize politics and gridlock.

Be sure to also time your projects in the broader context of your organization's bandwidth, making sure there is enough free attention to allow for adoptions and use of findings, or projects will die from neglect when more urgent, or noisy, factors intercede. There are always many initiatives going on in an organization at all times; only a few of them are with analytics.

It is also important to consider politics. Though many analysts consider politics distasteful, they do have an impact. At a recent conference, I heard an analytics executive talk about prioritizing according to business needs and aligning projects to strategy, similar to how prioritization is presented in this chapter. The presenter noted how hard it was to manage stakeholders to keep them focused on executing on the strategy they had developed while minimizing distracting projects.

The analytics executive also confessed that sometimes the executive directly above him comes up with a project he is curious about and wants investigated, even if it is not on their strategic road map. Here the analytics executive stated, "I am not dumb," implying a keen awareness that there was a time to keep the boss happy, even if it meant a detour or two, in order to maintain support for analytics across the firm, and perhaps also enhance job security.

Sometimes those tasks are designed for the analytics professional, especially if they are hired to do something that has already been decided. For example, Albert Owusu, who specializes in government contracting, talked about how in nearly all cases the government has already defined and prioritized projects through the political process, and there is little flexibility or opportunity to prioritize on your own. Cecil John, of Virtual Developer, shared something similar in building cloud and analytics solutions for clients. In these cases you can sometimes share your thoughts, which the client may listen to, but your focus generally becomes executing well on what was already prioritized by others. Both talked about the importance of seeking clarity in requirements for these types of projects.

According to management legend and guru Peter Drucker, "Efficiency is doing things right; effectiveness is doing the right things."[15] By taking time to use the DAD framework to find the right approach to actions and synergies and to screen and prioritize problems, your analytics projects will be much more effective. The tools provided at the end of this chapter are designed to help you succeed and be more effective with your analytics.

CHAPTER SUMMARY AND EXERCISES

Task 1: Summary

It is tempting to dive into analysis before taking time to find the right opportunities, screen them for viability, prioritize them, and make sure they are properly defined. But it is an inefficient and ill-advised approach. Even if you come up with something that is eventually useful, it is likely less useful than what you could have done by better exploring, planning. and prioritizing.

The first step is to identify which approach or approaches to use, and how to apply them effectively, preferably in a way that creates synergy. The DAD framework can be used to help guide action, which is the key way value is created. It consists of these analytics approaches:

- **Decision centric.** Approaching analytics with the goal of solving a defined problem and finding a path to do so effectively
- **Data centric.** Starting with exploring data as a resource and assessing its value to help with an undefined problem
- **Action centric.** Starting with a defined action believed to add value and then using analytics to encourage those actions through guidance, control, persuasion, and monitoring

Decision-centric analytics needs clear problem definitions, clear enough that a child can understand, including defined goals and metrics of success. Data-centric analytics requires clearly defined and understood data. Action-centric analytics requires a clear understanding of what actions are to be encouraged, for whom and when.

Leaders should make sure the projects are viable, meaning they have data, supportive team members, strong business impact, and more. The projects also need to be rigorously prioritized to meet business needs.

Task 1: Exercises

1. Consider the DAD framework with its focus on decision-centric, data-centric, and action-centric analytics and their potential synergies.

    a. Give a one or two-sentence description of each.

    b. Share a real or hypothetical example of each from a domain area in which you are familiar or have an interest.

    c. Discuss how each approach could be used synergistically in the domain area of your choice.

2. Because most organizations begin with decision-centric analytics, we will start by going through the five-step process for finding decision-centric analytics opportunities described in this chapter to find a valuable problem to solve with analytics.

    a. Think through each of these five steps to look for a promising area for pursuing analytics in an organization familiar to you.

    b. Write down three promising areas you find. Be sure to describe the organization and how analytics can be helpful in these three promising areas. Be prepared to share your ideas and observations.

3. Pick one of your most promising areas and convert it to a crystal-clear analytics problem statement. Make sure you explain how it meets each of the criteria listed in Table 1.1.

    Use Table 1.1 to score from 1 (needs improvement) to 5 (excellent) on each dimension. If possible, do this exercise with a classmate or friend and have them review and give feedback on each of the five criteria and how they could be improved while you provide feedback for their problem statement.

4. Check to make sure that your problem is amenable to an analytics solution by going through the Tool 1.1: Screening Projects for Amenability. Be sure to write down your scores for each question, report where it ended up on the scoring rubric, and share your observations from this exercise.

Table 1.1 Scoring the Problem Statement

Attribute	Description	Score (1–5)
Outcome focused	A problem statement that is clearly expressed in outcomes, not activities or intermediate outputs	
Measurable	A problem statement that is specific and measurable wherever possible	
Decision-maker values	A problem statement that explicitly addresses the decision-maker's values and boundaries, including the accuracy needed and the scale of aspirations	
Creative flexibility	A problem statement that is structured to all sufficient scope for creativity and unexpected results because too narrowly scoped problems can artificially constrain solutions	
Organizational level	A problem statement that is solved at the highest level possible and works for the organization as a whole, not just a locally optimized one	

5. Use Tool 1.2: Project Prioritization Matrix to assess where your idea fits on the scale. If possible, do this exercise in a team or with a partner to assess and rate all projects against each other, and make a recommendation for which one to move forward when. Write up and share your observations and learning experiences from this exercise.

Tool 1.1: Screening Projects for Amenability

To assess whether your project idea is likely amenable to an analytics solution and can add value to your firm, please follow the steps outlined here.

1. Create a clear picture of your project and make sure you can describe it simply and clearly with a focus on action. Write it in the space here.

   _____

   _____

   _____

   _____

   _____

2. Rate each of the following questions on a scale of 1 to 5, with 1 being no way and 5 being yes absolutely and 3 being neutral. Circle (or click on) the best answer.

   a. **Business impact.** Is this problem one with the potential for significant business impact if solved?

1	2	3	4	5

   b. **Data availability.** Do you have easy access to quality data that can help solve this analytics problem with known analytics approaches?

1	2	3	4	5

   c. **Stable environment.** Is the data you have access to likely to be consistent to similar data you expect in the future?

1	2	3	4	5

   d. **Data culture.** To what degree does your organization trust data and data-driven solutions?

1	2	3	4	5

   e. **Executive support.** Are your executives supporters willing to use their leadership position and political capital to lobby for and support this project from start to finish?

1	2	3	4	5

3. Add up your score for each of these questions. Write it here: _____

4. Review where your score fits on Table 1.2 and determine if the idea is worth taking to the next step to project prioritization.

Table 1.2 Scoring Project Amenability

Score	Rating	Sage Advice
23 to 25	Outstanding!	Run, do not walk, to your colleagues and recommend exploring this idea.
20 to 22	Very Good!	Tread cautiously because you may have a winner. But first check whether there are any fatal flaws, where one of the questions has a score below 3. If so, carefully review if there is a way to improve that score before continuing. Otherwise please discuss the idea with appropriate colleagues because a very low score in even one area can be fatal to your project's success.
17 to 19	Deeper Consideration	Check if you have scores of 4 or 5 for executive support or business impact. If so, dig deeper before walking away to see if there is a way to salvage the project. If those scores are 3 or lower, consider whether it is time to move on.
14 to 16	Lifeline	Notice whether executive support is at 4 or 5 for this project. If so, call in a lifeline from a few friends to see if you missed anything before trying to shelve the project in a politically correct way.
13 or lower	Out of Luck	Note your unlucky number and try to find a more suitable project that can meet similar or better business objectives. Also, seek strong executive support.

Tool 1.2: Project Prioritization Matrix

Here we introduce a tool and framework to help you prioritize among your good potential analytics projects. To use the tool, first go through the following steps:

1. **Identify must-dos.** Determine if this is a must-do project. If so, categorize it as a foundational must-do project and write it in the foundational must-do box.

2. **Estimate likelihood of success.** Assess the likelihood of success for each project under consideration because not all projects will be successful. It does not have to be 100%, because some projects promise enough value to warrant taking a risk. Your task is to balance these factors so you are always bringing value to the organization. A thoughtfully created scale of 1 to 10 can help sort your projects.

3. **Quantify visibility.** Take note that to build a data culture you need quantifiable, visible business impact. Focusing on these properties improves the likelihood of action resulting from a project. Engage your team in quantifying the business impact using established key metrics or KPIs. Doing so will increase visibility and trust. Does a project have these properties? Once you have some numeric estimates, standardize them to a graphable scale, such as the 1–10 scale mentioned previously.

4. **Estimate speed to value.** Determine how long it will take to start seeing value from a project. This estimate can depend on a number of factors. To speed it up, consider including the use of fast iterative development methodologies, such as agile analytics. Whatever the source, do your best estimation. If it is quick it will be more visible, so add a few points to your visibility score. Deduct a few points if there is a longer time to value.

5. **Seek synergy.** Review each potential project to look for synergies. Does doing one project make doing other good projects more feasible? If so, you can estimate the collective time savings (time to impact) on other projects and the increase in visible impact and add it to this project as a synergy bonus, which could lift or slide it to another level.

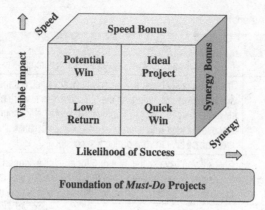

Figure 1.4 Analytics Project Prioritization Matrix

6. **Graph.** Take the scores on visible impact and likelihood of success and graph them on the core 2 × 2 matrix as shown here. Next, add a bonus or penalty if appropriate by sliding or lifting a potential project if there is significant synergy or speed.

7. **Assess project location.** See where each project ranks on your scale in Figure 1.4, which is designed to help prioritize viable analytics projects.

Based on where your projects land on this matrix, you can prioritize them with this list:

- **Must-do.** Start with the must-do projects, but beyond those the following categories can be quite helpful.

- **Ideal project.** Note whether projects deliver high impact in a short time. They should be prioritized very highly.

- **Quick win.** Consider projects that can give some value very quickly. They can be useful to build success stories and make allies by helping solve their annoying problems quickly, even if not as deeply as other projects. They are often worth doing early on to build momentum.

- **Potential wins.** Remember there are often longer-term strategic projects that are quite important for the business, but they take a greater amount of time to demonstrate value. They are important, but consider completing a few projects with faster value to help maintain support for these other types of problems.

- **Low returns.** Consider that these projects are often not worth your doing because they provide low value for your time, so they are best discarded.

NOTES

1. https://www.statistics.com/type-iii-err/
2. https://www.hivetracks.com/post/2022-hivetracks-outlook
3. F. Davis, *Perceived Usefulness, Perceived Ease of Use, and User Acceptance of Information Technology* (Minnesota: Management Information Systems Research Center, 1989), pp. 319–340.
4. E. Hassler, P. MacDonald, J. Cazier, and J. Wilkes, "The Sting of Adoption: The Technology Acceptance Model (TAM) with Actual Usage in a Hazardous Environment," *Journal of Information Systems Applied Research* 14, no. 4 (2021): 13–20. https://jisar.org/2021-14/n4/JISARv14n4p13.html.

5. L. Cech, J. A. Cazier, and A. B. Roberts, "Data Analytics in the Hardwood Industry: The Impact of Automation and Optimization on Profits, Quality, and the Environment," *International Journal of Business Analytics* 1, no. 4 (2014): 16–33.

6. M. J. Wooldridge, *A Brief History of Artificial Intelligence: What It Is, Where We Are, and Where We Are Going* (New York: Flatiron Books, 2021).

7. F. Davis, R. Bagozzi, and P. Warshaw, "User Acceptance of Computer Technology: A Comparison of Two Theoretical Models," *Management Sciences* 35, no. 8 (1989): 982–1003.

8. Uday Kulkarni, "Customer Relationship Management at Capital One," Arizona State University MS-ISM Program (2019).

9. https://gizmodo.com/amazon-amazon-prime-warehouse-workers-1849920947

10. https://www.goodreads.com/quotes/449969-a-problem-well-stated-is-a-problem-half-solved

11. Roger Hoerl, Diego Kuonen, and Thomas C. Redman, "Framing Data Science Problems the Right Way from the Start," *MIT Sloan Management Review* (April 14, 2022).

12. Uday Kulkarni, "Customer Relationship Management at Capital One."

13. F. Benford, "The Law of Anomalous Numbers," *Proceedings of the American Philosophical Society* 78 (1938): 551–572.

14. Andrew Scott, Ed Hassler, Giovanni Formato, Max A. S. Rünzel, James Wilkes, Awad Hassan, and Joseph Cazier, "Data Mining Hive Inspections: More Frequently Inspected Honey Bee Colonies Have Higher Overwinter Survival Rates," *Journal of Apicultural Research* (July 2023): 1–9. https://doi.org/10.1080/00218839.2023.2232145

15. https://www.goodreads.com/quotes/31286-efficiency-is-doing-the-thing-right-effectiveness-is-doing-the

TASK **2**

The Team

BUILDING A WINNING ANALYTICS TEAM

A shortage of good analytics talent is often the weakest link in many analytics projects. You may have heard that data scientists were named as having the "sexiest job of the 21st century" in a well-cited *Harvard Business Review* article[1] due to their high demand, ability to add value, and the difficulty in finding them. Data scientists, analysts, data engineers, and similar flavors of dedicated analytics professionals have a critical role to play in doing the analytics that businesses need to succeed, and they are often hard to recruit and retain.

Yet, as discussed in Task 0: Analytics Leadership, for analytics to take hold and succeed in a business, it takes more than a team of data scientists. It takes analytics-minded talent at many levels in the organization to truly succeed in this arena. Recall the McKinsey report,[2] which we referenced, that signaled a shortage of 250,000 data scientists and an order of magnitude larger (2 to 4 million) shortage of data savvy business leaders to lead and support their organizational analytics efforts.

In order to succeed in analytics, we must think about teams more broadly than just the technical team. Yes, there are many data scientists, engineers, analysts, and others who play a role in the mix. But we start with a broader view of the team by going deeper into the Pleines's minimal viable team, which you need for analytics to succeed. In the next section, Dr. Rudi Pleines, head of business transformation at ABB Robotics, provides the definition of the minimal viable team.

Pleines's Minimal Viable Team

Pleines breaks the team down to a minimum of at least one member of each of three categories needed for each analytics project. These categories include an executive champion who sponsors and supports the project politically and financially and who also drives change to improve the business area they are responsible for by making sure the analytics is integrated into a clear process, and at least one technical team member who does the analytics. These are the minimum mandatory team members who are needed for a team to succeed.

Executive Champion

The executive champion may or may not be a senior executive team member. However, they must have some management role and sufficient authority to act as an executive champion. Their role is to find resources, remove obstacles, communicate the analytics value broadly, and enforce adoption and use. However, this alone is not enough. They must also lead by example and actively demonstrate the use of analytics and request/enforce the change through the use of the analytics. In short, their role is to drive change at every level of the organization.

Although all of the roles enumerated in these sections are critical components in doing analytics, the executive champion has an outsized role in analytics success. No project will succeed for long without the support of the executive team, and the executive champion helps acquire and keep their support throughout the entire analytics process. Let us take a moment to understand their key functions.

- **Vision.** Executive champions need to guide and provide vision for analytics projects to ensure they ultimately add value to the organization. This function is critical in the development and ongoing review of the business problem through its final implementation. The executive champion helps engage the various business process owners needed for the project to succeed effectively.

- **Drive.** Beyond vision, executive champions need to actively drive the project forward, keeping it on task and fueling it with their energy and resources. They need to actively provide the support and muscle to make sure things move in the direction most needed by the business to ensure value. The executive champion helps keep the various business leaders focused on succeeding and moving forward.

- **Change management.** Executives have the power to drive change. If they do not use that power, little will actually change. They need to look for implementable solutions that make a real difference in the business and then ensure the business uses them. The executive champion communicates the results and helps drive change throughout the organization with the help of other business process owners.

The executive champions have a key role at the beginning of a project by providing vision, in the middle by removing obstacles and driving the project forward, and at the end by making sure the project gets implemented and used by the organization. Figure 2.1 summarizes the executive champion's role at each phase of the project.

The role of the executive champion is so important that Dr. Karl Kempf, who identified the five manageable tasks and is head of a large analytics team at Intel, shared how a majority of his time is spent working with executive champions. Kempf finds it essential to spend considerable time continuously building and maintaining support, listening to their priorities, making sure the team stays in sync with them, and helping these executive champions see and understand the possibilities of what analytics can do.

This is the area where I failed. Maybe not the only place, but it was the biggest cause. I failed to build and maintain proper support from potential executive champions in my organization. We had plenty of strong support outside our organization—great

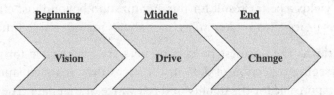

Figure 2.1 Role of the Executive Champion

sponsors and supporters lined up and good technical staff members ready to do their jobs—but I lost the support of those willing to defend our analytics efforts. But when one executive decided to kill our project, for mostly political reasons, without another strong executive to champion our project in that environment, it did not have enough support to continue and died.

This lack of an executive champion was partly due to leadership changes, because the person I usually worked with, who had always guided, championed, and supported our work in the past, moved to another position, and a new person took their place in a temporary appointment. We did not have that history of shared success that builds strong supporters, and I neglected to build that type of relationship quick enough or communicate proactively with other stakeholders to bring together broader allies. When that support was not there and the politics shifted, regardless of the prestige and value of the project, it died.

What was much worse was seeing several of my team members lose their jobs, having their work shut down, and shouldering the impact on the broader international team of supporters and friends who were let down and hurt by the failure after they had invested so much to support it. Seeing their loss and disappointment in the failure was the hardest part, especially as my team, our supporters, and allies scattered to the winds, never to come together the same way again.

I should have prepared better, built better relationships, and paid more attention to the politics to maintain that executive support, but I did not. Perhaps you already know about the importance of an executive champion, but if not, hopefully my story will be helpful to you in some way. The important message is that it takes more than doing good work, more than creating value, more than generating great ideas. It takes forming a team of allies, being politically aware, and especially building and maintaining strong executive support. Interestingly, all of the senior people I interviewed knowingly spoke about this problem. They must have learned this lesson faster than me, but my hope is that now you will learn it, too.

Business Process Owners

Business process owners and their staff members are the ones who perform the core functions of the business. This work might be in accounting, finance, marketing, manufacturing, supply chain, IT, or any other core business function. For many of them, analytics can help them work more efficiently or more effectively and sometimes both. Efficiently means helping them do what they are already doing quicker and cheaper in a more automated way. Effectively means helping them do it better or differently in some way that yields a better result for the organization beyond just efficiency.

The business process team's key roles in analytics include these functions:

- **Collect data.** The business process owners are responsible for participating in and overseeing collection of data in the areas they manage, and they are ultimately responsible for the quality and relevance of that data. They need to work collaboratively with the analytics team and executives to make sure that the collected data is useful, relevant, and available for analysis and use.

- **Support data cleansing.** Although the technical team will do most of the data cleaning, they have to know what needs to be cleaned and have verified that it has been cleaned in a business relevant and useful way. The business process owners are often the only ones in the organization that truly have deep enough domain knowledge to know what the data means, what is relevant to the job, and how to make it useful. They must actively participate in this process for the data to be in the right form, quality, and shape to be useful.

- **Sense check results.** It takes deep domain knowledge to sense check the applicability, quality, and relevance of results. This is more than business knowledge; it is the deep technical process knowledge that is nearly impossible to get without years of working in this area to truly understand what is happening and seeing if it makes sense. Even if the analyst was right and the business process owner's team wrong in some way about the results, they will never adopt unless that discrepancy is resolved. It is not only making sure the results make sense and are useful but also building trust in those results.

- **Design and adapt training protocols.** Every highly skilled business process has its own vocabulary, culture, and understanding that outsiders without that training and experience struggle to understand and integrate with. Even if the analytics team were explaining the analytics in the right way, a simple way that many could understand, without linking it to the vocabulary and culture of that process, adoption will be slowed due to the extra training friction in getting up to speed on the new protocols. If the training is adapted to the business process owner's vocabulary and way of thinking, there will be less friction, more trust, and quicker understanding, and adoption will be more likely. Thus, the business process owners team should actively, collaboratively help design any training materials and related protocols to minimize the friction to learning the updated processes that integrate analytics tools.

- **Adopt.** The business process owner's team are the ones that need to change by adopting the new or updated systems with the analytics. If they do not change and adopt, little, if any, value will be created, yet costs will still have been incurred, leading to a failure to generate a significant business return, which will likely generate a negative reaction and increased resistance to analytics.

Most of the value from analytics comes from improving business processes that are owned and managed by the business process owners. If, as noted, business process owners do not change, there will be little impact from the analytics initiative on the organization. For this reason, it is the responsibility of the technical team to take time to really understand the business process owners, what they do, and how analytics can offer improvement in a way that fits into the current process. If the technical team pushes for radical change immediately, it is likely to be rejected; but if they listen, learn, and help business process owners do what they need to do better and easier, the analytics is more likely to succeed.

The analytics team should see where business process owners get their answers now and see how to improve that process. However, just because they come up with something analytically better, that does not mean it will be adopted. The earlier and more effectively the technical team can engage the business process owners, building trust and support, the more likely projects are to succeed.

Likewise, the role of the executive champion is also critical here. They have the ear of the team that leads the organization and often controls key parts of it. They can help manage the process by using their power and influence in an appropriate way to encourage adoption and change. The more effective this collaboration is, the more likely it is that future projects will also have a chance to succeed.

Skylar Ritchie, a data scientist in the financial services industry, shared a story about working with business process owners. Ritchie was asked to build and automate a model for one of the financial support functions of the organization. The data scientist carefully listened to what the analytics director wanted, and they both attended several meetings with the leaders of the affected divisions to understand the process, how it worked, and what needed to be done to add value. They even reviewed the written documentation and procedural manuals for the affected tasks to make sure they understood them, and crafted the models accordingly.

Next they built a great system the executives said they loved, and pushed it out to the business process owners. As they monitored for the impact, they were both surprised and disappointed to learn it was not being used, at all. They did not, at the time, understand why. They checked on a few things, made sure their models were right, and reviewed the written procedures and notes from the division leader. They could not find anything wrong.

Finally, they started talking to the business process owners about it. At first, the business process owners did not want to share anything. Fortunately, Ritchie is one of the friendliest, most personable, and disarming data scientists I know. The business process owners eventually warmed up to Ritchie and they started sharing why they had not adopted and integrated the new system into the business process they owned and managed. There were two problems the analytics team had not anticipated. The first was the process that was written down, which was the one the leaders of the division thought was being used was great in theory, but did not work in practice, especially as market conditions had evolved, making the original documentation outdated.

Over time, the business process owners had adapted and improved their processes to handle an increased load more efficiently, to account for new rules and regulations, to integrate new helpful information into the process, and to adapt to a changing environment. These adjustments were exactly what an executive would want them to do. However, they were so busy doing it, surviving, they had not updated the process manuals, and the senior leaders they interviewed had not kept up with or recalled the details for all of the changes.

Why would they? It was working well, better in fact than the old process, and updating manuals does not always feel like an understaffed department's highest priority. Richie was able to address this situation, after listening to them and building a nonthreatening relationship. Once Richie's analytics team finally understood the new process that had been developed, the one that had not been written down, and saw it was actually better, they updated the models and process flow and finally had a system that followed the actual decision-making process instead of the written decision process.

At this point, the business process owners encountered the second problem: their employees were still not using the new analytics system, at least not as much as was expected. When the analytics team demonstrated it, everyone agreed it seemed to fit the process. There was no indication it was wrong in any way; the business process owners had now agreed they had the right process and it would be helpful. They were using it, just not as much as desired, with no obvious problems they could find, even with the full support of the executive champions.

It might have been left there with them always wondering what went wrong, when the relationships and trust that Ritchie had built with the business process owners came to their rescue again. One of the business process owner's staff members, confidentially, shared with Ritchie that several in the department were secretly afraid that the newer, better, more efficient model could do what they had been doing, only better, and they were resisting out of fear of losing their jobs. Now it made sense to Ritchie why the business process owner's staff members were so reluctant to adopt and use the system, even though, or maybe especially because, it was better.

With this insight, Ritchie was able to reach out again to the executive champion and the business process owners to find a way to address their concerns. The executive champion gave the business process owners' staff members some assurances, recognized their great work in improving the old processes, and assigned the area additional responsibilities. As the business process owners' staff members felt more understood, were recognized for their contributions in improving the process that also helped build an even better model, and felt more security in their jobs, they fully integrated and used the model and the company achieved the full expected benefits with a successful project.

Technical Team Members

The technical and analytics teams' roles are to work together to build a solution that the executive champion desires and that the business process owners will use in a way that adds value. Recall that although there is often significant overlap, the technical team generally focuses on supporting operations and building new tools and the analytics team focuses on discovery and designing more valuable processes for the business. The technical team's collective role is to do the following tasks:

- **Project consultation.** The technical team will often be called in early, and should be called in early, to review and evaluate ideas from executive champions, business process owners, and others that could be done. The technical team should provide a realistic technical view on the potential project, including how achievable it is, the cost, the infrastructure needed, potential data and security risks, and resources required to do it, including staff members and skills needed. This accurate assessment is very important to the project prioritization and feasibility process discussed in Task 1: The Problem.

- **Design.** Design a technical solution for an analytics project/task that adds value by improving, enhancing, or replacing a current business process, or, sometimes, creating a new one. This takes much more than just technical skill; it takes collaboration with those who desire it (executive champion) and those who will use it (business process owners) to design and build something useful. Yes, of course they need technical and analytical skills, too, but without the full participation and guidance of the other groups, their efforts are likely to be wasted.

- **Ensure efficiency.** If the new system is more work than the old or current system, it will encounter resistance, even if it is better. The technical team needs to make sure the system they build is efficient and integrates well in the business process owner's team processes and avoids extra or unnecessary work.

- **Avoid errors.** Dr. Pleines has observed that errors are as effective as poison in killing otherwise valuable projects. Avoiding errors is a very high priority, even if it may delay the project, and it is more likely worth it to take time to eliminate them to enhance the chances of successful adoption and use.

- **Provide technical support.** As much as errors need to be avoided, there will always be some issues the technical team will need to address, especially during the early phases of adoption. Even if everything is going perfectly, updates will be needed as systems evolve and technology changes, people will move on to other roles and functions and new ones hired, regulations and data needs will evolve, all of which will require ongoing technical support forever. Good documentation throughout the entire design and build process can make this burden much easier for both the technical and business process owner's teams.

As a way to scale and increase efficiency, several specialized technical roles are now emerging, partly due to the evolving nature of technology, which requires more specialization for different tools as the technological universe expands. These advances make it inefficient and impractical for any one person to truly master them all.

The other reason is to support more expensive and harder-to-find deep data scientists by bringing in more supporting roles to do aspects of the analytics process, such as cleaning and preparing data, building common dashboards and reports, and implementing robust solutions across the organization. This approach leverages the data scientist's time and talent to focus on more advanced modeling and discovery efforts and scale their impact across the organization much more quickly and efficiently.

The names for these critical support roles change quickly and will continue to evolve. Although it is and will continue to be impossible to keep up with and cover them all, here are the most common ones:

- **Data engineer.** The data engineer focuses on the data in a very technical way. Their job is to make sure the data flows freely and securely through the organization, and especially to the data scientists, in a trustworthy and usable way.

- **Data analyst.** The data analyst is skilled at building reports, dashboards, and basic models based on organizational data. They typically have a good understanding of business needs, enabling them to provide immediate value to the organization with quick answers to common questions using readily available historical data.

- **Implementation engineer.** The implementation engineer has a deep technical knowledge of how to use information technology across the organization, coupled with expertise in model deployment and optimization. They focus on operationalizing proven models across the organization at scale to maximize value and impact.

Together, these roles create efficiency and scalability by enabling the data scientists to be more productive so they can focus on their unique area of contribution. Whereas in the past up to 80% of a data scientist's time might have been spent gathering and cleaning data, much of that work can be automated and supported by a good data engineer. Data analysts cover common and urgent business questions, letting the data scientist focus on deeper questions and discover more ways to add value, enabling the implementation engineer to help deploy and optimize the solutions at scale across the entire organization.

Although there are other roles that can and often do come into play, such as a project manager to coordinate everyone's activities, these roles currently serve the three most essential technical functions in supporting the data scientist. By preparing the data at the front end, meeting immediate business needs in the middle, and implementing scalable solutions at the end, they all play a critical role in growing the organization's analytics efforts.

Even in cases when the data scientist could do all of these functions, and might do them in the beginning, it is not efficient or productive for them to continue these tasks for long. Their job satisfaction will wane and their impact will be diminished if they do not have time to use their core skills where they can add the most value, potentially leading to slower discoveries and even to high turnover. The team should strive to include each of these roles as soon as they have proven the value of that analytics stream and reached a level of maturity and analytics acceptance to justify it.

It Takes All Three

All three groups are required to work together for success. Sometimes more are needed, as discussed in the section on contingent team members, but executive champions, business process owners, and the technical team are required for businesses to realize value from the analytics project. Here is what happens when any team is left out:

- **No technical team.** The project will remain a dream that cannot be fulfilled without the team with the skills to build it. The executive champion and business process owners may identify a valuable area that could be improved, they may even greatly desire that it be done, but they simply cannot build it without technical teams doing the work.

- **No business process owner.** The executive champion and technical teams may build a very nice, advanced, and visually appealing system that will never be adopted because it does not fit into the business process owner's way of doing business. Many important features and processes will likely be missed. Even in the case when the new system is built perfectly it will still likely be rejected because there will be no buy-in or trust from the business process owners' team, who will resist the system because they were excluded from the process.

- **No executive champion.** Sometimes a technical team member and a business process owner or member of their team come together with a valuable idea for improving their business processes. This can be a great start to a valuable project. However, if there is no executive champion found to support and, well, champion the project, there is still a high risk of failure to generate business value. They need the executive champion to provide funding and allocate staff members for the project, which is likely to run out or disappear without these resources. They will also run into the roadblock of not having sufficient authority to implement and use the project.

All three groups—executive champions, business process owners, and the technical team—are required for a successful project, which is why it is called the *minimal viable team*. If there is no executive sponsor to champion change, little will happen. If there is no business process owner open to change, it will be resisted and little will actually change. Yes, the technical team is needed, but it needs to exist in a larger environment where others are ready for change and willing and able to apply the insights from analytics. If there is no change or business improvement, it is hard to define the analytics project as a success even if potentially useful models and insights were generated, as Ritchie's story illustrates.

Contingent Team Members

Next, Pleines's minimal viable team includes contingent team members, who may be required for certain kinds of projects. The first is an outsourced external partner who provides needed expertise, a faster turnaround, or enhanced scalability depending on project needs and the skills and availability of your internal team. The second is a legal team who reviews potentially sensitive initiatives. Note that even when a legal review is not required, an ethical review is an essential part of the analytics process that should be built into the planning phase for every project. This process is discussed in detail with Task 7: Responsible Analytics.

Beyond the Minimum

Pleines's minimal viable team is a great way to think about who is essential to the analytics process. Indeed, it is difficult to envision many analytics projects succeeding without this talent base. As organizations mature and seek to grow their analytics functions, additional roles beyond the minimum and contingent team members become important. Let us discuss a few additional options of helpful roles as the organization scales analytics.

Analytics Translator

During the interview for this book, Bill Franks, chief analytics officer for the International Institute for Analytics, shared a personal passion and insight regarding the importance of having an effective analytics translator.

The analytics translator has emerged with a new and critical role as a catalyst in helping analytics expand and succeed across the organization, and even in society. These effective communicators bridge the gap between the business and analytics sides of the organization. They clearly communicate the business needs to the analytics team in an actionable way they can translate into an analytics plan and effective model. They also share a vision with the executive champions and business process owners of what can, and cannot, be done in a way that shapes strategy and effectively prioritizes objectives effectively and communicates results in a way that leads to scalable implementation.

These change agents can greatly accelerate both the effectiveness and the adoption of analytics across the organization. However, they can only be effective if they have a deep understanding of each side and credibility with both. Consequently, they should be in senior positions with experience on both sides, delivering results the others can believe in. This role is critical in an organization that is approaching and striving for analytics maturity. As such, it should be filled with a senior highly paid resource and not a junior, low-paid resource.

An analytics translator should never be confused with a project manager, which is a separate and distinct function and a more junior role to what is needed to be an effective translator. Sometimes the role of analytics translator is filled by former executives with a deep understanding of what analytics can do and how it works. Other times a senior analytics team lead who has a deep understanding of the business and solid reputation with the business side of the organization is a good option. Occasionally, a trusted consultant or other expert can fill this role. However, they are always an essential part of scaling and growing the analytics function across the organization.

The Analytics Team Summary

Many team members from inside and often outside the company need to come together with a common vision for analytics to succeed. Table 2.1 summarizes the key players.

Table 2.1 The Analytics Team

Title	Description	Role
Pleines's Minimal Viable Team		
Executive champion	Powerful executive with influence and resources	The executive champion provides vision that aligns with key business goals, removes roadblocks to drive the project to its conclusion, and ensures change takes root to achieve lasting impact.
Business process owner	Person responsible for a core business function, like accounting, manufacturing, or sales	The business process owner needs to implement the analytics in their system and change what they are doing based on the results. It is essential to include them and build to make their tasks easier and their work more effective.
Technical team member(s)	The person or team doing the actual analytics work	The technical team member provides high-quality, relevant insight that leads to action to improve performance.
Contingent Members for Pleines's Minimal Viable Team		
External partner	Outside experts, consultants, or developers	The external partner brings in needed expertise, staff members, or other resources to help build and scale the analytics and its impact.
Legal team	Qualified expert(s) in relevant legal and ethical areas	The legal team reviews the analytics to help foresee and avoid legal or ethical problems. It is a growing concern today with diverse international laws and hidden biases in black box analytics and legacy data.
Expanded Team for Growth and Maturity		
Specialized technical roles	Diverse technical experts to support the data scientist and analytics process	The specialized technical roles expand the quality and productivity of the data scientist by supporting them on the front, middle, and end of the project. Typically these roles include data engineers, business analysts, and implementation engineers, though titles are multiplying.
Project manager	A project manager with an understanding of both business and analytics	The project manager coordinates team members, executive champions, and business process owners; manages resources; and oversees schedules and budgets. This role is not the same as an analytics translator.
Analytics translator	Senior leader with expertise and credibility in both analytics and business	The analytics translator communicates the power and potential of analytics to the business, aligns business needs with analytics capabilities, and steers around business and analytics pitfalls and traps. This role is not the same as a project manager.

Figure 2.2 provides a visual summary of the most common analytics team and those who support them. The functions in the three circles constitute the Pleines's minimal viable team. The analytics translator is critical in helping them understand one another and work together more effectively.

Now that we know the important players on the analytics team, we turn to building and managing your team. Although the advice and framework in the next section can be helpful to all members of the analytics team, it is especially critical to the technical team doing the analytics work.

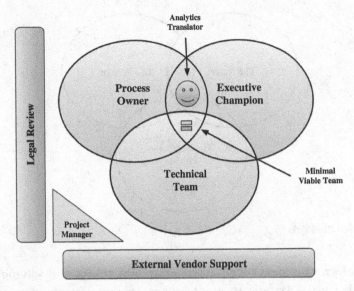

Figure 2.2 The Typical Analytics Team

BUILDING AND MANAGING YOUR TEAM

The first step in building and managing your team is understanding them: who they are, what they can do, and why they do it. From there, you can more readily find the right people, keep them focused, and help them succeed. We start with why people do analytics and how understanding their motivation can help you manage and retrain them.

Why People Do Analytics

There are many reasons why people might do or become involved with analytics. Let us call this their *analytics orientation* or the *primary* way they approach and think about analytics. Knowing an analytics team member's analytics orientation provides insight into how they can best help with analytics in the organization and how to manage them in a way that keeps them engaged and focused on project success while improving the retention of a scarce talent resource.

Although there is some overlap, most people's analytics orientation falls into one of three categories: the native, the seeker, and the businessperson, as seen in Figure 2.3. What follows is a brief introduction of each type.

- **The native.** For the native, data and analytics is who they are. They love its fit with their skills, abilities, temperament, and personality. They often take joy in cleaning, managing, and optimizing data processes and/or analyzing data, and finding useful answers to relevant questions. For the native, managing the flow of data and analyzing it is as natural to them as a violinist playing the violin. The topic of analysis is less important to them than the craft of doing it right.

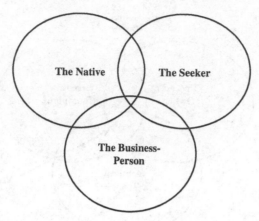

Figure 2.3 Analytics Orientation

- **The seeker.** The seeker loves discovering new things and solving problems in innovative ways. Data is an input for sensemaking, discovery, and knowledge generation. For the seeker, the topic of inquiry invigorates their natural curiosity and is central to the experience.
- **The businessperson.** The businessperson sees data and analytics as a tool to have a measurable impact on their organization's performance by helping them make better decisions with data and persuade others to take action. For them, analytics benefits their company and them in a direction they are already traveling. For the businessperson, arriving at their destination is their key driver and the topic or process to get there is much less relevant than the impact on their goals.

By managing the team in a way that takes advantage of the strengths of each contributor's analytics orientation, while staying focused on achieving a useful business purpose, executive champions are more likely to achieve their business purpose while also reaping several other benefits.

I had the pleasure of working with and getting to know several incredibly talented, successful, and inspiring people working in or near to data science, and having an incredibly positive impact on the world, from each category. The following list includes many who agreed to be interviewed for this book. I would classify a few of these experts into these categories for their primary orientation, which I share here to illustrate and personalize the type.

Native Experts
- **Josh Belliveau.** Belliveau, a principal solutions engineer at Tableau, is one of the most naturally talented technologists I know. I have always been impressed with the way Belliveau can mentally envision entire systems, how they fit together, what could go wrong, and how they can be used for operational excellence. To me, Belliveau appears to be a classic technical native.
- **Stephen Kimel.** Kimel, now a data scientist at Red Hat, was one of the most naturally gifted students I met, with a special faculty for math and music and a

deep set curiosity to understand everything. I would classify Kimel as a mathematical native, who is also talented in many other areas.

- **Dr. Wayne Thompson.** Thompson, former chief analytics officer for SAS, is highly gifted in math and coding, and with entire systems; he has developed analytics products and even holds a couple of patents. Thompson can solve almost any problem as well or better than anyone I know, with a heavy focus on the applied and practical side of analytics. I believe Thompson embodies the very best that natives have to offer.

Seeker Experts

- **Lindsay Marshall.** Marshall, director of data and analytics at Gilbane Building Company, mixes being a trained experimental psychologist and talented data scientist. Marshall loves to ask why, always seeks to understand things, and strongly believes in discovery, and searches for "truth through proof."
- **LeAnne Hill.** Hill is an analytics manager at FORVIS LLP. I first met Hill in a graduate class I was teaching in analytics. Hill was a liberal arts major with an incredibly strong desire to make the world a better place and also had an aptitude with technology, financing college by repairing computers in IT support. Hill switched to analytics after seeing its potential for helping us discover ways to benefit humanity. Hill is currently leading efforts to understand and manage risks related to climate change.
- **Dr. Beverly Wright.** Wright, head of data science at Burtch Works, is a lifelong, self-described "truth seeker." It is one of the main reasons Wright does analytics and loves it so much. Wright leads many "analytics for good" initiatives, including for INFORMS and the State of Georgia, and goes out of her way to always be honest about findings, even when it is politically unpopular.

Businessperson Experts

- **Tim Rahschulte.** Rahschulte has proven to be an inspiring businessperson with the vision to see what is possible and the skill to execute well by driving action to success. I have often been impressed with Rahschulte's ability to blend careful listening and data in a holistic way that advances and motivates others to move effectively in a better direction.
- **David Houser.** Houser is a very accomplished businessperson with decades of experience in technology and logistics; he is also a good friend. Among other things, Houser has a special fondness for anything international and a great respect for all cultures and practices. Houser also has a keen ability to stay focused and move the needle with incredibly impressive business results, whatever the setting.
- **Rudi Pleines.** Pleines is one of the smartest, most practical, and strategic business thinkers I know, and he is a natural leader, especially when it comes to implementing change. Pleines loves and understands technology and analytics and approaches it with deep domain knowledge and practical business understanding that amazes me every single time.

I could name many others in each category, but these people really personify the types of analytics orientation for me. It is worth paying attention to the behaviors of people to understand their analytics orientation.

When analytics team members are able to fulfill some of their inner desires consistent with their analytics orientation, they have greater job satisfaction, higher engagement, and lower job turnover. This benefit lowers business costs and improves quality and innovation. The result is that the analytics team members work more effectively with each other and with the business side, thus reducing friction and increasing analytics success. A particular best practice for seekers is having time set aside for them to innovate during regular business hours, as many tech companies do. Sure, all orientations like this, but seekers crave it.

For example, my assistants and volunteer reviewers for this book, Sai Kollaparthi and Keerthana Bandlamudi, are a self-identified seeker and native, respectively. Both of whom have been incredibly helpful to me and I believe will be very successful in their careers. I always think carefully before assigning Kollaparthi or Bandlamudi a task and consider their analytics orientation, which I think has led to better work and learning for both of them, more loyalty, and better performance for me and our work together.

Conversely, there are dangers in letting people's primary orientations run too wild and going off the rails by focusing only on their natural tendencies and ignoring business needs. It is therefore important to understand and manage both the strengths and weaknesses of team members by ensuring proper alignment and knowing where to focus your management efforts.

Strengths and Weaknesses

A good analytics team needs the strengths of all three analytics orientations to perform at their best. However, it is not just their presence that matters. They need to be managed in a way that takes full advantage of their strengths while mitigating the impact of their weaknesses. Even though each individual is unique in their own way, here are some of their common strengths and weaknesses.

The Native

Some common strengths:

- **Operational excellence.** This group sees analytics as a process from beginning to end. They know where the data comes from, how it is transformed, and what is done with it. They seek to optimize and improve the process for efficiency and impact.
- **Topic flexibility.** This group loves the act of doing analytics well. The topic is less relevant as long as it is a good fit for their skill set. Thus this group can be deployed on a variety of problems others might find boring or mundane, as long as they can do it well.

- **Deep knowledge.** This group gravitates to depth over breadth. When they commit to something, they go all the way and seek to master it. They may not know everything, but what they do know can be relied on.
- **Quality focused.** This group enjoys the analytics journey and avoids taking shortcuts to get to the end. They are intrinsically motivated to do quality work and push back strongly when pressured to compromise.

Some common weaknesses:

- **Clear objectives.** Because this group favors excellence over creativity, they need to have clear direction. They execute well on projects, but their impact is largely determined by the directions given. Although they will push back on method or quality shortcuts, they generally do not do so when business objectives are clear and valuable.
- **Inflexibility.** More than any other group, they hate project changes once the project has begun. This challenge can mean missed opportunities when a new direction is actually needed. Some may perceive them as stubborn and unwilling to adapt.
- **Business communication.** This group tends to live deep in their technical and mathematical worlds. As such, they often struggle to communicate outside of that group, especially in business terms to executive champions and other stakeholders.

The Seeker

Some common strengths:

- **Visionary.** This group is often the first to spot new opportunities, maybe even before they are ripe for picking. Inherently, this vision often gives them a long-term focus with a view of many intermediate steps needed to get there.
- **Intrinsically motivated.** Although all these groups can be intrinsically motivated, this group is a little different in that they are driven by vision. When they catch the vision and see where it can go, they thrive and pursue it no matter how much the odds may be stacked against them.
- **Objectives over orders.** This group needs clear objectives and the freedom to reach them in their own way. They love to explore creative ways to meet objectives and often change direction in the middle of a project to deliver something more useful.

Some common weaknesses:

- **Boredom.** When the vision is lacking, they flail in the wind. A vision to make something better or discover something new is the key to their engagement. This boredom often leads them to jump to many areas, giving them great breadth but only a few areas that are truly deep.

- **Lost in quest.** Sometimes their vision exceeds current technological capabilities. They may be right about where things can and should go, but wrong about the timing and market readiness, leading them to struggle with implementation and kill projects too slowly, meaning they keep investing after the point of being able to get a reasonable return.
- **Strong boundaries.** Because of their need for vision, they can get distracted by something new, but that is out of scope. They need clear boundaries for the problem with lots of leeway in how to achieve it.

The Businessperson

Some common strengths:

- **Results driven.** This group never forgets about impact. They excel at strategic alignment of project outcomes with business goals.
- **Prioritization.** This group excels not just by aligning projects with business goals, but also by prioritizing when best to address which goals with specific projects by accounting for risks, budgets, and time constraints.
- **Implementation.** This group is generally the most likely to implement their project, not for technical reasons but because of its alignment with business goals.

Some common weaknesses:

- **Low tolerance for failure.** Because they want results, they tend to have a very low tolerance for failure. This weakness leads them to focus on short-term sure bets instead of game-changing advances, which they may kill too quickly.
- **Short cuts.** Because this group is most attuned to business pressures, including politics, they are also the most likely to take shortcuts and succumb to political pressure or groupthink.
- **Breadth and depth.** The trade-off for being so attuned with the business needs is that there is less time to go deeper and broader on the analytics side.

Alignment Advice

Here are some best practices in aligning your team, based on their analytics orientation.

Diversity

The most important advice is to ensure you have a diverse team, including in their analytics orientations. Together, they can naturally complement each other's strengths and weaknesses. Teams dominated by any one orientation can stagnate and lose adaptability and flexibility to meet changing business needs.

Leadership

Although you need all of them, some types of projects may need to be led by, or have more (or less) representation from, different orientations than others. For example, long-term technical projects with concrete objectives benefit when led by natives. Faster tactical level analytics benefit from the leadership of a businessperson, and long-term visionary or innovative projects benefit from seeker leadership.

Matched Support

It is important to ensure there is enough representation on each team to support the nature of the project. Mission-critical technical projects benefit from more natives. Dynamic tactical projects benefit from business orientations with strong native support and some seekers to keep them adaptable. Long-term visionary projects benefit from a healthy dose of seekers strongly supported by natives with regular consultations from businesspersons.

Review Audits

Seekers benefit from having natives review their technological ambitions and businesspersons review their impact. However, timing also matters. Be sure to give seekers a little space to run and envision what could be done first, then do a technical feasibility check. If that check looks good, give them a little more time to work on the business case with support from the businessperson orientation. Likewise, natives and businesspersons benefit from a visionary push from a seeker's review audit, which may prompt them to consider emerging alternatives.

Portfolio

Each organization should have a blend of mission critical, tactical, and visionary projects under way. The mix of these projects will vary with the type of organization and their level of analytics maturity. Not only does this blend help the business innovate, but it gives them a place to align their team members' orientation with the type of projects they do best, improving retention, performance, and job satisfaction.

Analytics Orientation Summary

Table 2.2 provides a summary for each of the primary analytics orientations, including what drives them, how to identify them, their common strengths and weaknesses, and specific advice for managing them better.

A person's inner analytics orientation matters to them and should matter to you, too, if you want to succeed in analytics. Given the short supply of analytics talent and high failure rate for analytics projects, managing retention, engagement, and analytics orientation can create a competitive advantage for your analytics team. Please consider these factors as you recruit, manage, and grow your analytics team. A more detailed description of the topic of analytics orientation is available in a research article I published with the International Institute for Analytics (IIA).[3]

Table 2.2 Common Characteristics and Advice for Each Analytics Orientation

	The Native	The Seeker	The Businessperson
Key Driver	*Excellence*	*Discovery*	*Results*
How to identify	• Maintains deep focus, hates interruptions • Dislikes changes • Asks for clear objectives • Loves math/technology • Stays focused on process • Embraces structure	• Is invigorated by the question • Will change for better question • Loves learning, very curious • Likes to tinker and experiment • Holds optimistic vision of future • Loves unknown solutions	• Likes known methods and tools • Will only change plan for better ROI • Always measures impact • Excels at prioritization • Seeks quick ROI • Focuses on known problems
Common strengths	• Strives for operational excellence • Has topic flexibility • Has deep knowledge in area • Enjoys clear directions • Handles routine tasks well • Stays quality focused	• Finds new opportunities • Is intrinsically motivated • Is engaged by the right project • Values objectives over direction • Loves the new and novel • Stays focused long term	• Is results driven • Values prioritization • Strives for strategic alignment • Looks for practical solutions • Manages implementation well • Stays focused short term
Common weaknesses	• Has method or tool inflexibility • Needs clear objectives • Needs assistance with business communication • Dislikes project changes • Favors depth over breadth	• Can get lost in the "quest" • Needs clear boundaries • Struggles with implementation • Succumbs to boredom with routine tasks • Favors breadth over depth	• Focuses on short-term gains • Misses out-of-the-box solutions • Has low tolerance for failure • Lacks deep tool skills • Can kill projects too quickly
Alignment advice	• Assign to concrete projects • Focus on core business • Provide stability and clarity • Have businessperson present • Allow to screen innovative ideas • Help develop technical depth	• Give space to dream and test • Validate impact as progress • Support with businessperson • Encourage to share vision • Give complex problems • Help develop breadth	• Lead tangible business projects • Allow to evaluate new projects, after some progress, for impact • Lead communication with business side • Engage in prioritization • Help deliver immediate value

MANAGING THE TECHNICAL TEAM

Many of the skills that executives and managers learned from leading other projects will help in leading analytics teams, but a few things will require additional attention due to the complexity and specialization of analytics work. Fortunately, several of the experts interviewed for this book shared helpful advice for managing the technical team, and their advice is summarized here.

Dr. Bill Disch on Job/Skill Alignment

The importance of aligning analytics orientation job goals and tasks was detailed previously in this chapter. Here, Dr. Bill Disch, a former chief analytics officer and now an analytics educator for Data Robot, adds another dimension regarding the importance of job tasks and skill alignment. Disch shared some experiences concerning dissatisfied analytics professionals because managers put them in the wrong category, leading many to quit or scale back in their commitment to work.

Because analytics can be a highly technical and complex area that takes deep specialization, your technical team will have spent years developing their skills and then continuing to invest significant time keeping up with technical advances and learning new techniques. Just like any business, they want a return on their investment of time and resources by being given the chance to use these new techniques in the field and keeping their skills sharp.

Because most of the people attracted to analytics tend to be very bright lifelong learners, they can usually succeed, for a short time, at tasks adjacent to their core area of expertise. However, they tend to become dissatisfied during prolonged periods of not being assigned to tasks in their core area of expertise and start to look around for opportunities to apply their hard-won skills elsewhere.

Disch was able to increase both job satisfaction and retention of the analytics team by carefully aligning them to their skills and hiring to match the organization's needs. Disch noted that many organizations relatively new to analytics do not really understand the different flavors of analytics professionals and how to align them with organizational needs, creating unnecessary expenses with productive bottlenecks in the analysis process by misaligning skills and task to be done.

Therefore, it is worth understanding a few of the broad areas that make up the technical team and common mindsets associated with them.

Although there are many titles associated with analytics, most of them fall into one of three core skill categories: technology, math, or business knowledge. A few so-called unicorns have skills in multiple areas, but even they tend to have a dominant core area. These areas are described here and represented in Figure 2.4:

- **Technology.** Technology enables analytics to be done and applied at scale. It takes many individuals with this background to succeed in analytics, and technology is the dominant background of many in the analytics space. However,

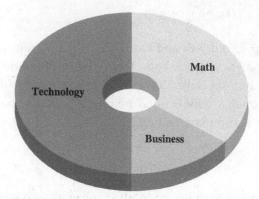

Figure 2.4 Common Analytics Talent Backgrounds

this space is very broad and specialized. Even within this space, there are many titles and backgrounds, and it is important to align their work with their specialty and interest as much as is practicable.

- **Math.** Math is another area central to the analysis technical team. These individuals generally use code and technology to build and apply very complex mathematical models to data at scale. This skill is enabled by technology, but the model is designed by those with a deep understanding of math, modeling, and solid data practices. Most individuals on the mathematical side will have learned some coding in order to clean and analyze data, but do not mistake them for software or data engineers or ask them to perform this function.

- **Business knowledge.** The technologist and mathematicians exist, in a sense, to serve the business's needs, and the technologist and mathematicians need to be supported by those needs to ensure success. If they do not know what the business needs are or how the models they create will affect the business, the analytics is not likely to succeed over the long term. Every team should have a few people with business or domain understanding embedded in their process to ensure their work is adding value.

Figure 2.4 illustrates these three types of technical team members in rough proportion to how many businesses deploy them.

Although it is important for the technologist and mathematicians to develop an understanding of the business outside their core discipline, and essential for analytics leaders, the more you can keep these types working and contributing primarily from their core area, the more productive and happy they will be. Similar to many areas, the 80/20 rule seems to work well here. That is, core analytics team members should spend about 80% of their time and effort working in their primary discipline and 20% in supporting areas. Analytics leaders should follow closer to a 60/40 ratio, with more business knowledge and work effort being required the higher up the leadership ladder they go.

Businessperson orientation team members usually come to analytics with experience in another business function. Dr. Karl Kempf described the importance of having "refugees from finance" or other business functions embedded within his team at Intel. Unlike the other two areas, this group is most helpful when they actively develop a deeper understanding of the other areas. Though they may never code or build fancy mathematical models, they are critical to the success of the project and generally enjoy diving into, working in, and learning as much as possible about the other areas in analytics.

Table 2.3 summarizes the key categories, common titles, and backgrounds associated with each type, and key things to remember about managing these team members. Because different companies and industries often use differing titles, and people evolve throughout their careers, there will be some overlap in titles and backgrounds in the table. Of course, this discipline is rapidly evolving and growing. Therefore, the table is meant to give just a flavor for each team category.

Table 2.3 Primary Technical Team Members by Discipline

Category	Common Titles	Typical Background	Management Advice
Technology	<ul><li>Computer scientist</li><li>Data architect</li><li>Data engineer</li><li>Data scientist</li><li>Database administrator</li><li>Developer</li><li>Information scientist</li><li>Machine learning engineer</li><li>Security analyst</li><li>Software engineer</li><li>System architect</li></ul>	Some come from very deep in the technology space, others from hybrid areas such as information systems. All of them love and use technology nearly every day and spend a great deal of time staying current in their fields.	Technology experts need opportunities to use the skills they spent years developing, so cultivate areas where they want to grow. Learn the difference between the varying areas in the technology space and what they do and try to understand technology experts' mindsets to support their needs, both by aligning skills and considering their analytics orientation.
Math	<ul><li>Data analyst</li><li>Data scientist</li><li>Modeler</li><li>Operations analyst</li><li>Researcher</li><li>Statistician</li></ul>	Typically mathematicians have masters or doctorate degrees in a math or stem topics, such as physics, management science, statistics, or other variants.	Mathematicians tend to have high-quality standards and ethics regarding proper process. Support this process by keeping them focused on end goals while allowing them to rigorously test ideas to help achieve those goals.
Business	<ul><li>AI ethicist</li><li>Analytics translator</li><li>Business analyst</li><li>Domain expert</li><li>Data governor</li><li>Data steward</li><li>Legal expert</li></ul>	Most of these workers come from a quantitative side of the business, such as finance or accounting. A few started in analytics and moved into business through management.	Those who are business centric tend to be easier to manage, provided they focus on their areas of competence. However, they crave growth opportunities and generally love discovery and impact. The more you can help them achieve these goals, the more engaged they will be.

Dr. Arora's Recipe for Successful Analytics Team Management

Dr. Hina Arora, clinical associate professor at Arizona State University and former senior data scientist lead and analytics group manager at Microsoft, shared a recipe for successfully managing an analytics team. Arora's recipe will be especially useful for those on the technical side moving into management.

Embrace Failure

When you do new things you often fail. No one wants to fail, but if you play it safe by running from the possibility of failure, you also run from the possibility of big wins, limiting you and your team's activities to safe incremental improvements. When you make it safe for your team to fail, you also make it safe for them to try new and risky approaches that can have a big payoff. Embrace the risk of an occasional fast failure for the possibility of a big win by making failure safe for your team.

Encourage Planned Obsolescence

Encourage your team to work themselves out of a job. Do not make them fear for their job security. By encouraging them to work their way out of a job, you free them up to work on bigger, better, and more impactful solutions. Encourage them to automate, improve processes, and tackle bigger problems. Even better, provide incentives to do so.

Support Multidimensional Lifelong Learners

Technology, in general, and analytics in particular, is a field full of rapid change. It is very difficult to stay current, but essential that your team does. It is not that the latest technology is always the best, but if you do not know what it is and what it can do, how can you make the best choices going forward?

Most analysts, data engineers, data scientists, and other team members will naturally continue to learn inside their domain. This pursuit often takes place through training programs, conferences, and natural job demands. It needs to be encouraged and embraced at every level to not only keep top talent but also to keep them in top shape.

To bring even better value to the organization, your talent needs to expand their horizons and learn and grow beyond just going deeper into their technical or specialty area, without being pushed too far out of their core area, as noted in the last section with the 80/20 rule. Some of this desire for growth may happen naturally, but might not be fast enough for most.

To better increase the analytics team's impact, job satisfaction, and effectiveness, you need to find ways to encourage and support the development of their deep technical skills and other, broader business skills. I present a few ideas in Task 6: Analytics Maturity.

Here are several focus areas:

- **Tool flexibility.** It is certainly advantageous to know one or two tools extremely well. Be aware, however, that doing so can limit the type of projects team members work on and who they can work with. Sometimes it is better to know several tools a bit, rather than knowing only one tool a lot. This strategy enables them to better match the tools and work more effectively with other team members, vendors, and groups. Although there may be sound business reasons for members to focus on a limited number of tools, when possible, you can encourage tool flexibility, build it into your processes, and reward this cognitive flexibility in your analytics team.

- **Domain expertise.** Analysts cannot, and should not, model what they do not understand. Otherwise, they risk doing more harm than good. By investing time in their understanding of the business and what drives it, they can be much more effective in their job. A side benefit is they will feel more fulfilled as they can see more impact from their efforts.

- **Communication skills.** Good communication skills are always essential. Yet, those skills are generally less common in technical hires. It is therefore important to help your analytics team develop these skills. It is especially critical because so few people outside of technology and analytics really understand what these groups know and do every day. By increasing their communication competency, you not only improve employee effectiveness but also you help your organization grow and mature as collective understanding for what analysts and their tools can do for the organization expands.

- **Project management skills.** As discussed, most IT and analytics projects fail. There are several reasons why this outcome can occur, including technology changes, scope creep, and new and untested approaches. Good classic project management skills can help increase the chances of success, so every team member should be encouraged to grow and develop project management skills.

Guard the Ecosystem

Because many executives and business process owners do not fully understand the analytics process, what is involved in it, and how it actually works, it is common for analytics teams to be assigned trivial, low-value work. Consequently, the team is demotivated, which too frequently results in losing valuable team members as they find other opportunities. This cascade then undermines important big-impact projects.

It is important for managers to guard the ecosystem to enable analytics team members to flourish and grow and to maximize the company's value. Managing the ecosystem requires executive champions and other business leaders to run interference for the team. They need to push back by saying no to less important work as they help the organization prioritize what matters most.

ENGAGING YOUR TEAM

We wrap up this section with a couple final nuggets of wisdom for attracting and retaining your team.

Challenging and Meaningful Work

Patrick Getzen, retired chief data and analytics officer at Blue Cross Blue Shield of North Carolina, shared how it was possible to attract and retain top talent by challenging them with complex problems that were invigorating, meaningful, and impactful. Because it usually takes a bright person to do well in analytics, most relish the challenge of using all of their faculties to solve a big hairy problem and find it intrinsically motivating to wrestle with it. This maxim is even more true when it connects their actions to impact, especially for a societal good.

In Patrick Getzen's case, the complexity and importance of improving health care engendered an obvious societal benefit. Dr. Daniel Cohen-Vogel, former VP of data and analytics for the University of North Carolina System, shared a similar perspective regarding the complexity and meaning of work in education: helping students graduate and succeed. I could share similar stories regarding some of my team's work with pollinators, sustainable energy, and poverty reduction, which were outcomes from my team's work while directing the Center for Analytics Research and Education at my former university, where I retain the rank of emeritus professor.

Although it may not be as obvious as it is with health care, education, or poverty, most organizations wrestle with complex problems, or will as they grow in their analytics complexity. As you master the low-hanging fruit, what is left are inherently complex problems to solve. Additionally, the majority of organizations serve society in some useful way, which is why people pay for their goods and services.

Find the challenging impactful story of your organization and make sure your current and potential analytics team members understand the big picture, the complex problems you are trying to solve, and the difference it makes for the world. When possible, make sure team members have time and resources to wrestle with big intractable problems and can see the impact of the results. This approach will help you attract and retain analytics talent by increasing their engagement, their commitment to the organization, and their productivity.

Engage the Ecosystem

Most of us tend to think about analytics as a team of nerds, working in a closet somewhere doing techno magic. Although this view is not completely untrue, it is not entirely true either. The reality is that there is, and needs to be, an entire ecosystem to support analytics for it to succeed. Josh Belliveau shared the importance of engaging the entire expanded ecosystem and leveraging everyone's talents and energy to succeed. Belliveau includes product power users, vendors, vendor networks, external partners, managers, data producers, and businesspersons to create a win.

For example, Belliveau shared the story of his coming to use Tableau because of the ecosystem. Belliveau's supervisor had met with Tableau representatives at a conference when the company was still very new and was impressed with what it could do. Subsequently, Belliveau and the team began using it quite effectively and were impressed with how easy it was to use and how effective it was built to convey complex information in real time. Serving in a new role, Belliveau has been able to see a variety of enterprises leverage the ecosystem on Tableau. These enterprises take advantage of the many vendors and supporters that know how to use the product, integrate it into other systems, offer training and support, and share best practices. This expanded ecosystem, beyond Tableau, magnifies the usefulness of the product alone.

We have talked about many roles inside the organization in this chapter, and will share more about external partners in Task 6: Analytics Maturity. Yet, the ecosystem is much broader than what we were able to share here.

Leadership with Dr. Dan Cohen-Vogel

Dr. Dan Cohen-Vogel is one of the most enlightened analytics leaders I know. With a breadth of experience, Cohen-Vogel strives to help other organizations develop successful data and analytics strategies and products. He is someone who excels at managing staff members with reciprocated respect and devotion, is passionate about leadership, and readily follows the motto: practice what you preach.

Here are a few of the principles and insights from the interview I found useful and expect you may benefit from them, too.

Mission, Mission, Mission

Just like the most important phrase in real estate is location, location, location, the key phrase in public institutions and nonprofit organizations, such as those Cohen-Vogel works with, is mission, mission, mission. For these types of public service organizations, you must start with and stay focused on the mission at all times. Everything should advance the mission and be understood as mission relevant, or it is a distraction.

It is easy to forget the mission in the rush of day-to-day duties, and different people in different parts of the organization may see the mission differently. They may, for example, focus on the part of the mission they are responsible for, and sometimes forget the bigger picture. It is important to have both. We all do better with more meaning in our life. If you are helping someone, whether a for-profit business or a public service, centering the mission can be helpful to maintaining engagement and focus.

Compelling Story

Still, it is not just the mission that motivates the team and stakeholders. That is the start. The mission should be wrapped into a compelling and authentic story that motivates and communicates clearly why you do what you do and includes specific examples of real people and real impacts. This is your elevator pitch. Always have a few versions ready to share with the appropriate audience on a moment's notice. The story also serves another purpose: it helps you recruit the right people, those who want to contribute to the mission and be a part of that story.

And within the data and analytics function, a compelling data story is part and parcel to how we go from actionable information to organizational action. Packaging information in a way that is consumable and compelling and explaining results in a way that engages the decision-makers are critical to an effective analytics team.

Humble Smart

Cohen-Vogel advised to be humble, recruit people smarter than you, and point them to the mission with your compelling stories. When hiring, do not just look at an HR requirements list, checking boxes and verifying qualifications. Yes, those qualifications can help sometimes, but they can also lead you astray and cause you to miss golden nuggets. Look at the whole person, what they bring to the table, their drive, intellect, eagerness, and ability to learn, desire to be part of a team, and yes, commitment to the mission, too.

Cohen-Vogel's Rules for People

Cohen-Vogel also has a few rules of engagement, which I found insightful. Here are a few highlights:

- **Gardener versus chess master.** Cohen-Vogel loves and lives by this quote, from US Army General Stanley McChrystal, "Many leaders are tempted to lead like a chess master, striving to control every move, when they should be leading like gardeners, creating and maintaining a viable ecosystem in which the organization operates."[4] It is especially relevant to developing cross-functional or inter-organizational teams.

- **Lead by example.** You cannot expect your team to do what you do not do yourself. Show, do not just tell, how you want them to work. This ability to model collaboration and communication is particularly important for team leaders' interactions with colleagues and stakeholders because they are essential to successful engagement.

- **Align incentives.** Make sure all incentives are aligned to the mission. Though obvious, sometimes this rule gets lost. An obvious but often overlooked opportunity to align incentives is to compensate the team sufficiently to retain them and also to create an environment that reflects the unit's values (e.g., collaborative spaces, family-friendly expectations).

- **Empowerment.** Build a culture where your team will be comfortable, even eager, to come forward and tell you things, even unpopular things. You do not want them to say, I saw this problem but was too afraid to tell you about it. Even better, make sure they know to tell you early. And this extends beyond simply the team's reactions to the boss's ideas. It is just as important to empower team members to bring their own new ideas to the table. Many of the changes Cohen-Vogel, as team leader, made in the working environment and projects were the result of subordinates bringing their best thinking forward, whether for resources needed or approval to "run with it." Communication needs to go both ways.

- **Take blame, share credit.** As the leader, take the blame for your team's mistakes; you should have managed better. Always credit team members when things go well. The recognition is deserved and is also a motivator.

- **Focus on the problem.** Problem first, technology second. Today we see too many cases in which someone knows a given technology, or wants to sell it, and focuses on the technology. If you stay focused on the problem, you will be able to see more clearly, and not be fooled about whether the technology will really solve your problem.

- **Relationships.** Continuously build relationships, share visions, and build understanding, not just with your team but also with the broader community of stakeholders. I wish I had learned this rule and put it into practice earlier! Cohen-Vogel is quick to point out that many of the relationships cultivated as part of Cohen-Vogel's "team of teams" have been foundational to a private consulting practice. Always strive to do more and do it better.

CHAPTER SUMMARY AND EXERCISES

Task 2: Summary

For any project to be successful, it requires what Dr. Pleines refers to as the minimal viable team. It consists of an executive champion or business leader who is willing and capable to champion, promote, fund, and drive the project and its adoption. It requires a business process owner who is responsible for a relevant business process that can be improved. Their role is to guide the analytics and technical development in a way that ensures it integrates into their process and is adopted. It finally requires the technical and analytics team who work with all parties to make sure the project meets the requirements, is easy to use, is error free and useful to the business process owner and their staff members, and aligns with the executive champion's objectives.

By understanding the notifications and characteristics of those that engage with analytics, namely, the native, the seeker, and the businessperson, you can better manage the strengths and weaknesses of each group, improve engagement, and ultimately achieve success. In addition to understanding their analytics orientation, it is also important to align their skills and training appropriately.

Finally, Dr. Arora presented a recipe for better managing analytics teams and Dr. Cohen-Vogel shared principles for leadership and engagement with all stakeholders.

Task 2: Exercises

1. Although all team members are important to the analytics process, the experts interviewed for this book universally agreed that without an executive champion and broad executive support, the project would almost certainly fail. Take a few moments to describe the executives role and why it is important to analytics success.

2. Since the beginning of this book, we have shared the importance of the minimal viable team developed by Dr. Pleines, which consists of an executive champion, business process owner, and the analytics or technical team. Yet, sometimes you need more than the minimum. Please list and describe two or three scenarios when this might be the case, whom you would need, why you need them, and what their function would be.

3. An analytics translator has been described as a key catalyst who can accelerate analytics adoption and use. In your own words, describe the key characteristics needed for an analytics translator to be successful and why these translators are so important to analytics adoption.

4. Understanding why people love or do analytics can be helpful in managing them and keeping them excited and engaged with the team and the various projects in which they might participate. Please describe each of the three common analytics orientations, namely, the native, the seeker, and the businessperson. Next, identify which orientation you believe you most closely align with and whether the strengths and weaknesses for each orientation align based on your experience and observations. Finally, consider how aligning training and skills can also help with managing an analytic team by sharing a few thoughts on the matter.

5. Drs. Arora and Cohen-Vogel both shared valuable advice for managing and leading teams. Pick the three most interesting management concepts to you. List and describe them and try to make it real by either describing how you have seen one used or how you would like to use one and then describe how effective it was or whether you believe it would be.

NOTES

1. Thomas H. Davenport and D. J. Patil, "Data Scientist: The Sexiest Job of the 21st Century," *Harvard Business Review* 90, no. 10 (October 2012): 70–76.

2. McKinsey Global Institute, "The Age of Analytics: Competing in a Data-Driven World" (December 2016). https://www.mckinsey.com/capabilities/quantumblack/our-insights/the-age-of-analytics-competing-in-a-data-driven-world

3. Joseph Cazier, "Aligning Team Members' Analytics Orientations with Project Characteristics," *International Institute for Analytics (IIA): Research Brief* (March 2023).

4. https://www.forbes.com/sites/danschawbel/2015/07/13/stanley-mcchrystal-what-the-army-can-teach-you-about-leadership

TASK **3**

The Data

AMORPHOUS ASSET

Data has become one of the most valuable assets of the 21st century. Indeed, we have reached the point that sometimes a company's data can actually be worth *more* than the entire company, as *Forbes*[1] shared in a news report in which both United Airlines and American Airlines were able to secure multibillion-dollar loans based on lenders valuing their data two to three times more than the value of their entire market capitalization. Yes, that is right. You could purchase either major airline and all of their assets, including the data they owned, for less than half the value of the data alone.

This type of valuation of data, especially for a traditional company, would have been unimaginable just a few decades ago. The message is clear. Data is an incredibly valuable asset. However, it is also a very amorphous asset. It is one you cannot see that often lives in the cloud, one that many do not really understand, and one that is difficult for executives to manage effectively, especially traditional ones trained before the age of Big Data.

This chapter focuses on helping you understand the source of your data's value and what attributes it has compared to traditional assets to manage it more effectively. First, we show how you can identify where that value is and what it is worth followed by how to harness and enhance that value. Finally, we show how you can safeguard the value of your asset by more effectively managing and improving your data's quality.

UNDERSTANDING DATA'S VALUE

A century and a half ago, the industrialization of oil opened the doors to a new era of energy. Fortunes were made and lost and massive changes flowed through society as the value of affordable energy changed how we live and work, and indeed who we were as a people of the modern world. It truly was the dawn of a global energy revolution that would have far-reaching consequences.

Today, we are in another revolution. This time it is a data revolution thanks largely to improvements in storage systems, processing power, and accessible algorithms. We can now collect, process, store, and analyze more data than most imagined a few short years ago, giving us results that are being used once again to change our world in novel ways.

These advances have turned data into one of the most valuable and dynamic assets of the modern organization, as shown with the airline example. Data is reshaping our fortunes and the world, just as oil did for our ancestors a few generations ago. It seems that everywhere we turn we hear pundits and technologists shouting "Data is the new oil!" due to its untapped potential to add value to a company. Comparing data to oil is useful in that both have incredible implications for everything we do. Yet, they are also fundamentally different in how they are doing it; the comparison is only useful if you dig deep enough to understand the similarities and differences and learn how to use them to navigate how things are changing. This analogy is designed to help executives understand where and how data can add value and identify where and what that value is.

Data Is Like Oil

Here are a few ways that data and oil are similar:[2]

- **Finding.** Data is like oil in that it starts with discovery. Not all land or all data are equal. Just as only a fraction of the world's land has oil underneath, only a fraction of the world's data holds transformational value. A great deal of thought, investigation, and sampling needs to be done for both data and oil to get a sense of their value.

- **Failure.** Even when members of the geological team believe they may have found oil, after careful searching and evaluation, 85% to 90% of test wells fail to find a commercially viable product. This is similar to the 80% to 90% failure rate in analytics, after a leader or analyst believed there was enough possibility of finding something useful to start a project. This fact underscores the critical importance of careful thought and value assessment before starting a project, with better prioritization and screening for amenability.

- **Moving.** Just as oil needs to be extracted from the ground and moved to the refinery before it can be processed, valuable data needs to be collected into a central point that enables it to be accessed by your analytics team. There are many technologies that can facilitate this process, but leaving it in hard-to-find and not readily understood data silos will not bring significant value to the organization.

- **Processing.** There are a number of very important steps in the oil refining process, including distilling, segregation, cracking, reforming, blending, and treating. Although the steps in processing data are a little different, they can also be very complicated, technical, time-consuming, and costly. Still, just as the oil reaches its full value only after processing, data must be cleaned and processed in order to be used effectively.

- **Positive and negative societal impact.** Although there are many benefits to using oil and data, they both have a dark side. The negative impact of oil acquisition, processing, and use on the environment has been well documented. We are still learning about the long-term negative impact of data and analytics on society, but it is clear that issues like privacy, security, unethical manipulation, environmental impact, and biased data are matters to be handled with great care and concern.

Data Is Different from Oil

Here are a few ways that data and oil are different:

- **Reusable asset.** Oil can only be used once. Data, however, can be used an infinite number of times. In fact, as you use it and learn how effective various parts of it are, or are not, it may actually become more useful to your organization.

- **Commodity versus differentiated asset.** Oil is a commodity, maybe the commodity of the last century. Anyone who finds and processes it to the global standard can sell it on the open market to anyone who uses oil. Aside from political and logistical concerns, it does not matter who produced it. Any barrel from any producer can be easily interchanged with any other barrel of the same type. It makes very little difference to the end customer. Data, however, is a highly differentiated asset that is mostly unique to that organization and market. Its value is not so much determined by what it is as by what can be done with it. This means its value depends as much on the organization's resources, commitment, and expertise as it does on the data itself. Who produced and owns it matters a great deal to the value that can be harvested from it. Companies should exercise great care in designing and managing their data collection and processing in a way appropriate to the organization.

- **Competitive advantage.** Because data is a differentiated asset unique to a given organization, it offers a greater ability to achieve a sustainable competitive advantage than commodities, at least without becoming a monopoly. Yes, it needs to be used effectively, but if done wisely, it is much harder for competitors to replicate.

- **Value opacity.** With oil, the value of the asset can largely be determined by applying some common evaluation methodologies. This is true within the firm itself and also by competitors and other interested parties outside the firm. Alternatively, the value of data is largely opaque. This is often true inside the firm and even more so outside the firm. This opaqueness changes the strategy for firms, giving them more possibilities to delight customers and surprise competitors. Because the value of the data is based on what you do with it, no firm can ever extract all the value from their data, as they can never do all things they want to do with it. Sometimes the act of doing one thing with the data changes what other things can be done. Actions taken change the balance of resources in the firms and influence what happens next.

- **Customer.** Oil ultimately needs to be purchased and used by the end customer to have its value realized. Conversely, although there are a few firms that sell data directly, most of us want to use our data to improve our operations to create value in other ways. The value either comes from selling something directly to a customer or by improving the value proposition of other products or services to current or future customers. Either way, there is an endpoint beyond which the firm is the source of that value. This is true even for process improvements that enable you to improve the efficiency, quality, or scale of your offering.

- **Market stability.** The customers who use oil have products from power plants to furnaces, to cars and airplanes, that are designed to last decades. Although the price may go up and down, the market will only change slowly due to the heavy fixed investment in durable assets. The market for data products, conversely, can change in days.

- **Process uncertainty.** With oil, the uncertainty is largely in the discovery process, which is in finding and testing oil fields. Once discovered and evaluated, oil shifts to a known production process based on operational logistics and proven industrial processes. Although the market retains some uncertainty, as all markets do, most of the risk is in the discovery process as the oil has intrinsic value and the uncertainty is mostly driven by supply and demand, not the usefulness of the product. With data, there is uncertainty at every step in the analytics life cycle, from finding data that is valuable, to processing it into something that can be analyzed, to assessing the actual usefulness of the model to the business, to determining the length of time it will continue to be useful. Thus, much greater care needs to be taken throughout the entire analytics process, compared to oil. The complexity of the entire process creates many more potential points for failure.

- **Controlled generation.** The creation of oil was determined by mother nature, outside the control of the firm. The most the firm can do is harvest what has been created in a profitable way. They cannot make more, change its innate quality, or easily alter its underground location to be more convenient for extraction. With data, the firm does have a high level of influence in creating the data they model. They largely control or can control the generation, storage, and quality of the data. This control can be used as a valuable tool to reduce the uncertainty in the analytics process, enabling the firm to collect relevant and useful data, the primary ingredient of analytics.

- **Quality.** Although the quality of oil reserves can be reliably estimated, the quality of data is highly variable over time, location, and type. Data that gets used frequently for decision-making and important operational functions is likely of reasonable quality. Data that is seldom used is often of poor quality.

- **Organizational change.** There is more to data science than cleaning and processing the data. You also have to build useful models and adapt your business practices to take advantage of them. Analytics is about making better decisions, but you only get the value if you are willing to change based on the insights you learn. You can find brilliant insights, but if you do not adapt and build them into your process, they are of little value. This is one of the hardest parts of succeeding in analytics and an important topic in later chapters.

See Table 3.1, which summarizes the key attributes of oil and data, along with their implications for executives.

Table 3.1 Oil to Data Comparison and Implications

Attribute	Oil	Data	Implications
Reusable	One and done	Unlimited use	Data can be used many times, and may actually become more useful as you observe what works and refine your approach.
Commodity versus differentiation	Commodity	Differentiated	Maintain a clear strategy customized to your firm and market. Analytics strategy must not only align with the general business strategy but also the general business strategy needs to be informed and crafted based on what is possible with analytics now and in the future. Only by working together, and continually adapting your strategy based on outcomes and changing market conditions, will you succeed over time.
Value opacity	Clear	Opaque	Note the challenge of valuing your data for you and others. You have to focus not so much on the data itself, but the value that can come to your firm by using it. Its value changes as your firm and market conditions change, making it a moving target.
Customer	Final Product	Enhancement of other products and services	Focus on how the analytics will change your business process or the offering of your products and services to your customers, not on selling the analytics product directly.
Market stability	Stable	Volatile	Stay attuned to market conditions and likely changes and categorize projects based on their durability or volatility for differentiated management, given how quickly the market for data products can change and evolve.
Process uncertainty	Uncertain discovery, certain processing	Uncertainty throughout all steps of process	Watch for careful alignment with business strategy and cross check for value at every step in the analytics process. This focus also means continual iteration on the analytics problem you are trying to solve as you learn more about what can be done and how it will affect the firm.
Generation	No control over natural resource creation	High level of control over quality and relevance of data	Maintain a high level of control over how your asset is generated. But, it also means that careful thought needs to go into this process and that competitors who design their data thoughtfully from the start may have an advantage. So always look for ways to improve the quality and relevance of your data by managing the generation of that data, not just passively analyzing what you already have.
Quality	Consistent	Variable	Take steps to improve the quality of data believed to be relevant to the firm's goals before it is needed. The quality of your data will largely be influenced by the frequency and importance of its use. The quality of data you have not previously used should be viewed with skepticism until tested and evaluated in the analytics process.
Organizational change	No change	Value depends on change	Accept that you have to change to get significant value from analytics or you will only find incremental process improvements. When modeling something, always ask if your organization will be willing to change based on what you find. If not, go back and reassess your goals.

IDENTIFYING VALUABLE DATA

The first step in identifying valuable data is finding relevant data to evaluate. The second step is to put a monetary value on that data so you can manage it appropriately.

Identifying Relevant Data

If the data is not relevant, why collect it? The most important way to enhance the value of your data is to make sure you are collecting the most relevant data to support your mission and goals. Unlike with oil, organizations do have a great deal of control over the generation of their data, so they should first design their data to be relevant from the start.

Sometimes business operations depend on data being collected a certain way, but many times a minor change can still serve, even improve, those needs while also making the data more relevant for analytics uses. We can learn from scientists who spend a great deal of time designing and testing various approaches to data collection with a mix of theory, intuition, testing, and validation. Designing data for relevance, and reducing collection of irrelevant data, can improve your analytics and business operations.

With a deeper understanding of the attributes of data, it is easier to go to the next important step where business leaders should play an active role, which is in identifying, and eventually helping create, data that is valuable to the business. The underappreciated reality is that most of the data in a firm today has limited value beyond supporting current business operations. The reason is simple: that is what the data was designed to do—support current operations. Until recently, it came at a very significant cost, and it would have been seen as an expensive distraction to do much more than that.

Yes, supporting current operations is critical, and a clever data scientist can often use some of that data to improve business operations and help you do what you are doing better. However, that data is seldom transformational and mostly leads to incremental improvements. This is still very much worth doing, but it may not be worth the current level of hype around it. You have to know where to look to find value, just as you would not find oil on every piece of land where you could drill an oil well, especially without due diligence.

Pareto's Principle Applies to Data

Most operational data is still best served by supporting and improving current operations and then managed and analyzed accordingly. Yet, some data can do much more. Most organizations will find that the Pareto principle,[3] or the 80/20 rule, applies to their data as much as to many other things they do. Somewhere in the vicinity of 10% to 20% of your data will have significant value beyond sustaining current operations. The rest will not and should not be treated or managed as such.

For example, Piyanka Jain, CEO of the analytics advisory firm Aryng, shared how to help clients set up their data structures and analytics process in months instead of years by working with them to prioritize their data. By identifying the 20% or so of their data best suited to support their strategy, Jain found that data governance being put in place to improve data quality and analytics to sit on top of it was much more effective, had an improved time to value, and was more likely to be used by the organization because they could understand it instead of being overburdened by trying to manage all of their data equally well.

Steps to Finding the Most Relevant Data

The key is identifying which data is, or can be, the most valuable to your business and managing it such that the value can be readily harvested in a way that supports your business strategy. The steps outlined here can give you a road map to identifying this data:

1. **Identify and communicate business strategy.** Fully understand your *business* strategy, how your business functions, and how it competes in a competitive market. What is the primary focus? Data professionals can help identify how data can support your strategy, but they need to know clearly, at a granular level, what it is. Better yet, they may be able to help shape it based on what could be done in Step 2. Analytics professionals can get a head start on this by listening and paying attention to which KPIs leaders talk about the most. They can then look at data likely to influence or be indicative of those KPIs and have a good place to start prioritizing based on where the executives seem most focused.

2. **Explore possibilities.** Take time to understand what is possible with data and analytics technologies. This statement is generally true, but is especially true as it specifically relates to your organization. It is important to look at both what can be done now and what could be done later with the right data curation and analysis. Most possibilities will have limited value, but a few will have exceptional value that supports a winning strategy important to your firm. To have this data focus, analysts need time to play with the data, conduct exploratory factor analyses, and create models that test correlation, impact, and potential value.

3. **Develop data strategy.** Identify (or adjust) your data strategy for now and later. Consider what it is you want to do with the data. There will be many possibilities in many places. You have to focus on the 20% that is the most important, and then focus on managing that 20% effectively to generate value.

4. **Engage theory and intuition.** Published theory is often high-quality analytics that has been demonstrated repeatedly in a controlled environment and has been vigorously peer reviewed. It is not perfect or all inclusive, but it is an excellent place to augment your analytics journey by identifying what has already been proven to work in similar situations. By building on proven theories, and building your own by following your intuition, you can build more stable and generalizable models of higher quality and durability, avoiding many data traps along the way.

THE DATA ◀ 99

5. **Use theory to prioritize data.** By starting with theory and intuition, as opposed to blindly following the data, you can avoid many data traps and spurious correlations. Use the theories identified in Step 4 to identify and prioritize the data you likely need to succeed, based on your strategy. For example, I found the technology acceptance model very relevant to encouraging adoption of our technology at HiveTracks.

6. **Design data collection efforts.** Scientists put a great deal of effort up front to design data collection mechanisms to collect relevant data. By following a similar strategy and carefully designing or redesigning data collection efforts to be more relevant and of higher quality from the start of the process, where the data is generated, it can usually be made much more valuable and useful.

7. **Enrich with secondary data.** Secondary data, or data collected for another primary purpose but that has other uses, enriches the data you own and multiplies its utility. It can add different and sometimes explanatory data that improves your models. For example, weather may have a strong impact on sales of certain products and could likely be used to better predict those sales. Demographic and socioeconomic information may largely explain certain consumer behaviors. There are many free sources of secondary data (e.g., government data) and other sources to purchase data.

8. **Experiment.** Following established theory, intuition, and exploration is a good place to start. Confirming those hunches and looking for new ones through experimentation and exploration is even better. Using experiments, maybe even thousands of micro-experiments, can confirm and better target which data is valuable and which is not. However elegant your theory is, it is worth looking around to make sure it is actually working. Once tested and validated, you can see more clearly where the value is.

Valuing Data as an Asset

Ahmer Inam, chief data and artificial intelligence officer at Relanto and former head of analytics for several other well-known organizations, shares how important it is to put a tangible value on the data, just like you would for any other asset. Only when you learn to treat and manage data with the same processes and techniques you use for other assets will that data be able to compete appropriately for resources in the firm. Trying to put a value on your data, a potential monetary value, will force you to think carefully about your data's value and learn to prioritize projects accordingly.

Granted, putting a value on data is not an easy task. There are books on this subject, such as *Infonomics* and *Data Juice*, both by Douglas B. Laney, which Inam recommended. However, it is still much more uncertain and complex than putting a value on a building or oil reserves, even though it is no less important. It may be tempting to outsource this activity to the data scientist, but although they need to be included in the process, this is a core business activity that should be supported, led, and validated by executives and business process owners in a way that leads to proper management and investment in data technologies.

There are several critical reasons that executives and data scientists need to work together on this task. The data scientist should be able to advise about the current quality level of the data, what it could be used for, and what investments in technology it might take to make it happen. Executives understand the value of those actions to the business and can adjust for the probability of success and impact. They can also help assess what would happen given competitive challenges in the marketplace in terms of downsides if they fail or choose not to proceed, both of which can influence investment decisions.

Still, it is much more than just placing a value on an asset. Executives and business process owners should actively engage in the analytics process by helping to identify and map data to value. Because they know the business needs and often have valuable insights on business pain points and how certain actions would likely affect the business, they can help identify the types of projects likely to be the most relevant and urgent to the business.

Patrick Getzen, retired chief data and analytics officer for Blue Cross Blue Shield of North Carolina, shared an important approach they used to drive adoption and change from analytics that I believe could also be used to put a value on data as an intermediate step to adoption and help quantify the value of your data. They used a concept they called *identified value*, which is easy to understand, is focused on executives, and drives action.

First, they would look at their data and determine something they could do with it, something valuable to the firm that it could in fact adopt, that would be in line with their mission and strategy, and that would very likely be the best thing for the firm to do. They would then use a range of analytics techniques to estimate the impact of adoption on the value of the firm.

For example, the firm had premium levels of roughly $10 billion at the time, if Getzen identified analytics that could theoretically deliver $100 million in value from analytics that in turn would help motivate adoption, especially when those numbers were shared with the board, which could influence action. It would also provide a measuring rod for how far they came to achieving that value by showing they achieved $10 Million of the $100 million in identified value. It might be used to motivate them to increase adoption and to fulfill their potential. It could also be used as part of project prioritization decisions.

This method could also be used to put a value on your data, to add quality improvements to your data, data you may enhance or enrich, or for data you may want to collect. If you can adapt Getzen's concept of identified value, you can estimate the impact of the various analytics possible with the data, estimate its impact on your firm, and maybe adjust for a probability of success. A simple equation might look something like this:

Identified Value = (Likely Value of Use × Probability of Success) − Cost to Achieve

It is important to note that this is not really the use of one project, because it would take a stream of projects working together to harness the value of your data, along with a considerable investment in infrastructure (see next section). It would therefore be important to sum the identified value from the various uses with the data. A process like this could be used for general approaches and likely uses of data to help put at least a relative monetary value on your data that can guide data stewardship, enrichment, and use. However, see an adjustment I recommend in the section on data versatility.

Their knowledge of the business enables executives to share valuable hunches and intuition regarding where the value is and how to use it in the firm, and to estimate identified value. As they identify where value is likely to be, they can help map that value to specified data the business collects that may be relevant with their knowledge of how the business processes work. There are several more steps the data team would need to take to validate and harvest that value, but this step can get the process started in a beneficial way.

For example, it was Getzen's knowledge of the business that allowed Getzen to share the identified value with the board and other leaders, encouraging action. The data team will generally be able to tell you what is possible, tell you how likely it is to succeed, and offer new approaches and ways to use the data to support business goals that the executives and business process owners can assess and help prioritize. Working together, they can accomplish much more than working separately.

HARNESSING DATA'S VALUE

The classic five Vs of Big Data (volume, variety, velocity, veracity, and value), and the infrastructure associated with them, are essential to implementing industrial scale analytics. Indeed, a recent article in *CIO Magazine*[4] reported on a survey of more than 2,000 executives who indicated that, "the lack of proper infrastructure [was] a primary culprit for failed AI projects."

Yet, it is not easy to know what infrastructure is needed and how it fits into a comprehensive analytics strategy for harvesting the value in your data or enhancing and preserving that value. Trying to maximize all of the Vs of Big Data is costly, inefficient, and unnecessary. Indeed, sometimes there are trade-offs where increasing one V decreases another. For example, increasing volume and variety often lowers velocity.

It is not an executive's role to understand everything about Big Data technology and how it works. They have technical teams to help. That said, it is an executive's role to know what that technology needs to accomplish to benefit the firm and make the cost benefit trade-offs associated with them. The classic Vs of Big Data, and a few less well-known smaller Vs that can help enhance or preserve your data's value, can be a nice road map for executives to use in identifying what the infrastructure needs to accomplish.

Each of the classic five Vs[5] of Big Data has an important role to play in realizing your data's value. Here are a few thoughts for executives to be mindful of for each one.

Volume

Volume is the amount of data you have, and it matters because in having more data there is greater statistical power and opportunity to find possibilities that are interesting. This is especially true for machine learning models that use extensive amounts of data to build custom algorithms. In most cases, more data is more important than fancier algorithms. This is a salient point because, in machine learning, you are building a custom algorithm unique to your dataset, as opposed to statistics where you use prebuilt algorithms that were built and vetted on thousands of datasets.

All of this means that the more and varied the data you have, the more customized and accurate your algorithm will likely be, and the better job it will do. Quality, variability of the data, and other factors come into play, as does the job you are trying to do with your data. But, in general, more is better. Of course, more data is not free, so executives should evaluate the business benefit to make sure a reasonable payback is likely for their investment.

However, I have seen many analytics team members overlook the other reason that more data is so valuable. Depending on what the data is, it can give you more power to act. For example, if you discover a certain type of customer would likely respond to a given promotion, increasing the relevant volume by having more of that type of customers in your database increases the payout for executing on that insight.

Having a good algorithm is great, but acting on that insight depends on what you can do with it, which largely depends on the volume of relevant data you own. If you are a small firm with only a few thousand customers, the total possible value will be limited to the value you can receive from those customers. However, a large firm with millions of customers can apply that value to them, and even if the value is smaller per customer, they will have a much greater overall value because they have a much greater ability to act.

Unfortunately for small firms, this circumstance often gives large firms an advantage when it comes to data, if they are nimble and skilled enough to use it. They have more data to build better algorithms and have more ways to act on that data. What they lack is the ability to learn and adapt to data quickly, that is, organizational learning, as discussed in Task 0: Analytics Leadership in the book. Just as organizational learning is a competitive advantage when it comes to data, organizational unlearning can be a competitive hindrance.

Larger, more established firms are also less likely to be able to sacrifice current business lines to build new ones, what Clayton Christensen, a late Harvard professor and author of the *Innovator's Dilemma*,[6] termed *corporate cannibalism*. Much of the advantage of industry disruptions we see from the start-up universe is because those firms do not have to sacrifice old lines of business to build new ones, and tend to be more nimble at learning and changes because they do not have to unlearn old ways of doing things first.

If traditional firms could master those same skills, and put the advantages of their data endowment to better use, Silicon Valley would have a much harder battle for the future of industries. But once a new firm proves the value of an approach, and larger firms feel threatened and motivated to change, the larger firm often acquires these smaller start-ups, creating value because of their ability to scale across larger datasets to gain a larger benefit.

This is another reason that volume matters, making it essential to compete with the bigger fish out there over the long term, because those with a larger data endowment will likely catch up soon, or acquire you, if there is more value in doing so. Because variety, veracity, velocity, variability, and other Vs also matter, it is not just volume alone that gives you an advantage. So please stay tuned for the rest of the Vs before going all in on volume, making sure to consider the trade-offs between them that we discuss later.

Variety

Whereas volume influences the depth of your insights, variety influences the breadth of those insights, and expands what you can do with your data. Increasing the variety provides more context to the data you already have, giving a broader range of potential hypotheses that can be tested for insight. By introducing variety, meaning more and different types of data, there are more possibilities that can be analyzed.

Much of the progress in the Big Data era is from learning how to add structure to unstructured data (such as text files, GIS coordinates, or social network connections, and image and audio processing) and add that variety to the analysis. Another source of variety is in looking for secondary sources of data, often from outside your firm, to add more context and awareness to your data. Examples might include adding weather data for store locations, images of the number of cars in a parking lot, and demographic or other useful data to generate broader and more actionable insights.

But that is not the whole story. Yes, we can and should use this unstructured data to great effect. Yet, many firms overlook other sources of data that can also add significant value. Some of it is publicly available, structured, or semi-structured and can be added to models more easily than some of the more advanced techniques, making it a good place to start.

Dr. Bill Disch, data science educator for DataRobot and former chief analytics officer for various firms, talks about the value of secondary data in enriching variety. In Disch's experience, enriching your primary data with secondary data always leads to better analytical models. Examples include using public sources like the US Census data and county, city, state, and federal records for free or low-cost data. Additional sources include data you can buy or collect from other third parties or track across the web, including partnership with Google, Facebook, and others for single sign-on services that also inherently share data.

Similarly, Joshua Cazier, an executive at Qualtrics whom we introduced in Task 1: The Problem, shared another type of secondary data: experiential data. This is an area pioneered by Qualtrics that collects customer data based on their experience when interacting with your firm. This type of planned and intentionally collected data helps you not only understand what your customers are doing in their transactional data but also gives clues as to why they may be doing it.

Cazier shared a story of working with an internet service provider (ISP) who wanted to know why some customers were dropping their service. Cazier and Cazier's team worked with them to collect experiential data. They found that many of the customers who dropped had left comments such as "smoking" or "dirty" as reasons why they left. Further investigation revealed that some technicians had, in fact, been smoking at or near the property, leaving a less desirable customer experience, which caused many customers to turn over. Now, with proper policies and training the ISP was able to reverse the trend and reduce churn.

Personal note. I have a lot of respect for Qualtrics, partly because my brother works there, partly because I find the data they collect to be incredibly useful in opening up new insights and plans of action. Most of all though, I will always be grateful to their founder, Scott Smith, whom I admire for being one of my favorite professors while working on my MBA, for advising on the board of a start-up I was involved with circa 1999, for writing a letter of recommendation that helped me get into my PhD program, and especially for calling me up and convincing me to change my mind when I was thinking about dropping out of my doctoral program and going back to industry due to financial pressure. If you ever read this book, thank you, Professor Smith!

Enriching your data by increasing variety with these sources will, almost certainly, increase the accuracy of your analytics models and expand the types of things you could do, not just improve what you can already do. It opens up unexplored doors to do new and potentially valuable things. This can also enable you to not just compete better but also to serve your customers better, be more sustainable, and improve business operations, among many other benefits. Many customers would want you to use secondary data so they get better, more tailored products, messages, and services, especially now that we know what is possible today.

There are a few cautions to consider, however:

- **Speed.** As variety goes up, it often reduces velocity, the next V, so make sure it is adding enough value to compensate for any loss (see the trade-off discussion that follows).

- **Theory.** Using theory to guide you, from someone somewhere who looked at a related idea before and tested it, can help you pick what is most valuable. Do not just throw everything in or you will likely find results that are not true or do not hold up over time.

- **Unobtrusive.** Some data collection efforts are more obtrusive than others and may annoy more than they help. It is usually more effective to keep your data collection efforts as invisible or unobtrusive as possible.

- **Ethics.** Some people may look askance at unobtrusiveness, but wise firms always think of the ethical implications, including perceptions, not just the immediate benefits. See Task 7: Responsible Analytics, for a deeper discussion of this topic.

Velocity

Data is moving faster than ever before. With real-time data processing and analysis, we can often react to situations in time to capture value. For example, if you know what a customer really needs while they are on your website, the phone, or in your store, you have a chance to make a sale you might have missed or add value in other ways. Likewise you might better find someone hacking into your system while there is still time to respond, before they find the keys to the kingdom, or you may better detect where crime is most likely to happen so you can respond. Although the variety of the data helps you discover new insights, it is the velocity that helps you act on it in time to capture more of the value.

In addition to the benefits of reaching your customers in real time, Patrick Getzen shared a story about how you can get answers much faster. In a test, Getzen pulled some code written 20 years before, simulating insurance claims for stop-loss insurance. Getzen recalls it took 10 computers working simultaneously for about two weeks to run that same code in the past. This time, the entire code was executed in less than $\frac{2}{3}$ of 1 second.

It is this speed to answers that enables speed to execution. However, even fast computers may not be fast enough if you slow down your analysis with too much volume, veracity, and variety, each of which can slow velocity. It is important to balance and prioritize technical and business needs and optimize for value as opposed to maximizing everywhere.

Veracity

Veracity is the trustworthiness, truthfulness, and accuracy of your data. Joshua Cazier has frequently observed that if your data is not trustworthy, executives will revert back to their own opinions and old ways of making decisions. I am sure many others have noticed this behavior as well. Veracity is important for building a foundation of trust in your data.

Veracity lays the foundation for quality data, without which it is impossible to have high-quality data. According to Steve Stone, former CIO of Lowes, if you want to have value from data, quality is job number one, and that includes improving the veracity of your data. Yet, Stone notes you can go too far with veracity and reduce your realized value because nearly everything you can do to improve veracity slows your system down, reducing velocity. Nevertheless, without it, nothing else matters because there is no real value. So again, executives should strive for the right balance.

Note that veracity is necessary, but not sufficient, for quality data. Quality data also requires a degree of validity, versatility, variability, relevance, availability, and the proper structure, which are discussed in more detail later in this chapter.

Value

Value is the most important V, without which none of the other Vs matter. Executives care about data because of the value it creates, not just to have it. Every other V is a tool that executives can use to manage the value of their data. All of them focus on increasing or harnessing the value of the data in ways useful to the organization.

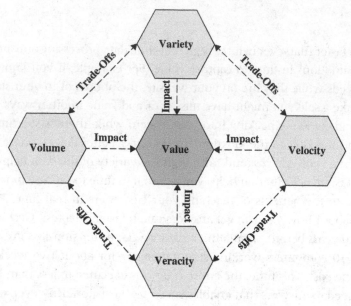

Figure 3.1 Five Vs Interactions and Value

Value is not about maximizing all of the Vs. Nor is it just about increasing volume, variety, velocity, and veracity, though these can help at the appropriate time, done the appropriate way. Value is about getting the right mix for your organization at the right time and managing the trade-offs among volume, variety, velocity, and veracity, as shown in Figure 3.1.

Each of the first four of the classic Vs of Big Data have the potential to increase value for the reasons mentioned previously. Still, there are trade-offs you have to manage to realize the value, which must be aligned with your business strategy. For example, adding verification systems to ensure higher veracity for your data is likely to reduce your velocity, just as the requirement to react in real time lowers your ability to use the most accurate data, often forcing you to settle for proxies that are faster and more readily available. Similarly, more variety of data may take longer to process, reducing velocity and taking up volume, raising the storage cost and affecting the volume of data that can be economically stored. Higher volumes of data to process can also reduce velocity.

As each of the Vs can increase your ability to harness value, they each come at a cost. Steve Stone inspired and expressed this interaction in Table 3.2 as well as the explanatory text for an article that Stone and I are working on.

Here is how Stone explained it: The three icons represent increase (arrow up), neutral (side-to-side arrow), and pressure (down arrow).

- **Increasing volume.** The common scenarios for increasing volume include retaining additional history, enriching core data, or adding new use cases. Although new use cases will likely increase variety, there is no certainty that additional history or enrichment will change data patterns (variety). In all cases, additional volume will pressure velocity and veracity.

Table 3.2 Interaction of Five Classic Vs of Big Data

Increasing	Impact On			
	Volume	Variety	Velocity	Veracity
Volume		↔	↓	↓
Variety	↑		↓	↓
Velocity	↔	↔		↓
Veracity	↓	↔	↓	

- **Increasing variety.** Increasing variety almost always requires an increase in volume. As such, velocity and veracity are often pressured when data variety is increased.
- **Increasing velocity.** Increasing velocity often does not affect volume as a whole, though it could require changes in the overall data storage architecture. Velocity increases have no impact on variety, but can place new pressures on veracity protocols to operate in a real-time or near-real-time manner.
- **Increasing veracity.** Increasing veracity can reduce data duplications and data noise, reducing overall volume. Usually, changing veracity has a negligible impact on variety, but it places more pressure on velocity as more time is often needed to verify the data.

As we see, all of these Vs can help harness the value in your data and put that value to work, but you cannot and should not maximize them all at once. There are trade-offs that need to be made. The wise executive will work closely with their technical teams to understand and develop a business and operational strategy that optimizes the Vs in alignment with the business strategy to harness the most value for their firm. Table 3.3 summarizes the key points of this section, and presents, without making any recommendations, some common tools or concepts associated with each V to get you started on your journey.

A FEW VS TO ENHANCE VALUE

The five classic Vs of Big Data can provide a useful guide to using the data you already have more effectively. However, there are a few other Vs that can guide you to enhancing the intrinsic value of your data, which we cover in this section.

Validity

Validity is a term we use in science to make sure that we are actually measuring what we think we are measuring. Although relevance focuses on getting the right data, validity ensures we are measuring that data the right way. Traditional researchers spend a lot of time thinking about validity before collecting data to analyze. Organizations that

Table 3.3 Summary of the Classic Vs of Big Data

Vs	What It Is	When to Use It	When Not to Use It
Volume	The quantity of data you have available for analysis	When additional data gives better coverage, statistical power, or the ability to use a more advanced algorithm	When increasing the amount of data costs more than the value created or exceeds computational capacity or skills available to analyze
Variety	The breadth or relevant data sources available for analysis	When theory or intuition suggests a different type of data can improve analysis	When the infrastructure is limited, when following a "kitchen sink" throw-everything strategy (unguided inclusion), or when speed is of the essence
Velocity	The speed in which the analysis happens, often in real time	When speed in processing an analytics application can add business value, such as responding while a customer is in your store or on your website	When speed adds little business value, when the data is not designed for speed, when the algorithms would be too slow, or when application is not effective
Veracity	A measure of how trustworthy the data is, if you know what it means, and if you believe it	When concerned about data quality, when validity is important, or when legal issues may arise	When speed matters more than quality, when data has shown significant reliability in the past, and when the data management process is mature
Value	The value you have in your data in terms of how it can be used to advance your mission and goals	When you believe there is useful potential value from relevant data, working to optimize and use it effectively	When owning, using, or collecting the data is illegal or unethical

neglect this forethought might end up with data they think is relevant, but if it does not measure what they think it does, it is not likely to be as relevant as they hoped.

Because of the rapid growth of data science, a shortage of skills, and the heavy reliance on secondary data collected for other reasons, I believe our field grew faster than proper training and best practices were able to keep up. Therefore, data scientists and executives are missing an opportunity to improve their results by testing and improving the validity of their data.

Many analytics professionals end up having to contort, combine, and transform the data in a variety of ways to turn it into a useful feature they can model. To some extent, this situation will always be true. However, if we went back to our roots and took time to improve the various types of validity of our data, using approaches borrowed from science, we would need to contort less while learning more.

Here are a few ways you can improve the validity of your data:

- **Design for validity.** Think carefully, from the very beginning, if it is clear that your data means what you think it means. Look at it from different perspectives; ask different groups, from different backgrounds, what they think it means; bring in a consultant or other expert to help in the design to help make sure it is well designed from the very beginning. For some data, you should also check internationally to see if international colleagues interpret it the same way, especially if there are language issues or different customs and norms.

- **Collect a representative sample.** Part of validity is not just measuring how it should be done, but that you are also measuring who or what most matches the intended use. If the sample does not represent the audience fairly, or the groups measured are disproportionate to what they will be, bias will likely result. See the discussion of data variability later in this chapter, and survivorship bias in Task 5: Execution for related concerns. In some cases, synthetic data can help, also discussed later in this chapter.

- **Conduct performance testing.** Conduct tests on your data to make sure it is performing as hoped and intended. Also check the shape and distributions of your data to make sure they represent what you think they do. You can also use statistical tools to measure the reliability and validity of your data, using well-developed techniques evident in many peer-reviewed journal articles.

- **Compare to a benchmark.** Compare your data to samples of other external data you may be able to acquire. See if they look and behave similarly. Check the properties, distribution, ranges, and other profile factors. If they are significantly different, you should seek to understand why.

Vocabulary

Data standardization is not exactly the same as vocabulary, but they are highly related and interact with each other. Both are important and often confused with each other. Each has its place with their unique advantages and disadvantages. I learned this lesson well when I led the International Working Group for Bee Data Standardization, and will share a few insights for both vocabulary and data standardization from that experience and others and then discuss the synergies and trade-offs between them.

Shared Vocabulary

Vocabulary refers to how you describe the meaning of something you capture in your data, to create a shared understanding of that meaning across the organization. It includes a very precise and sometimes technical definition of exactly what that means, so that others who hear the word or phrase would very easily understand what it means, where it comes from, and how it can (and should not) be used for analysis. Vocabulary facilitates very precise and useful communication about the data that ensures everyone is on the same page and uses the word or phrase appropriately.

Vocabulary is essential for scaling your data capabilities across the organization, learning what data can do what, sharing important features, and enhancing the ability to build more precise models over time. Indeed, it is critical to learn from data and, ultimately, become a learning organization that consistently succeeds in analytics.

Without this clear vocabulary, any lessons learned about the data, its strengths, weaknesses, and other attributes are often lost and not communicated clearly to other analysts who may need to model something similar. Thus, a lack of a clear vocabulary can slow down growth, learning, and discovery efforts. In addition, without a clear vocabulary understood widely across the organization, at least for the important variables and data points, it is difficult to clearly identify where problems are in data collection and how to improve them for relevance and usefulness.

Data Standardization

Defining a clear data vocabulary is the first step to data standardization, but they are not the same. Data standardization also involves selecting one way (or at least very few) to record and use that data for the organization, whereas data vocabulary can still allow for many representations of a concept, as long as they are clearly documented, understood, and communicated. In other words, they can all coexist. With data standardization, all of you agree on one primary way to record something and do so consistently across the organization. You thus have fewer vocabulary definitions but can better merge and aggregate the data with a deeper shared understanding of what it means.

In reality, sometimes data that should mean the same thing may not mean the same thing in different parts of the organization. There are many ways data can be coded, especially when people are involved and different practices and cultures emerge. Some differences are driven by custom or convenience, others because there is some local advantage or law to code data a certain way.

Although there may be good reasons for the differences, whatever they are, it is important to know what the data means so it can be modeled correctly. It is also important to standardize or harmonize the data so that (1) it can be aggregated and (2) the data has similar meaning after it is aggregated and can be correctly used in models.

Measurements are designed by people and eventually turn into data. Many measurements were created years ago, which may or may not be relevant to today's business challenges. Business process owners started with a concept that needs to be measured and operationalized for that purpose. There are usually several ways to measure a concept, and each way to measure it has its own strengths and weaknesses. For this reason, many social and data scientists try to find or design multiple ways to capture and model an idea because it lets them test multiple approaches.

However, there is a cost in collecting the data, difficulties in harmonizing different approaches, and loss of focus and understanding across the organization of different measures. Although in the beginning it may make sense to test and validate a few ways to measure a concept, inasmuch as one or a few are proven to be good indicators over time, the data should be standardized to improve access, efficiency, scale, use, and understanding across the organizations.

Sure, there may be occasional exceptions where a deep data scientist needs something a certain way, but most of the time having well-chosen, common standards accelerate access, use, and trust in the data as everyone knows what it means, how it was collected, and what uses have proven most appropriate, enabling everyone to focus on using it for action.

Take for example, the idea of collecting debt from someone who purchased a car. When would you say that someone is in default? Is it when they are 3 days late on a payment? 30, 60, or 90 days? What if they made a partial payment? What if they made this payment, but have been routinely late several times over the last year? What if they are a few days late and they happen to have other credit difficulties on other accounts you can see on their credit report? What if they are late, but you can see that they just moved, reported a salary increase, and maybe are just getting organized?

Do all of these possible definitions, and many more options, have the same relevance and usefulness for the business? There may be a legal or historical definition, but it is also important to use a definition that is relevant to your business operations, one that can help you make decisions and take action in a timely way. The most useful definitions should be identified, tested, used, standardized, and shared.

Data Documentation

Similar to the concept of data standardization is data documentation. This concept addresses the need for clear definitions of attributes or measures, but it should also include its lineage, origin, and history of any changes or updates made to it. Data documentation should also be searchable and easy to find by those authorized to use it. It should include the origin of the data, its intended use, and, where possible, descriptions of where and how it has been used well and where it has not proven so effective. This level of documentation and discipline is essential to maintaining and communicating data vocabulary and data standardization.

Manage Trade-Offs

A good, clear data vocabulary is essential for doing analytics at scale to improve quality, consistency, and repeatability. When you are new to modeling a concept, it can be helpful to have a range of related variables, each with their own definition and vocabulary, so you can test them and see which ones are more useful and for what purposes. However, there is a cost. Expanding data vocabulary with more data types increases the sparsity in your data, reducing the volume of a particular defined variable, which reduces what you can do with it. It reduces the ability to aggregate, and when you do aggregate, it requires an extra step so meanings can be harmonized, when possible.

Conversely, data standardization allows for greater consistency and scalability of your data, making aggregation easier, and increases volume. But you lose richness and variety. Without the variety, there is also a danger the metric on which you standardized may not be the most relevant and useful one. Thus, standardization, although valuable, should be done with care.

My recommendation is to use a mix of history and theory to identify a few likely candidates; test them in a variety of situations, even if this is with simulated data; and see which are more useful. In terms of base data, which is the primary data you collected, I recommend the following after testing: standardize on one or two promising definitions and try to minimize the variation, but have a wider range of features built on various transformations and permutations of that base data the data scientists can then field test.

Versatility

Steve Stone introduced me to the importance of data versatility. Versatility is a measure of the adaptability of your data, its ability to be used in many different contexts and for different uses. When prioritizing your data needs under limited resource constraints, data that can be used in a wide range of applications should be prioritized over data that can only be used for one. Even without constraints, having a few versatile data points readily available that can be used for many purposes in which people can become familiar and learn to trust is a worthwhile investment.

When putting value on data, the value for those data that can be used for multiple purposes should be added together for each purpose rather than just giving it a value for the purpose at hand. Even more, I suggest adding a synergistic coefficient to the total identified value estimate for versatile data, maybe by 1.5 or more times depending on the range of uses and likely synergies that would result from the multiple uses. Data versatility increases quality, and versatile data should also be prioritized over other non-versatile data you might collect, unless that data is extremely valuable.

Variability

Previously we discussed the importance of the volume of data. Although it is indeed important, there are limits to the value gained from increasing the volume of data. Not all data, even data of the same structure, is equally valuable. More of the same data will add limited marginal value beyond the increased scale of your ability to act; it just tells you more robustly what you already know.

For example, if you are trying to make better movie recommendations, more data from a particular demographic may help you with that demographic. But eventually you have enough data on that demographic that there is little practical increase in the quality of new insights made with additional data. You reach a point where additional investment in data and time do not yield better decisions, outcomes, or value. You reach a point of diminishing returns.

Increasing another V, the variability of your data, enables you to develop new insights if you can bring in data from groups that are underrepresented in your current data, and are likely to be different in a way that enables you to act on that insight. Variability gives volume with more coverage, that is a greater variability in the data, while retaining the same data structure and format. This step assumes you have, or plan to try to acquire, customers from that underrepresented group or you would have insights with no ability to act on them.

The point is, even for a given structure in a database, not all data is equal and there are blind spots. Many ethical issues have arisen on datasets that have very high volume but have low coverage or variability. They may be more valuable for one group but not apply to another. Of particular concern with this type of data is racial profiling, where models were inappropriately applied to situations outside of the data on which the models were trained.

A good principle to remember is that the models and insights generated from your data are only as applicable to new data as that new data is similar to the data on which the model was trained. Executives should consider not just the volume of the data they have, but also its variability and the coverage it provides and judge its relevance to current and future business applications. Rather than blindly increasing volume without purpose, executives should carefully consider both the depth and breadth of their data along with how and where it might be used. Instead of treating all data equally, when the value varies based on its variability and potential use, the coverage should be considered along with the volume. It is not just about having more data, but the right range of data that should come with that volume.

Availability

No matter how valuable the data, if it is not accessible to those who need it, it cannot be used. It is more than just making a data file available for use. Data needs to have its meaning and history (data lineage) well documented and internally marketed to those who could use it and for its intended purpose. Even inside the company, there are different priorities and inertia. People, even data scientists, all have their biases and often go for what is convenient over what is valuable. Focus your energy on making quality and valuable data available to those who can use it so it can be prioritized and used to advance business goals.

Data is an asset that largely loses much of its relevance as it gets farther from the circumstances or the time in which it was generated. It is not because the data itself changes, but rather that the context and environment often changes in a way that makes the data less relevant.

Data Silos

It is common for most organizations to have data scattered across different departments, platforms, business units, and systems. Sometimes the data is siloed due to legacy data systems, acquisitions, changing data formats and geography, or political considerations. Occasionally there are good reasons for data to be siloed or protected in some way, such as for security concerns or regulatory rules.

In general though, data is more valuable together than apart, especially when it is data relevant to an important business problem. Therefore, most of the time it is better to have relevant, usable data together in one place for easy access and analysis. This proximity allows for more use and potential synergies between related data to be analyzed.

The thoughtful executive will find ways to overcome obstacles to integration and put most relevant data together in a place where it can be easily and efficiently accessed. It may be a cloud-based solution or another localized solution, but having the data available is essential for analytics success.

Dark Data

Even harder to find and use than siloed data is dark data, which is data that you do not even know you have. It can also be buried deep in silos, but the difference is you do not even know to go look for it. It may have been left there because it was hard to analyze. However, with more advanced tools and techniques, data that was once hard to use can often be quite valuable today. If it is relevant, you should have and use it. If it is not relevant, you may be unknowingly spending resources on something of no value. Regardless, if you do not know about it, you will not be able to manage it appropriately. Here are a few tips for finding dark data.

- **Know where to look.** Dark data typically resides in databases, archival storage systems, log files, emails, text, social media posts, stored documents, or data warehouses. It tends to be unstructured, incomplete, or hard to access, making it more challenging to use, which often leads to it being forgotten.
- **Take inventory.** Just as you would with any asset, taking an inventory is critical to managing dark data effectively. You could ask various departments to take a data inventory and file a report, but analyzing logs of data access can also help to identify data that is being stored but not accessed.
- **Use data discovery and profiling tools.** Data discovery tools search for data across different systems to identify patterns and relationships within the data that can help you find new sources of dark data. Data profiling consists of analyzing your data's structure, content, and quality, which can also help you identify incomplete or inconsistent pockets of dark data in data you already use.

Table 3.4 summarizes these Vs for enhancing value and whether to use them.

QUALITY DATA

Nearly everyone interviewed for this book talked about the importance of having quality data. LeAnne Hill, a manager at the accounting and advisory firm FORVIS LLP in the enterprise risk and quantitative advisory practice area, shared that at a firm she worked for earlier, 90% of the complaints they received were about data quality, which is mostly controlled by the business side. Most called an improvement in data quality an investment for the future. Steve Stone went so far as to say it is job number one for executives to ensure quality data, just as they would care for any asset. Indeed, this statement makes a lot of sense given how valuable data is. However, because data is an amorphous asset, different from most other assets within an organization and less familiar to executives, it is hard for them to know how to do this job number one well.

Table 3.4 Summary of Vs to Enhance Data's Value

Vs	What It Is	When to Use It	When Not to Use It
Validity	The degree to which your data measures what you think it should be measuring	When you have substantial control of the data generation process, make sure it measures what you need. Test it when it is important, but you cannot change it.	Do not use validity when you have little control over the generation process. In those cases, focus on evaluating what it does measure and seeing if that is useful in some way.
Vocabulary	Standardized definitions for important data that everyone understands	When you know the concept you need to measure, take care to define it well so it can be accepted, communicated, and shared effectively in the organization.	Do not use vocabulary early on when you are still exploring and seeing what is useful. If testing and exploring shows promise, then you can develop and share a standard vocabulary. But broad sharing too early, when its usefulness is still speculative, creates an unnecessary cognitive burden on others that will lead them to tune out future updates.
Variability	The range of instances of data and how much it varies within a given attribute	When the variability of the data matches the current and desired use, it should be used. In general, variability builds robustness and adds value while reducing bias. Synthetic data may be helpful in expanding data to match desired uses in otherwise sparse datasets with low availability of expanded use.	Do not use variability if the intended use is highly focused on a certain population. It can sometimes be useful to have a very narrow dataset focused on a very important population that you need to study carefully, without potential noise from other groups not deemed relevant to the problem.
Versatility	A concept to capture the variety and value of uses for a given piece of data	When versatile data is prioritized, it creates synergies and people learn what it is and how it works. If they can go back to the same data for multiple uses they become more familiar with it and will use it more often and more appropriately.	Do not focus on versatility when highly specialized data with just one use may be a critical use. When that is the case, it will bump that type of data up in priority.
aVailability	A measure of how available data is to those who need it and how useful those features derived from the data actually are.	When data is available, it can be used. In general, the more available and understood the data is, the more likely it is to be put to a valuable use. But ease of access and use are important. Decision-makers need access, but data should also be in the right format they can use and be reliably available when needed.	Do not use availability if it causes too much data to be made available. Some data is confidential or has risks to sharing, so controlling access is important, too. It is also important to not overload people with too much irrelevant data or it will hide the valuable data and reduce its use.

This section focuses on understanding what quality is, why it is so hard to maintain, and how to improve and measure it.

Defining Data Quality

You would be forgiven if you equated the concept of veracity, discussed previously, with data quality. Although veracity is an important part of data quality, it is only a part of it, though a critical, foundational one. There are a few more things to think about when it comes to quality. Most were previously discussed independently as dimensions of quality, but all of them fit together to form a foundation of quality, more or less in the order I list and describe them here:

- **Relevance.** Relevance is the first, and one of the most important, factors in data quality. From an executive's perspective, the data only has quality to the degree that it lets you do something useful with it. If it is not relevant data to a problem you can solve or value you can create, the rest of the attributes do not matter.

- **Validity.** Validity is the accurate measurement of what you think you are measuring. Even if you have relevant data for a concept you care about, if your measurement is significantly wrong, the quality and usefulness will not be there.

- **Veracity.** Assuming you have relevant data that measures what it should be measuring, it is important it is true and accurate. Perhaps not perfectly so as we can live with a little dirty data in exchange for speed for some, but not all, applications. Yet, having too much dirty data renders it useless. It is important to judge the harm of dirty data and benefit of clean data when optimizing for veracity. When in doubt, try to improve veracity.

- **Variability.** Quality data represents the audience or concepts you are trying to model. Although it does need to be relevant, valid, and true, it also needs to have enough representation to cover what it is you are trying to analyze because you cannot, and should not, extrapolate the findings beyond the data you have. The more variability in the data, the greater the quality because its applicability to more potential uses goes up.

- **Availability.** If the data is not accessible and available to be analyzed and used, the rest of the features do not matter much. However, availability is not just about technology, it is also about the structure of the data and how it is stored that affects quality the most. The same data, structured differently, can be used much more efficiently in different ways. The structure of the data should be appropriate to the use. Figure 3.2 introduces a conceptual map of the most important attributes of data quality.

Law of Data Entropy

Unfortunately, the dirty little secret of data is that it is, well, dirty. It is actually much dirtier than you would expect or likely believe. Patrick Getzen talks about how surprising it

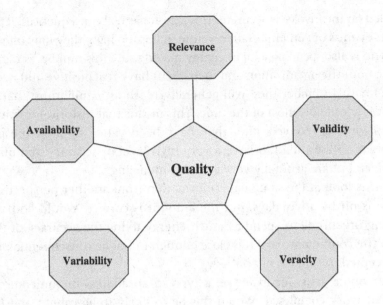

Figure 3.2 Attributes of Data Quality

was to discover how dirty some of their data was when Getzen became a chief data and analytics officer. The early stages of analytics maturity is also what most teams spend their time doing: collecting, cleaning, and managing data. Estimates are that up to 80% of an analytics team's time is spent managing data, leaving much less time than desired for analysis and impact. Even more, no amount of cleaning can completely compensate or compare to getting better data at the start.

What I have found particularly interesting is that your data is likely dirty in largely predictable ways. This is due to what I call the law of data entropy. The term *entropy* can be thought of as "the amount of order or lack of order in a system,"[7] where in this case we think of the system as our data. In physics, the second law of thermodynamics says that entropy always increases with time.

This law applies nearly as well to data as it does to physics. Unless energy is being spent designing data quality and even more energy is spent keeping quality data, your data quality will inevitably degrade. I have never seen or heard of a bona fide exception to this law. As with any physical system, it takes energy to bring order to it, and even more energy to keep and maintain its quality. You have to continuously invest in data quality. It is never a one-and-done investment.

This principle of energy determining your data quality also enables you to predict where you likely have quality data and where you do not. You follow the energy. If there is little energy going into keeping the quality up, it will not last. Even for data on the same type of system or fields in the very same data table, certain elements will have very good quality, and others will have less.

It is not just energy, but energy with real consequences on something that matters, positive or negative, with a mix of both that is best. For example, let us look at client invoicing. Someone at the firm will spend a lot of time and energy making sure that the amount billed on the invoice is accurate. This action has real consequences. If the amount is too low, they miss out on important revenue. If it is too high, they may often anger the customer who is also spending a lot of energy making sure this number is right.

Because both the organization and their client have real positive and negative consequences, for this number they will generally reach an equilibrium that is close to the number it should be, most of the time. This means that historical invoice amounts billed and payments received, after they have been vetted by both the paying and receiving organizations, tend to have a very high level of accuracy and quality. They are not perfect, but are generally very good for modeling.

Now, let us look at the same data information from another perspective. Say the service date is off by a few days, but the amount is correct. Would both the paying and receiving organizations spend as much energy fixing the accuracy of the date? It depends on the consequences. If it is close enough to not be consequential, it will generally be accepted, regardless of accuracy.

Consider other parts, for example, a typo in an address or someone's name, or description of work completed. Would this be as likely to be caught and fixed as an error in the payment amount? Not likely. Sure, if someone saw it they would likely fix it, but they would not go out of their way because the consequences of being wrong and the benefits of being right are much lower than with the amount.

From a practical value standpoint, this means that you can largely predict the quality of your data by the nature of the consequences to the firm or to the person responsible for the data. The more the data is relied on for important business operations, and the greater the reward or loss if it is wrong, the more likely it is to be corrected and accurate. Without that consistent pressure, the quality will not be there.

Note, this is not just about investing in data strategies. Even a significant investment in data quality, without natural consequences occurring when there are errors in the data, will also drift into disorder. The consequences are an important signal to the organization of an error, and one that needs fixing when the organizational pain is high enough for it to be adjusted. However, a firm can spend a lot of resources on data quality, thinking they are making progress, and maybe they are, but if they are not using the data in meaningful ways important to the organization, there is still a risk the data is not accurate.

Doheney's Axiom

This leads to what I refer to as Doheney's axiom, named after Shaun Doheney, who first shared the idea with me while he was taking the Leading in Analytics course offered by the Professional Development Academy, which forms the foundation for this book. Doheney, who is currently an analytics manager at Amazon, gave me permission to use this quote.

"The best way to improve the quality of your data is to make decisions based on it."

—Shaun Doheney

Although there are many methods and paradigms regarding data quality, and they should be used, Doheney's axiom is generally the best way to get started. Once you start making decisions with data, there will be consequences and feedback for data quality, which not only gives a motive to improve data quality but also gives valuable signals of where and how the data needs to be improved with energy and resources behind it to get the job done.

Quality will improve where it is most relevant for the decision, based on the data. If the decisions have any consequence, energy will naturally go into the parts of the data most needed to improve the outcome. Yes, that energy still needs to be directed into proven ways to design, monitor, and improve data quality, but without that energy and focus driven by the pain and reward of decision-making, there will only be marginal improvements in data quality, even if funds are spent without consequences. One big advantage to this approach is the data that is most important to whatever decision-making is at hand will naturally be improved because of its impact on the outcome.

In addition to using the data to make decisions, there are also many systems and practices in place for managing data quality that should be used, including data observability, data stewardship, and different ways of capturing, storing, and collecting data. Our focus here is on what executives can do to ensure decisions are made on the data. This focus will put pressure on the organization to ensure quality data is kept and made available for decision-making. Executives and business process owners can then work with the various technical team members and outside consultants to determine the best path for them in terms of operationalizing quality data.

Data Minimalism

The more data you have, the harder it is to ensure it is quality data. "Don't boil the ocean," says Piyanka Jain. Instead focus on the most relevant data to your business today and where you want to go tomorrow. Rather than focus on increasing data volume and variety, as powerful as those features are, it is often more fruitful and less costly to focus on increasing data relevance. When we recognize not all data is equally valuable, nor is all data worth storing or using, and that some data is actually harmful to even own or collect, we can design a mature data management strategy focused on value, the most important V.

More irrelevant data will not save you or help your situation. Sometimes the answer is not in Big Data but is more easily found in a smaller highly relevant and focused dataset designed to meet business needs. There is also a cost to collecting, storing, and processing data. This cost is in money and lost focus due to the lack of prioritization of data relevant to your needs. Here are a few reasons not to collect and store every piece of data you possibly can:

- **Storage cost.** It is true that the cost of storage has dropped dramatically, but it is not free, and the amount of data companies are collecting is rising just as fast, if not more, than the cost of storing it is falling.

- **Risks.** Some data is risky to have, and if you do not have it you cannot be charged with using it wrongly or get into trouble for a data breach.
- **Loss of focus.** Having irrelevant data distracts you and gets in the way of paying attention to the relevant data that matters.

As a data scientist I often want to collect and analyze as much data as possible. However, the quality and relevance of the data matter a great deal and are often confused for each other. If I have very high quality data that is exactly what it reported to be but it is not relevant to what I am modeling, it is of no use. If, however, I have low-to medium-quality data but it is highly relevant, I can usually clean and enhance it to the point of getting some use out of it. Not as much use as if it was high quality, but much more use than from irrelevant data.

If I instead focus on identifying and collecting relevant data, and deprioritize other data, it is much easier to have high-quality and relevant data because I can devote more energy to maintaining and improving data quality when there are fewer distractions from the noise of irrelevant data. It is generally better to have less data with greater quality and relevance than more irrelevant data. Task 7: Responsible Analytics presents another dimension of data minimalism that includes the ethical aspects and risks associated with the collection and use of irrelevant data.

ALCOA

Ahmer Inam, referenced previously, advises that the responsibility for the stewardship of the data, for ensuring good quality, should rest with the source where it is generated. Executives should measure the quality of these dimensions and hold those who influence data generation accountable for improving that quality.

Johann Vaz, with his decades as a CIO and technology executive in the pharmaceutical industry, shared a useful way to think about capturing data quality at the source, where it is generated. It does not cover all the dimensions of data quality, because some factors are outside the control of where the data is generated, but it can be a very good place to start in training the people or managing the processes of what they should be thinking about during the data quality process to increase the likelihood of quality data downstream in the data pipeline.

Executives can use the ALCOA checklist to train those responsible for generating quality data from their area to know what it looks like and how to audit their data quality and make sure they are on the right track. Executives should be able to ask those responsible for data generation specific questions about each of these dimensions of their data to make sure it is captured. Here is a quick ALCOA primer:

- **Attributable.** Do you know where it came from, its origin and process? A data scientist will often extend this to the broader concept of lineage, which includes knowing not just where it came from but also everything that has been done to it since initial collection.

- **Legible.** Do you know if the data is precise, understandable, and unambiguous? When you look at the data, you know what it means, which requires having clear, standardized definitions. In addition, this includes appropriate meta data, or data about the data, that gives you context to better understand its meaning and how it can be used.

- **Contemporaneous.** Do you know if the data was collected at the time the event happened, which increases the trustworthiness of the data? The farther from the time of the event the data was collected the more opportunity for errors, intentional or not, to creep into the system.

- **Original.** Do you know if you have the original recording of the data or if it is a copy? Having the original record increases trust in the quality of the data. Your data scientist will do some cleaning and transformation to prepare it for modeling, but tracing the lineage back to the source will give them more confidence in the quality of the data.

- **Accurate.** Do you know if the data is accurate? Is this the correct information that matches reality? Errors can creep into the process from a variety of sources. Making sure the data is accurate can go a long way to building trust and usefulness in the data and the solutions it produces.

The data scientist will add a few more checks and controls once they get the data for a project. But those post-collection measures will not catch everything, so addressing the ALCOA conditions will go a long way toward providing high-quality inputs for the analytics' models. This, in turn, will build trust in the process and the outcomes on the business side.

CHAPTER SUMMARY AND EXERCISES

Task 3: Summary

Data is at the heart of most of the analytics we think about today and essential to its success. It is an incredibly valuable resource that has often been compared to oil and the economic revolution that resulted from the discovery and use of oil more than a century ago. Data is like oil in that it takes skill and effort to identify, extract, and harness that value effectively. Data is unlike oil in that it is a reusable asset, it usually improves a business process instead of being sold directly, it is highly differentiated for each firm, and its quality and generation can be largely controlled by the firm.

Not all data is of equal value. All data should be prioritized for relevance and managed for quality. Valuing data as an asset with a monetary figure placed on it can help data be prioritized more effectively. The five classic Vs of Big Data (volume, variety, velocity, veracity, and value) can be used as a framework to manage and harness the value of your data more effectively. A few other, smaller Vs can help enhance data's value.

Left alone, the law of data entropy posits that data quality will decay. It requires constant energy to maintain data quality and integrity. The best way to improve data quality is to make decisions based on it, as noted in Doheney's axiom, because this provides the needed energy to reduce, halt, or reverse the decay. ALCOA is one framework that can be used to assess some data quality measures. However, the focus should be on keeping relevant data in good quality, but some data should not be collected or stored.

Task 3: Exercises

1. Consider the comparison of data to oil, as summarized in Table 3.1. Reflect on your experience with data and select three key attributes of data that seem interesting or important to you. Write them down, explain why you find them interesting, and how they might or should guide your future interactions with data.

2. Consider the steps presented in the section titled "Identifying Valuable Data." In your own words, list and describe each step in the important process of finding relevant and valuable data.

3. Consider the concept of identified value as outlined in this chapter by Patrick Getzen. Discuss how you might use the concept to put a price or value on data you are familiar with and give an example. Discuss how this concept can be used to identify and value relevant data.

4. Consider the discussion on the five classic Vs of Big Data. Describe the trade-offs among these Vs and how understanding the trade-offs, as shown in Figure 3.1, Table 3.1, and Table 3.2, can help business leaders understand how to better manage their investment in data technologies when they are aligned with business strategy.

5. Ponder the importance of data quality to analytics and do the following:

   a. Write a paragraph or two about why this is so important and what characteristics make up data quality.

   b. Consider the law of data entropy and its Doheney's axiom and write a few paragraphs describing how they are interrelated and why both are important.

   c. Review the ALCOA and use Tool 3.1 to assess the quality of a dataset in which you are familiar or have access. Report on your findings and discuss the implications regarding the quality and use of this data.

Tool 3.1 ALCOA Exercise for Data Quality

Think about data in which you have some experience from your current or a past organization. Now, answer the following statements regarding that data on a scale of 1 (definitely no) to 5 (definitely yes).

■ **Attributable.** I know where this data comes from.

1	2	3	4	5

■ **Legible.** I understand this data and the context in which it was created.

1	2	3	4	5

■ **Contemporaneous.** I know this data was collected at the time of the event of interest.

1	2	3	4	5

■ **Original.** I know this is the original data that was collected.

1	2	3	4	5

■ **Accurate.** I know this data is a true and accurate representation of the event of interest.

1	2	3	4	5

■ Now take a moment to add up your score, and compare it to the rubric in Table 3.5.

Table 3.5 ALCOA Scoring Rubric

Score	Interpretation
20 to 25	Generally good, unless one or more categories is below 3
15 to 19	A good start, but must improve the weak areas
10 to 14	Needs serious improvement
5 to 9	Do not ask

NOTES

1. https://www.forbes.com/sites/douglaslaney/2020/07/22/your-companys-data-may-be-worth-more-than-your-company/
2. Special thanks to my colleague and friend Dr. David Darcy for helping me think through some of the comparisons between data and oil.
3. https://www.investopedia.com/terms/p/paretoprinciple.asp
4. BrandPost, "The Reason Many AI and Analytics Projects Fail—and How to Make Sure Yours Doesn't," CIO.com (January 20, 2023). https://www.cio.com/article/419552/the-reason-many-ai-and-analytics-projects-fail-and-how-to-make-sure-yours-doesnt.html
5. Special thanks to Steve Stone, former CIO of Lowes, for helping me think through how the Vs interact with each other to harness, enhance, and protect the value of data.
6. C. M. Christensen, *The Innovator's Dilemma* (Boston: Harvard Business Review Press, 2016).
7. https://dictionary.cambridge.org/us/dictionary/english/entropy

TASK **4**

The Tools

ANALYTICS MINDSET

There are many tools used in analytics. Some are algorithmic tools that do the analytics; others are computational technologies that enable analytics to be done at scale. All of them can be helpful at different times and places, depending on their use. Yet, the most important tool is your mindset, according to Aryng CEO Piyanka Jain, because with the right mindset you will find a way to make an analytically driven decision.

This concept was underscored to me while interviewing Dr. Karl Kempf, my personal analytics hero and the father of the concept of the five manageable tasks, which are central to the framework for this book. Kempf talked about not being able to share a lot of insights on the tools of analytics, because that was not his specialty. He described himself as being the "math guy," not the "tool guy." I just love Karl for his humility. Here was one of the smartest people I have ever met in my entire life in a field full of smart people, talking about how much he did not know about tools, in spite of his team's many billion-dollar successes shared in the introduction to this book.

If you are an executive, business process owner, or even on the analytics team, *you do not have to know everything*. In fact, that should not be your goal, as no one can know everything. At the exponential rate knowledge is growing, it is doubtful anyone will ever be able to know it all. Yes, everyone can know, should know, something. Even in one field, you cannot know it all, but if we have the right mindset, like Dr. Karl Kempf, we can work together by contributing what we do know to the expanded team and our organizations and collectively have the knowledge we need to succeed. We do this by having the right mindset when even if we do not know an answer, it can be found by working together, seeking the right data, and analyzing it the right way, with the right tools for the right types of problems.

This determination, resolve, and belief is central to analytics success in your organization. There are many vendors willing to sell you their tools. These tools can be helpful, but if you do not have the right mindset, these tools, as good as they may be, will provide little value to your organization. If you do have the right mindset and are genuinely ready to learn and change based on your analytics, these vendors and tools can help you succeed.

The right mindset is one that focuses on the problem, not the tool. Whatever tools you use need to meet your needs and match the size and complexity of your organization. Many vendors sell the sizzle of their tools, and some go as far as to spread myths. The right mindset is also a discerning one, one that takes time to investigate not just the tool, but how it can be used to affect the organization, and one that can put an economic or societal value on that impact, not just that it generated good statistical significance or that everyone is talking about it.

As some of our experts shared, AI and analytics are not always a panacea. Whatever the hype, you cannot just "sprinkle a little AI fairy dust and hope your problem goes away," as Polly Mitchell-Guthrie, VP of Industry outreach and thought leadership at Kinaxis, said. It has to solve a real problem to be valuable. AI is a valuable tool, but not the only one, and not always the best one. Analytics is a journey, one where you start where you are, with the problems and capabilities you have today, and grow and expand to address other areas according to your needs, market conditions, and maturing capabilities over time.

Tools are important, but they are not the most important element in the analytics process. That is because tools, on their own, do not solve problems. People solve problems using the right mindset, a well-defined problem, data, and, yes, tools, too. The correct tools simply make that process more efficient and effective.

This chapter starts with a focus on the executive's role in tool selection, inputs going into the tool, and the use of those tools. We then look at the various categories of analytics and how using this framework can guide you to the right task of the job you want the tool to do, followed by the jobs that different types of tools can do. We conclude with a discussion about tool synergies and limits.

EXECUTIVES' ROLE IN TOOLS

Executives have an important role to play in tool selection, inputs going into the tools, and tool use, which we discuss in this section.

Tool Selection

It would be a mistake to believe that executives have no role in tool selection. Although others in the organization might be more technical and fluent with analytics tools and techniques, executives must set the stage and work collaboratively to make sure the tools take them in the right direction, at the right time, and are focused on the right problems.

To do this selection well, it helps to follow the wisdom of another one of my intellectual heroes, the late Clayton Christensen, Harvard professor and author of the *Innovator's Dilemma*. Christensen argued that innovative firms learn from the concept of *milkshake marketing*, which was coined in the book. The point is that innovators should focus on the job the product is being "hired" to do, rather than the product itself.

Christensen gives the example of a fast-food restaurant that sells milkshakes and realizes that the job their customers were hiring the milkshake to do was not to be a great healthy breakfast, as they had assumed, but it was to distract them with something pleasant during their morning commute. The job in this case is not what it does for the company, but what it does for the people who buy it.

With this idea, the restaurant made the straws a little bigger, the milkshake a little thicker, and added in fruit and candies to increase the enjoyment and distraction the milkshake was hired to provide. Sales soared as the milkshake fulfilled its function better, thanks to focusing on the job it was hired to do instead of the product itself or its features.

In a similar way, this is how executives should think about analytics tools. It is easy to get lost in the product details, listening to all the things it can do and getting caught up in all the hype. Sure, it is great that a lot could be done, but the *tool is only as valuable as the job it is hired to do*. Do not get swept up in the marketing. Instead, focus on the jobs you need done, and the jobs the tool could do that you may not have realized you needed, but that add substantial value for a reasonable investment. By focusing on the job you need your tools to do, you can more clearly see through the hype and assess the fit and value of a tool for your organization.

Here are some additional roles for executives to consider:

- **Set objectives.** Given their knowledge of the business, executives need to set clear goals and objectives for what business problems they need to have solved. They should listen to input from the analytics team and others, and study what job various tools could do for the organization. Next they should set objectives and drive toward what a solution could look like and how to implement it across the organization.

- **Review recommendations.** Once the objectives are clear, executives should put the technical team(s) to work on finding and screening possible solutions that can meet those objectives. Then executives can review possibilities the analytics experts have vetted, keeping a critical eye on the needs of the organization.

- **Maintain focus.** It is often their ability to focus on details that makes technical team members so good at their jobs. However, it is also easy for them to get lost in the weeds, the details, as the process unfolds. Executives need to regularly ensure the focus remains on the needs of the organization. When identifying needs by job and objectives, they help the organizations stay focused on what is needed to be achieved instead of just looking at a portfolio of tools for general evaluation. Technical team members must also adhere to and focus on these objectives while exploring possibilities. Any deviation should be justified by business needs.

- **Match size and complexity of the organization.** There are many tools available that do similar things. Some are very complex, others are very simple. Dr. Rudi Pleines, head of business transformation at ABB Robotics, makes the point that organizations need to also match the size and complexity of the tool to the organizational needs; otherwise, there will be a poor user experience and/or costs will bloat. An enterprise tool used by a Fortune 50 company will not likely be a good fit for a midsize firm, and vice versa. Take care to match not just the job, but also the fit for the firm's size and complexity as you would check fit for any employee you hire.

- **Consider switching cost.** Most analysts will be focused on what the tool can do for them. This is their bread and butter and what they love to do. Executives should listen and understand with the right mindset, as described previously. However, they also need to look at the business impact, which includes switching costs.

- **Evaluate total cost of ownership.** Similar to switching costs, executives should look beyond the tool's function, and beyond the initial sticker price, to evaluate the total cost of ownership, including maintenance, training, and other possible costs. They should then evaluate the costs against the benefits. There are, for example, several good reasons to consider open source tools. However, the initial sticker price is usually not a sufficient reason alone because many other factors come into play when taking this broader view into account.

- **Focus on integration.** Absent a universal solution, the executive's focus needs to be to connect and automate the various platforms and products required by the organization. Without this focus, the likelihood of efficient and effective analytics is greatly diminished. It is easy for an analyst to get overly excited about a particular tool. Executives need to help keep the focus on the big picture for the entire firm and make sure the tool can integrate well into their systems and processes so value can be added.

- **Champion change.** Executives must make sure the suite of tools the organization uses line up with the needs and goals of the organization, and then they must champion change and the use of the tools that do support business needs and goals.

Executives' Role in Tool Inputs

Executives have much more control over the generation, relevance, and quality of the data than the analytics professionals do, and they are responsible for their part in getting better inputs for the tools. The analyst and data scientist can clean data, but there is only so far that cleaning can go after the fact. Alternatively, it is much better to build in quality and relevance from the beginning, as opposed to attempting to fix quality issues later.

We talked about the executives' role in data quality and relevance in Task 3: The Data. It gives a good base of data for the analytics team to work with. However, the analytics team seldom models the raw data. The raw data needs to be in the right format to more easily do transformations, create target variables, and engineer features that can be imputed or created from the raw data and therefore modeled correctly. Executives also have a role in this process, as outlined here:

- **Target variables.** The analytics team will likely identify a number of target values to address a given business problem. This is the variable they are trying to predict or model. Although executives should let them ideate on this, it is so important to the outcome that executives ensure they understand what the target variable is, at least conceptually, and how it is built. The executive team should then do a validity check to make sure, in their judgment, that it makes sense and is actually what the business is looking for. Executives can give the analytics team a little more freedom to explore what might affect the target, but getting this right is incredibly important to outcomes and is worth reviewing to make sure the target variable is, well, on target, and is likely to be useful to the organization.

- **Curate data.** Without data, only very limited analysis can be done. Data needs to be actively curated for value and relevance to the organizational needs, and that process should be largely guided by the analytics team based on organizational objectives. However, when executives have hypotheses based on their experience, intuition, or knowledge of what others have found useful, it should be added to the list of data to be evaluated for potential usefulness. Additionally, executives must help curate both relevant and quality data that can address their objectives, as discussed in Task 3: The Data. They also need to facilitate appropriate access to that data.

- **Use the right data structure.** The same data stored differently can vary greatly in terms of ease-of-access and usability, including speed and efficiency in use. Although executives may not be able to guide how the data should be stored, they can facilitate analytics by understanding that how and where the data is stored matters, and work with their analytics and technical teams to make sure it is stored in a structure and location that will best facilitate meeting business objectives.

- **Curate features.** Many executives may not be aware that the analytics team generally models features created from the raw data, rather than the raw data itself. These features are permutations, transformations, and aggregations of the data that represent important business concepts they put into models. Sometimes executives can have an important insight or hunch about a feature that might be useful. It may not always work, but it should be shared with the analytics team for evaluation and testing for viability and usefulness.

- **Frame the problem.** As noted previously, executives need to make sure they frame and communicate the organization's problems effectively and in a way that is understood and will guide to tools that can fulfill those needs. Any ambiguity can lead the company astray.

Executives' Role in Tool Use

"Data does not speak, it responds," says Piyanka Jain. This quote introduces the role that executives should have in tool use: to guide questions so you get a useful response and ensure you have the right resources in both data and tools. Here are a few thoughts to help with this role:

- **Hypothesize.** Executives are business leaders because they know the business. They are intimately aware of what drives the business and how to improve it. This means that they often have intuitive hunches and ideas that can point the data scientist and analytics team in the right direction.

- **Include business metrics.** Executives should help guide the analytics team to include business metrics, not just statistical metrics, in their modeling. Dr. Wayne Thompson, formerly chief data scientist for SAS and currently an analytics director at Chase Bank, has always championed the importance of quantifying and including business metrics in the model, not just plugged in after the fact. I am sure this is one of the reasons Thompson has had such an incredibly successful career.

- **Set success criteria.** Executives should set clear criteria for success. If the analytics team does not know the criteria very clearly, with numbers and appropriate metrics, they cannot tell if they can achieve success and know when they have done so. Having this clear criteria, up front, can better guide the analytics team to the right tools at the right time to help them succeed, or fail fast, if needed.

- **Consider explainability.** Executives should carefully weigh the trade-offs and business needs of explainability versus performance. Sometimes explainable models do nearly as well as black box models, especially factoring in speed and an easier adoption lift. But sometimes they do not. Executives need to think through those trade-offs from the perspective of the organization and provide leadership and guidance on those trade-offs.

- **Promote analytics literacy.** Executives should also promote a better understanding of what various tools can do and how they work, and help analytics and non-analytics teams continue to learn and grow. The analytics team will focus on learning more about how and where to use analytics, but other employees should understand what jobs they can do to foster a broad analytics mindset across the firm.

- **Lead by example.** Employees tend to follow their leaders so executives must set the example they want their employees to emulate, which includes developing an analytics mindset, being willing to change, asking for data, and expecting others to have analyzed a problem with data before making a decision.

CATEGORIES OF ANALYTICS

For executives and other leaders to better understand the job the various tools can do for them so they can help guide the selection of the right tools for their organization, they should first understand the various categories of analytics and then the jobs that can be done by different tools in each category. There are usually many different algorithms that can do a specific job and even more tools that can use those algorithms.

Executives do not need to know all the tools and algorithms. But if they know the types of things that can be done, the job they can hire the tool to do, they can better lead and guide their firm to analytics success. This section focuses on understanding the broad categories of how to think about tools. The next section gives examples of the jobs those types of tools can do for them. Once executives know the job they need done, someone on the technical or analytics team can recommend a variety of tools that could do it.

Most executives will already have knowledge of various reporting tools, some understanding of statistics, and awareness of some optimization-style algorithms that have been used by businesses for decades. A likely newer feature to most executives is prediction and various machine learning techniques, which only recently have been enabled at the scale needed to make an impact, thanks to technological advances.

This rapid change and growth in analytics can be confusing, even to the most attentive observer. Many find it useful to seek first to understand the types of analytics and the various classes of algorithmic tasks that can do them before trying to understand individual algorithms. Once armed with this road map of the space, they can then work with their technical and analytics team members to find the best approach for their situation.

Analytics by Time and Action

The first dimension is time. Many older algorithms look at the past, whereas many newer ones look at the future. The other dimension is action, which means the degree to which action is guided by a person's judgment or by the algorithm. These tools can lead to insight into a current situation or be a guide to actions that could change a current or future situation.

Although insights often do and should lead to actions by the people who see them, in this case we are referring to not just using analytics to provide insight into a given situation, but using analytics to help guide the best response as opposed to leaving the action primarily up to the individual. Let us call this analytics action, that is, not just giving a human insight into what has or will happen, but having analytics guiding how to act on it.

If you put one horizontal axis on the time dimension, labeled past and future, and another on the human insight to analytics action on the vertical graph, you can nicely organize the various types of analytics by these dimensions. Figure 4.1 was inspired by a similar approach proposed by Taras Kaduk,[1] and was adapted and modified here.

All of these dimensions are on a continuum, and usually start low on the one-way arrows from human action to analytics action, with various degrees of automation or

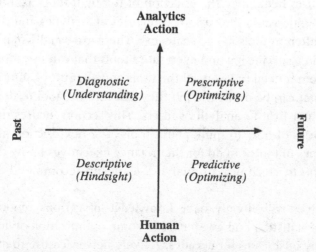

Figure 4.1 Categories of Analytics

guidance on that arrow, and the same from past to future. It is not that you stop seeing the past but that you see the past and more as you move to the future. It is not to suggest that humans cannot act. It is more that the algorithms give better recommendations and do better processing than leaving the data to a human to figure out the insight and how to act on it.

Descriptive Analytics

In the lower left quadrant, we have descriptive analytics, which are designed to give people knowledge and insight into what happened, sometimes referred to as hindsight. This insight can come from traditional reporting, data visualizations, descriptive statistics, or even some machine learning algorithms. What matters is that it is focused on seeing the past more clearly. This perspective may lead a person to take some action, but the analytics themself do not guide that action or direct what it should be. That action is left to a person. Example: reporting units of ABC products sold on Thursday at XYZ store for full retail price.

Most people are not big fans of raw numbers on a screen. Numbers can provide some of the information, but they generally are not intuitive or readily understood, and it is easy to miss important trends. Most important, numbers alone tend not to motivate action. You may have heard the saying that a picture is worth a thousand words. Although true, this expression underestimates the impact of visualizations. According to the International Forum of Visual Practitioners, human brains process visual information 60,000 times faster than textual information.[2] Since a picture is really worth 60,000 words, it will have a much bigger and more profound impact on understanding and action than text or numbers alone.

Josh Belliveau, principal solution engineer at Tableau, fell in love with Tableau and shared why. While working in the institutional research office of a university that was a very early adopter of Tableau, Belliveau was able to see firsthand how much more valuable and actionable descriptive statistics and related information, presented visually, had on their intended audience in terms of driving understanding and action. This software was especially important in showing important concepts and data such as student enrollment and retention, course completions, and at-risk students.

If you are new to analytics, visual analytics generated with products like Tableau are a great place to start your analytics journey. Even descriptive statistics can be much more effective visually because our brains are wired to process visual information much more efficiently then numeric or textual information. Even more, these visualizations need not necessarily be statistically significant to be impactful. Seeing trend lines and data changes that people can play with is another distinguishing feature of data warehouses and visualization products such as Tableau.

Both seeing and doing are key motivators to action. I believe the primary reason Tableau has been so successful is that it provides powerful visualizations and an easy-to-use interface enabling people to play with the tool and see the results for themselves, which makes action more likely. One of the early advantages of data warehouses, often built on allowing slicing and dicing of data by different dimensions, sometimes called multidimensional cubes, was that it allowed business people to play with the data in ways that were relevant to them.

In the early days of analytics, most of this complex but descriptive reporting was referred to as *business intelligence,* and it is. It gave early adopters a competitive advantage until others caught up and tools advanced to do other analytics tasks. However, it is difficult to effectively go to later stages of advanced analytics without having mastered these earlier tools. Just because these tools were descriptive and looked at the past does not mean it was unimportant. It is very important and helps build an analytics culture and a necessary stop on your analytics journey.

Diagnostic Analytics

The next quadrant up, diagnostic analytics, goes a step further in helping us to understand why something is, maybe even getting into causal analysis. The idea is to develop a deeper understanding that can guide actions to correct or improve a relevant situation. Example: figuring out why XYZ store sold 20% more units of ABC product at full price than DEF store last week.

Diagnostic analytics goes beyond seeing information to first proving it and to second (casually) understanding it, depending on how far along both arrows you travel. There are various tools for finding if something is statistically significant, which we take to mean as it is proven to be different or true. The first step to diagnosis is seeing what is, the second is understanding why with more advanced tools for causal analysis.

Predictive Analytics

As you shift farther to the right on the horizontal axis, you start looking more to the future than to the past. In the lower right quadrant, you have predictive analytics, which uses machine learning and similar analytics techniques to predict what will happen next. Although forecasting still fits in this quadrant, with advanced tools such as machine learning, prediction has become so much more functional than forecasting. Whereas forecasting looks at a few macroeconomic variables to estimate something like how many units will be sold, predicting uses millions of data points to develop a unique prediction for each one.

This functionality makes it much more useful for businesses by enabling them to differentially act based on each prediction. Example: predicting which customers will churn in the next three months, whereas forecasting might predict how many customers might churn, but not which ones. Predicting is inherently more actionable when you know which customers are likely to churn or turnover, and can therefore try to do something about it, rather than just plan for the loss.

Prescriptive Analytics

The final quadrant, in the top right, is for prescriptive analytics. These tools are designed to help you harvest or take advantage of a future situation that is guided by analytics. Although there are some concepts unique to this section, much of the raw material comes from insights from the other three quadrants, making it very difficult to succeed broadly without doing well in other quadrants. Example: optimizing the product price to maximize profit for XYZ store sales.

A few tools in this category have been around for decades, such as various optimization algorithms used in operational research. However, many more tools are still being developed and emerging, as prescriptive analytics is an area ripe for growth and change. Look for exciting new developments in the coming decades, some of which may lead to significant changes in business and society as these technologies help guide, optimize, and automate many processes with AI tools.

Algorithm Classes by Category

There are many algorithms used in data science and more are being developed all the time. Keeping up with them is a challenging task, even for data scientists, let alone everyone else! What is important for executives is understanding the jobs these algorithms can do for them and identifying how these jobs can benefit their organization. The analytics team can then find the best algorithm for the specific application of the job that needs to be done.

This section builds on prior work[3] organizing algorithms by their tasks and further categorizing a few of the more useful, newer ones by the categories of analytics they help (descriptive, diagnostic, predictive, and prescriptive). Let us look at a few of the more useful analytics tasks that machine learning and other popular analytics techniques help us do better than was possible in the past.

Descriptive Analytics Tools

Descriptive analytics is about seeing what is and is generally designed for people to act on, though it will continue to become more autonomous over time. How timely, intuitive, accurate, granular, and relevant this information is presented can make a big difference to success. This field is the foundation of all the other types. Without capturing quality descriptive information, you have nothing with which to build to do the other work. Common tools in this class include numeric reporting, visual reporting, multidimensional cubes, descriptive statistics, and visual statistics, as summarized in Table 4.1. Because these are the oldest tools and most business leaders will be familiar with them, I will focus on the executive's role in this section.

Organizations have been capturing some descriptive information for centuries. Using descriptive information well has been a source of competitive advantage in the past, such as when double-entry bookkeeping was first developed 500 years ago and increased the accuracy and resiliency in accounting and reporting systems. These tools were later digitized and scaled across organizations, increasing timeliness and scalability of accounting systems. These early systems formed the basis for many business intelligence tools we use today by increasing timely, granular, and intuitive reporting of relevant information people use to make better decisions.

Even today, there is still a significant opportunity for competitive advantage based on this category. Although double-entry bookkeeping, descriptive statistics, reporting, and monitoring systems have been in place in many organizations for a while, we are still gaining insight into how to see relevant information in more timely, granular, intuitive, and accurate ways. Indeed, there is still a vast frontier of opportunity for most firms to do better with descriptive analytics, which will also lay the groundwork for doing better in other categories later.

In this category, historically, machines would report and discover information that enabled people to act. However, some automation systems are starting to change this approach. The key is to focus on improving each of the attributes mentioned before in a way that helps a person act in a more beneficial way. Here are the attributes people need from these systems:

- **Relevant.** Take great care in identifying relevant information that really matters to actions that can be taken and sharing that information in timely, granular, intuitive, and accurate ways. Take equal care in removing irrelevant information so people can better focus on the relevant information that actually matters.

- **Timely.** The closer in time to the event the information is shared with a person who can act, the more opportunity they have to act in a useful and beneficial way. Not all decisions need to be instantaneous, but identify when and where timing matters and build systems to share the information within the time needed to allow for optimal actions to be taken.

- **Granular.** Sometimes general information is enough. However, it often requires being able to see granular information, organized in a timely and relevant way, to understand exactly where to act. For example, knowing sales are down is helpful, but knowing sales of XYZ products at ABC stores are down this week in a particular location gives the actor much more ability to identify the problem, understand why it exists, and intervene to correct it in time to make a difference.

- **Intuitive.** Raw information is not enough for human decision-makers. Even organized numbers are sometimes not enough. The information needs to be intuitive and clear, presented in a way for the human actor to easily see how and where to act based on the information. Tools such as Tableau have become quite popular in part because of their ease in creating intuitive, visual information that enables people to see it and then act.

- **Accurate.** If people do not trust the data, they will not trust the results and will not act to fix problems, leaving little room for action. Additionally, poor data quality will limit movement into any of the more advanced quadrants that look into the future or have more machine-aided actions defined or taken. Quality and accurate data is the raw material for success, and without it, the rest will make little difference. Data does not need to be perfect to be useful, but the better it is the more it will be used and relied on, increasing its impact.

Finding additional relevant information is the largest frontier remaining in descriptive analytics today. All of the other attributes (timely, intuitive, granular, accurate) help to operationalize relevant information more effectively, but without relevant information they make little difference.

The main focus for executives should be tying relevant information to important decisions where actions could be taken. Once identified, executives can then operationalize it by effectively using the dimensions seen in Figure 4.1. There is an explosion of information today. Even if your organization has historically used descriptive information very well, it is likely there is additional descriptive information that is or could be generated to better manage your organization.

For example, the firm Qualtrics grew and developed quickly by helping gather a new type of very relevant descriptive data. Sure they also use some of the other categories of analytics, but these others are based on descriptive data. In particular, their focus is on capturing customer experience data, which was largely missing or incomplete in many organizational data profiles. They could then use insights from this new class of descriptive information (experiential data) to drive better actions in humans and machines.

Apple is collecting valuable biometric data from everyone who wears their Apple Watch. This information contains a potential gold mine of relevant information, if used appropriately. Sure, it will need to be analyzed and processed using other categories of analytics, but if they do not collect heartbeat, blood oxygen, or other information, what can they base future analytics on without this data?

Self-driving cars are collecting similar useful information with cameras, LIDAR, and other sensors. Manufacturers are putting sensors in more machines and devices. Waze was born out of collecting information from mobile devices to monitor traffic. The point of all of these innovations is to gather relevant descriptive information that can be used to add value. But it first must be collected, after which humans and/or machines can act on it. Table 4.1 gives a summary of common descriptive tools by class and function.

Statistical Diagnostic Tools

If descriptive analytics is about knowing what is, diagnostic analytics is about first proving if something is (i.e., inferential statistics) and then understanding why and how it is that way. Diagnostic analytics is on a continuum from knowing what is to why it is, and it is not always easy to draw a clear line between the two. However, the more you process and analyze raw data, the more you can understand the data and the underlying situation of interest.

Processing and analyzing requires good descriptive data, some that you have and often some that you may not have, just like a doctor might order additional tests to make a medical diagnosis by gathering the descriptive information needed to explore or verify possible causes or explanations. As alluded to previously, diagnostic analytics often requires the collection and analysis of additional descriptive data, which may

Table 4.1 Descriptive Tool Class Summary

Tool Class	Function/Job	Common Tools
Numeric reporting	Numeric reporting provides information about observable events in a way that someone, or an algorithm, can act on them.	Databases Spreadsheets Monitoring systems
Visual reporting	Visual reporting, such as with charts and graphs, shows similar information to reporting, but generally summarizes it in a way that enables people to more easily process it and then act.	Excel Power Point Power BI SAS Tableau
Multidimensional cube	The multidimensional cube presents data and reports on useful dimensions of the data that are pre-identified as highly relevant to the business. A dimension is a way of looking or segmenting the data such as by gender, location, or time. These dimensions are carefully planned in advance and set up with a data structure that facilitates easy, self-service access to information a person would need to manage better.	Excel (Pivot Tables) OLAP Business intelligence Power BI Tableau SAS R
Descriptive statistics	Descriptive statistics focuses on describing the shape of the data with measures of mean, median, mode, interquartile range, distributions, and similar metrics.	SAS R Excel
Visual statistics	Visual statistics shows important information about the shape of the data, including key changes, visually. This visualization allows for quicker understanding and increases the likelihood of action.	Tableau SAS R

create a feedback loop by identifying additional relevant data that may sometimes be worth collecting and monitoring more frequently.

Diagnostic analytics involves processing and analyzing that data in a way that gives insight and understanding, usually within a proven and tested framework, and occasionally by creating a new one. The better you become at diagnosis, the more effective and successful it will be at guiding your actions in a way that has a positive impact on the organization.

Not only do diagnostic analytics tools help you better understand your data or a given situation but also they are helpful with more advanced modeling, where more advanced diagnostic techniques generate inputs for predictive and prescriptive models. This is an essential step in mature and reliable analytics, in addition to providing valuable insight and understanding in its own right.

However, too often insights from the diagnostic phase of the modeling process are not well documented or clearly communicated to the rest of the organization to build understanding. Sometimes analytics team members skip this step in a rush for speed or overreliance on supervised machine learning without seeking first to understand it.

It is risky to rely on modeling of data you do not understand. Although some predictive algorithms can generate predictions based on raw data or with little diagnostics being done first, these models are less stable over time, less generalizable to new situations, and more likely to have hidden ethical issues. It is almost always worth the time to explore and understand your data with descriptive and diagnostics techniques before jumping to prediction or prescription.

Listed here are some common tools used for diagnostic analytics. Most of them will just be introduced because they have been around for a while, and many of you will be familiar with them. We will cover the newer ones such as machine learning in a little more detail.

Inferential Statistics

Most of you will be familiar with inferential statistics, having taken a class or two using it and maybe even using it in your careers. I put most inferential statistics in the diagnostic category because it (1) focuses on the past and (2) helps guide actions by giving more insight and assurance about the facts. For example, descriptive statistics will give you numbers, which may or may not be statistically significant.

Inferential statistics can tell you whether something is significantly different from something else, and to what degree, guiding your action with greater confidence and precision. There are many tools here; most have been around for decades and a few for centuries. The key is they provide more certainty by separating out the true signal from the random noise that is often seen in descriptive statistics, enabling more insight and confidence in actions to take.

Several years ago, when personal medical devices like Fitbits and Apple Watches were just starting to become popular consumer products, there was a lot of excitement about their potential to encourage healthier behaviors by providing data directly to consumers on various health habits related to steps taken, sleep patterns, and a variety of exercise metrics. The sleep tracking feature, for example, could help people better manage their sleep schedule and at a much more affordable cost than using medical-grade devices that were many times more expensive and less available. However, there were also many concerns about the accuracy of these devices.

Thomas Cech, now a senior data scientist at National Council for Community and Education Partnerships (NCCEP), helped me and another researcher set up and administer a trial to see if in fact these devices were as accurate as the medical-grade options. Our goal was to see if the commercial devices were accurate enough to use for a larger study we had planned to assess the impacts of sleep on at-risk high school students and the possible interventions. Before we could begin, we needed to know whether these commercial products, which were more affordable and students were more willing to wear, were valid enough to use at scale in the planned intervention.

After Institutional Review Board approval, we paid college-age research subjects to wear both the medical-grade and commercially available products at the same time for several weeks to measure sleep cycles. Cech and a few friends collected regular data from both devices in a controlled experiment. When we had enough participants and data, Cech used inferential statistics to see if the various brands of commercial grade products we tested were able to track sleep patterns as accurately as proven medical-grade devices over the weeks of controlled testing.

Through the use of these statistical techniques, we were able to prove that most of the commercial products in fact were valid enough to use for our anticipated study of sleep on educational outcomes, at a fraction of the price and with much greater willingness by students to wear them given their social acceptance. Cech helped publish a well-cited peer-reviewed journal article on the experiment,[4] which helped many others who were also struggling to know how much to trust these more affordable and available devices.

Diagnostic Experimentation

By actively collecting data under different designed scenarios, experimentation goes beyond just applying inferential statistics to data passively collected in your firm. Sometimes the purpose is to test different approaches to objectively see which approach works better, sometimes it is a step to proving causation. The first approach is about testing to see what works; the second is about discovering and understanding why it works (or does not). This section focuses on the diagnostic experimentation, or the why.

The key difference between inferential statistics and experimentation is in the active design of the data collection. Inferential statistics can be used on its own passively or actively collected data. But with the active design in experimentation, you gather a custom dataset to test your hunches or hypotheses and then can verify them statistically with inferential statistics.

Experimentation with statistical verification is an incredibly powerful tool. It has been around for a long time. Scientists use it as an investigatory tool and a step toward building knowledge, theory, and understanding by identifying true causes and effects.

Occasionally businesses will use this approach, too, especially when conducting research and development, such as in the biotechnology industry. However, more often they do a de facto brute force optimization on the problem by trying many things to see what eventually works. It is still experimentation and creates some knowledge, but it is harder to discern the why and is thus inherently harder to generalize results.

The real advantage of experimentation today is the scale that it can be done across platforms and in real time, often referred to as A/B testing. Firms can run thousands of micro-experiments a day to determine the best approach. At some point, experimentation at that scale and speed shifts from diagnostic analytics to prescriptive analytics.

The difference is in the intent. Are you looking to build generalizable understanding and theory that can be used in many contexts (diagnostic), or to simply optimize a current situation with a (mostly) brute force application unique to your situation (prescriptive)?

To be clear, the knowledge gained from the experimentation for understanding can also be used in prescriptive frameworks, even beyond the firm, but its first goal is to build understanding that creates a more stable framework for future treatments and optimizations. Either way, this is a powerful tool.

The agriculture industry has *greatly* benefited from hundreds of thousands of experiments run across the United States over the last century as an intentional and successful strategy spearheaded by the government and supported by industry to improve our food supply. The end result has been a dramatic green revolution that has lifted many out of poverty by providing more abundant and affordable food sources.

This need to test and replicate trails in many diverse locations really laid the groundwork for the A/B testing that many organizations now use digitally to test people's reactions to some treatment, which can also vary quite dramatically from each other. Because climate and soil conditions vary so dramatically by location, this type of work had to be administered at scale in many diverse locations to see and measure the impact and showed the importance of this type of micro-level A/B testing.

It also inspired many, including me, to go into data-driven fields. For example, Wayne Thompson, former chief data scientist at SAS and currently an executive director at JP Morgan, shares that the primary reason for pursuing an analytics career was seeing how collecting data could improve the cow-calf operation on the family farm. This led Thompson to pursue a degree in plant sciences to rigorously design experimental trials to test different approaches farmers could take on the farm, possible decisions if you will, and evaluate the outcomes to improve the value on the farm. The importance and impact of the knowledge learned fueled Thompson's passion for what we now refer to as analytics.

Causal Analysis

Although experimentation can be used for causal analysis, there are also other techniques beyond experimentation that can be used to analyze various datasets, real or experimental, to determine cause and to what degree what causes what. Sometimes causal analysis can be done by looking for natural experiments that were not necessarily designed but are similar enough that conditions exist with a key difference where cause and effect can be determined.

One option is to build a model, such as with structural equation modeling; another is through the use of counterfactual analysis common in economics. The main point is that advanced statistical techniques exist for getting to causation, beyond correlations and basic inferential tests. They can help guide your decisions toward appropriate action. Many of these options start out as diagnostic exercises, but if something useful is discovered, it can lead to models that are predictive and sometimes even prescriptive.

For example, one of my graduate students, Keerthana Bandlamudi, is helping analyze data my team and a couple of professors were able to collect for a state university system. The dataset included over 50,000 anonymized at-risk students across a decade with the goal of finding relevant factors related to graduation rates. The following description is a simplified version of our study.

Academic theory suggests two factors that seemed relevant to this particular group but are not surprisingly related to employment prospects on graduation. These factors were the expected salary and likelihood of achieving that salary. Theory suggests the higher the salary and higher the likelihood of achieving that salary, the more likely these at-risk students were to stay in school and finish.

After setting up our hypotheses and running a number of tests guided by the theory, we found that these variables (among a few others) were in fact highly significant, predictive, and likely to be casual. However, the effect was the opposite of what we had supposed, at least for the extreme groups with very high salaries and a high likelihood of achieving them. We decided to dig deeper to understand this counterintuitive result.

Additional evidence supported the idea that, at least for the group with the highest salary, they were leaving school because their skills were in such high demand they could make a good living even without their full degree, based on the skills gleaned from their first few years of college. Most of these students were from very quantitative majors, with options to work. Many of them might eventually return to finish their degrees later, but not in the limited time window we tested. Results are still in the peer-review process, but we expect them to be published within the next year or so. Table 4.2 presents a variety of diagnostic tools by class and function.

Unsupervised Machine Learning for Diagnostic Analytics

Machine learning, and in particular, unsupervised machine learning, can provide very interesting descriptive and diagnostic insights. The unsupervised part of these algorithms means they do not have a particular target, such as predicting who will do something. Rather, there is more freedom for the algorithm to explore the data looking for certain types of patterns that give insight and understanding.

Unsupervised machine learning algorithms can look at millions of records with multiple variables and find patterns hard for humans and earlier techniques to effectively detect. We call them *unsupervised* because they are mostly exploratory, trying to discover hidden patterns, whereas we call many of the predictive machine learning algorithms *supervised*, which we explain later.

These unsupervised machine learning algorithms may not be frequently described as diagnostic, partly because these methods are often done as an early step to building a predictive model, so these two classes of tools are often thought of together. However, they can provide substantial value on their own, in addition to their potential to become valuable inputs for other types of modes.

Table 4.2 Statistical Diagnostic Tool Class Summary

Tool Class	Function/Job	Common Algorithms
Inferential statistics	Inferential statistics includes many algorithms and techniques, many of which focus on proving if something is statistically different from something else.	T-Test ANOVA Chi-square
Diagnostic experimentation	Diagnostic analytics focuses on identifying cause and effect. Although experimentation can be used just inferentially to prove what is, carefully designed and properly replicated experiments can also prove causation.	Carefully designed and validated experimentation
Causal analysis	Although diagnostic experimentation can prove causation, causal analysis often goes a step farther by measuring the strength and breadth of impact of that causation, improving precision, and eventually allowing for robust prediction after adequate experimentation and analysis.	Regression Structural equation modeling Machine learning

Unsupervised machine learning tools can provide important insights and understanding that can not only help with other models but also guide business, strategy, and outreach by aiding human understanding of cause and effect and identifying interesting opportunities to explore. They look deeper into the mostly descriptive data, trying to make sense of it, similar to inferential statistics and experiments.

These types of tools might be thought of like a microscope. They let you see hidden details that would be missed by other techniques by looking at minute details of the data in new ways, too complex for the human mind to discern unaided. They provide interesting insights that lead us to seeing things that were missed before, understanding useful relationships in the data, and forming ideas that can lead to action. Considering the framework of past versus future and human action to past action, this is the best and most useful quadrant for machine learning tools when used independently of prediction, or when insight is gained as part of the prediction process.

Here are some useful types of unsupervised machine learning applications. Each type has many algorithms that could be used for a given task. The technical team can help test and decide the best for a given task.

Clustering

Many of you will be familiar with the concept of clustering, which divides data into a small number of groups based on observed similarities in each record. Clustering has long been used by organizations to better understand their customers as well as other data. In addition to being able to provide understanding and insights executives can use, natural clusters are often used directly as inputs into predictive models by passing on these labels to another algorithm or by suggesting other data mining tasks and approaches.

However, clustering with large datasets using machine learning algorithms can be much more predictive than older traditional methods with limited datasets. I was fortunate to have a doctoral student work in my research center a few years ago. Dr. Rafael Braga, who came as an exchange student from a university in Brazil, was really a first-class data scientist, especially when it came to modeling biological data.

Braga was able to take some industry data from one of our partners that combined sensor data inside a beehive, carefully trained human observations on a standardized scale, and weather data and prepare it for analysis. When Braga teamed up with a few other researchers, they were able to develop a cluster-based method for mining and explaining seasonal patterns in honeybees, the results of which were published in a prominent peer-reviewed journal.[5]

Similarity Matching

Although clustering explores the whole dataset looking for general patterns that emerge, similarity matching looks for other records that most closely match a record of interest. Rather than identify a small number of big clusters for the whole group, this algorithm looks very closely at thousands of micro-clusters to identify records that most closely match behaviors to the record of interest.

Common business applications include what is sometimes referred to as *collaborative filtering*, such as a bookstore recommending a book other people deemed similar to books you also liked or an organization identifying their most profitable customers or donors and then looking at new and existing data to identify more like them to target for a business purpose. Similarity measures are also foundational inputs for other analytics tasks, including classification, regression, and clustering.

Similarity matching can be very much like prediction in effect and impact, and a credible case could be made to include it in that category. However, it is fundamentally about finding similar instances in data to other known instances of interest and then treating those instances in a similar way. A better way to think of this is as a machine learning application of clustering at the micro level helping to identify similar patterns in your existing data that can be harnessed, rather than predicting the future. What makes it useful is that it is more immediately actionable at a micro level than many other techniques.

LeAnne Hill, manager at the accounting and advisory firm FORVIS LLP in the enterprise risk and quantitative advisory practice area, shared how a previous employer used a type of fuzzy matching to clean data and detect fraud. Anytime you have human-entered data, the likelihood of mistakes is much higher. This situation is especially common when people spell things creatively. Hill would use a fuzzy matching algorithm to find names that were similar enough they could have been typos or creative spelling attempts, which Hill could then verify with a few other techniques to eventually get a cleaner dataset that would improve the quality and predictive power of their models.

Co-Occurrence Grouping

Co-occurrence grouping is conceptually similar in approach to some of the other techniques discussed here, but rather than focus on customers, the focus is on the products and services businesses sell to them. For instance, by identifying which products are often sold together, such as peanut butter and jelly, a store might be able to take advantage of that association in interesting ways. For example, they might discount one item knowing it will drive sales of the another, perhaps more profitable item.

A time dimension might also be added, which might reveal that someone buying grass seed might soon need fertilizer, weed control, or a lawn mower, all of which could be used to some advantage by a business. Common terms in this category include market basket analysis, association analysis, sequence analysis, and frequent item-set mining.

Although physical stores have used many of these approaches for decades, the power of these algorithms has grown in the age of internet commerce where the firm has more ability to dynamically react to insights and changing trends to take advantage of these insights.

Dr. Wayne Thompson really pioneered some best practices in co-occurrence grouping. I recall reading many use cases and examples of how SAS, in particular, made this type of analysis very easy to use and deploy in their software to great effect. I have even used it myself. Thompson shared how this was one of the go-to tools to really understand what was happening in data and various groups within that data, leading to many opportunities for deeper understanding. From my experience, I absolutely agree this is a powerful tool that is often overlooked by many organizations.

Data Reduction

It is easy, even for a machine, to get lost in a sea of highly detailed data, missing important patterns and observations, especially with data and computing power that is less deep than desired. Various techniques, including factor analysis, concept stemming, and others, can help reveal latent or larger hidden concepts driving the various individual variable's actions.

Although data reduction does involve the loss of information, the trade-off is that bigger picture patterns often emerge, which provide deeper understanding and more generalizable actions when the algorithm looks at the forest instead of just the trees. It reduces the risk of multicollinearity, where items that are too similar can skew results, while making analysis easier to manage and process and making it more likely for the algorithm to identify the big picture by building broader understanding of the data.

One of my former employees, Preston MacDonald, now a data scientist for Red Hat, worked with me and a few friends on a project for HiveTracks. The project sought to improve use and adoption of our software system and applications. As you might imagine, these databases, some internal from the business and other external sources such as weather data, held a great deal of information about user behaviors, attributes, location, and weather, which all needed to be analyzed for beekeepers.

For step one of this project, MacDonald dove into the scientific literature and with a little guidance was able to identify a good academic theory to guide this work. Next, MacDonald reviewed hundreds of possible fields in the data that might be relevant. Guided by the theory and a few extensions we thought might be relevant, MacDonald built a number of candidate features that might be useful, based on logic, intuition, and always guided by theory.

However, there were many features that could be used for analysis or fit the concepts identified in the theory. We needed to find the best ones that were most likely to be more predictive of the desired outcome. Therefore, MacDonald performed a factor analysis, a type of data reduction that identifies the most important factors of the problem you are modeling.

With this information, we were able to see, not just guess, which data points best lined up with established theory, and MacDonald was able to build a much stronger and more accurate model with the right factors. Factor analysis reduced the data to what was most essential and important. It also identified the most relevant data driving adoption in our system, allowing for the creation of focused dashboards to monitor that data's quality, its completeness, and its usefulness as a management metric. If you are curious, we eventually published a portion of this research in a peer-reviewed journal to help others trying to do something similar.[6] Table 4.3 shares a few unsupervised machine learning tools, functions, and algorithms for diagnostic analytics.

Table 4.3 Machine Learning Diagnostic Tool Class Summary

Tool Class	Function/Job	Common Algorithms
Clustering	Clustering breaks data into groups that are similar to each other, allowing for deeper understanding of natural breaks and affinities in the data and providing insights and strategies for working with those groups.	K-means Hierarchical clustering Self-organizing maps
Similarity matching	Similarity matching finds data points that are similar to a chosen data point of interest. It is different from clustering in that it is not putting them into natural groups, but identifying an individual data point, then looking for others that have similar characteristics to the one described.	Euclidean distance Cosine similarity Manhattan distance Pearson correlation
Co-occurrence grouping	Co-occurrence grouping looks for patterns of events that often occur together, either at the same time or with a time dependency. By identifying items or events that occur together, businesses can seek to capitalize on this value.	Market basket analysis Latent semantic analysis Association rule mining
Data reduction	Data reduction reduces data to core elements by identifying the most important features to model. Although there is some loss of information, it allows for focus on what is most important and enables new insights to often emerge.	Principal components analysis Factor analysis

PREDICTIVE ANALYTICS TOOLS

Although some predictive tasks were possible without computers, such as simple regression analysis and the application of proven formulas or laws (i.e., gravity), it was not until recent advances in computational power and increases in data availability that these tools could be widely adopted. The reason is based on how supervised machine learning, the primary tool of prediction, works.

Let us review a few proven laws and then move on to supervised machine learning.

Supported Theory and Natural Laws

The best predictive tools are those that have been proven to be useful over many trials and broad circumstances. These algorithms are generally based on natural laws that have been discovered about how the universe works. For example, if you were going to launch a rocket, you would not want to launch a rocket thousands of times to get data to develop a predictive algorithm when that foundational work has already been distilled into an elegant equation.

Similarly, though not quite as robust and accurate as natural laws, there are many causal and/or predictive theories that have been developed in medicine, the social sciences, and other disciplines. They can predict, for example, the odds of having a second heart attack given various criteria, or the likelihood of a given student dropping out of school.

Although not rising to the level of laws, these theories have been painstakingly built on years of data in broad circumstances and can be more powerful than building your own algorithm. I have often been surprised by how many analysts try to start from scratch rather than build on work that has been done before and is readily available in the scientific literature.

At a minimum, this body of work can guide you to important variables or concepts that can improve prediction. Sometimes, there are ready-made, proven formulas that are widely accepted and handily available. Why build your own when you can instead use, adapt, and maybe improve one that has been used and tested before? Although predictive tools are powerful and have many important applications, the journey should start with a search of what has been done before to see what can be applied to your situation.

Steve Stone shared a story of using published theory while serving as CIO at L Brands. Stone had a hunch they were losing important sales by not having the right number of registers open during Black Friday weekend. Having too many or too few were both problems. After getting the hunch, Stone spent the weekend analyzing the data, discovered there was a problem, and started looking for a solution.

Stone found a paper published by a professor at a top university that presented a version of queuing theory that matched what they were seeing in stores during these holiday sales events. Stone wrote some code that showed how much it would have saved if they had used the theory. The next Black Friday, they used this theory for register management across their stores. It worked beautifully with the result of adding $25 million in profit to the bottom line in one weekend.

Supervised Machine Learning

Because so many of data science's "new" tools incorporate machine learning, it is worth understanding what makes machine learning new or different from traditional analytics methods. In reality, machine learning has been around conceptually for more than 50 years, but it is only recently that we have had enough data along with effective computer processing powerful enough to take advantage of its potential.

What makes machine learning fundamentally different is how it learns. Both traditional analytics and machine learning require data, but the difference is in the algorithm and how the data is used. Traditional analytics takes a known algorithm, applies it to data, and gets a one-time result. The process usually stops there. Figure 4.2 shows a conceptual model for how traditional learning algorithms are applied to data.

Machine learning is the reverse. It learns by example and often never stops. In this case, you take the known results for a problem of interest to you, where you have created labels that flag the attribute of interest, such as identifying a profitable customer. By going through the manual or calculated process of labeling the result of interest in

Figure 4.2 Traditional Learning

Figure 4.3 Supervised Machine Learning

your data, you can then train and build a custom algorithm, unique to your data, that can be applied to similar new data to predict the result. Figure 4.3 shows a conceptual model of how supervised machine learning works.

This approach is very different from using standard, well-known algorithms on your data. It is learning by example. You first provide a large number of examples of the desired and undesired results, then use those results to create a new algorithm that will generate more of the desired results. You then use the new results for the desired purpose, assess their performance, and then improve the algorithm with the new results.

Of course, figuring out and labeling your desired results well is a key factor in success. Another key factor is to have a large enough volume of data of sufficient quality and relevance to build a useful algorithm. It also helps if you have reason to believe there are natural patterns and differences in the groups an algorithm would be able to detect with enough accuracy to be useful. Descriptive and diagnostic analytics, as well as theory, intuition, and prior experience, can help, but ultimately they will need to be tested for confirmation.

Now, we discuss some common classes of algorithms that focus on prediction.

Classification

The term *classification* has its roots in biology, where an early main task was to assign each life form to a class with similar life forms such as plants, animals, fungi, and bacteria. Once they were in a class, principles learned about how one member of that class could often be applied to other members in the class, accelerating learning as commonalities emerged. Understanding how the various class members were similar, and in what ways they were different, has been key to understanding life and finding ways to improve it.

In a similar way, classification algorithms sort items in your data into two or more classes based on the various attributes of those items. For example, suppose you were rolling out a new financial services product across the country and you had data from a region where you already tested the product. In the test group, some customers had turned out to be very profitable, but others were not. As you expand the new service, you want to selectively offer the service to those customers to whom it would most likely be profitable, and avoid offering it to those for whom it would most likely be unprofitable.

In this example, the algorithm would look at the most promising attributes in your data for those who were profitable and those who had not been profitable from your test sample. It would then compare the data in the two groups that you have already classified as profitable or not, identify what makes the two groups different, and then develop an algorithm to separate potentially new clients into the business-relevant groups you identified (i.e., profitable, unprofitable). In this way, you can selectively market to those most likely to be profitable customers and avoid marketing to those less likely to be profitable.

Executives will quickly be able to see the inherent advantage of differentially identifying groups who give them a cost or profitability advantage. In general, with enough data, two or more groups who are labeled with business-relevant data, such as the historically profitable versus less profitable, can be used to build an algorithm to distinguish between the two groups on new data. Quality and usefulness will vary based on data relevance and quality, but machine learning models excel at this capability.

However, the key factor here is having labeled data. This caveat means that someone needs to first identify and segment the group of interest in a given training dataset, which can then be used to train the algorithm and be applied to new data. Good-quality labels can be quite expensive to get, or make, and often require hiring people for that task. However, once you have enough labeled data, you can sometimes use labels to build algorithms to label more data that can then be used in models.

The advantage of machine learning is that it learns by example, allowing you to develop a custom algorithm unique to your data, which can make it quite useful at tasks like the one described here. However, it does take accurate and sometimes extensive labels in order to build a useful algorithm, which takes time and costs money. The result is a predictive label on new data that should behave like the attribute of interest. This can be achieved by assigning new labels to a classification group, or by giving a probability score for belonging to that group, enabling you to see the strength of the prediction for each row in the data.

Regression

Most of you will be familiar with classic linear regression. It was one of the first prediction techniques that was easy to calculate, interpret, and understand. It works well for predicting many linear relationships and gives a prediction number as a value, not just a label on whether it belongs to a given class. This capability is what makes it very different from classification and also quite valuable for some applications.

There are many different types of regression, but not all types of regression are really regression in the classic sense. In data science, additional algorithms have emerged that use different approaches to estimate values as regression does. However, we use the name regression more broadly to denote an algorithm that gives a prediction estimate, or number, beyond predicting the classification.

Stephen Kimel, then a data scientist for the cloud storage provider NetApp, shared a story about using this broad category of regression modeling to forecast sales for thousands of products continuously, using increasingly sophisticated data sources and algorithms to improve speed and accuracy of forecasts by product, location, customer, or other factors. This information was essential for budgeting, planning, technology load management, and more.

Link Prediction

Link prediction uses a variety of tools to predict connections. This capability is very useful in social media recommendations. For example, if you know Harry, and Harry knows Sally, you would be more likely to know Sally than someone without a connection to one or more of Sally's connections. The more connections, the stronger the recommendation. Thus, if you know eight of Sally's connections, the prediction would be stronger.

This capability is also very useful in making product recommendations based on social connections. For instance, if a significant number of your friends or connections like a given product or service, you are more likely to like it, too. Based on the old adage "birds of a feather flock together," if you do not currently use a product or service, it might make sense to recommend it to you.

This technique can also be used in information security. For example, Chris Pitts, an information security manager for TIAA, shared how this approach was often used to help detect fraud and hacking attempts. When one computer, account, or individual was flagged for likely fraud, you could use link prediction to identify other devices, accounts, or people who might be related and investigate further.

Behavioral Profiling

Behavioral profiling looks at the behaviors of a device, individual, or small group, not so much at their personal attributes or characteristics but how they behave over time, and gathers data. After enough time has passed, it develops a unique profile of behavior for that person or entity. Whenever behavior occurs outside of that norm, it can flag that behavior as an anomaly and shut down or investigate its behavior.

Note that this is not the same as demographic profiling based on age, gender, or race. It is profiling at the individual level based on observed behaviors. This class of algorithms uses that information to build a baseline, then flags any behavior that deviates too far from that individual baseline.

Many of us have personally experienced this activity, such as when a credit card was flagged for fraud and temporarily suspended due to the detection of unusual activity. This technology is also very useful in detecting cyberattacks and any other unusual behavioral change.

It can also be used to categorize and describe the complex behaviors of individuals, small groups, segments, or clusters. Behaviors are significantly more complex than descriptions based on characteristics or demographics. These algorithms can give insight into not just what something is, but how it behaves, which can have value depending on the context.

Because they can describe what is happening in terms of behaviors and look for changes in that behavior, they are useful in generating alerts anytime there is a change in the status quo. Changes in cell phone use might signal someone may need more services, or may be about to churn, for example, both of which enable the company to act.

Table 4.4 Predictive Tool Class Summary

Tool Class	Function/Job	Common Algorithms
Theory	With an estimated 8+ million active, full-time researchers in the world today, many potentially useful ideas have been explored and published by someone, somewhere. You can improve efficiency and effectiveness by building on proven knowledge and applying it to your situation.	Game theory Agency theory Queuing theory Stewardship theory
Classification	Machine learning techniques predict in which class a new instance of data is likely to belong. New multi-objective classification models are maturing, allowing for greater granularity and efficiency in classification.	Logistic regression Decision trees Support vector machines Naive Bayes
Regression	More than classic regression, the name has expanded in general use to mean assigning a number, as opposed to a class, to an item of interest.	Regression Decision trees Neural networks
Link prediction	Link prediction focuses on predicting connections or links to other people or objects that should be there, but are not currently recorded in the data. It is useful for recommending new connections.	Random walk Common neighbors Preferential attachment
Behavioral profiling	Behavioral profiling enables you to get rich granular data on a person or object to establish a baseline of normal behavior and then flag any unexpected deviations from expected behaviors. It is useful in security and fraud detection.	Markov chain analysis Collaborative filtering

Another advantage of these systems is that they focus on rich data from what is being profiled, as opposed to the often shallow breadth of a little data from many different items. This advantage makes it easier to deploy them for custom and unusual applications and to tailor and customize them to more applications. It is also a little more robust than many other machine learning systems and is able to add value with fewer data records.

Chris Pitts also shared how the team uses behavioral profiling at their financial firm to enhance security. Whenever a new device is active in their network, or a new employee is set up, they collect vast amounts of data about the behaviors of the person or device. After a few months, they are able to develop a baseline of clean behavior they know to expect. When a device or person begins to deviate from the behavioral baseline, they flag it for investigation, or shut it down if warranted, to prevent and reduce hacking and fraud. Table 4.4 presents these classes of tools with their common functions and algorithms.

PRESCRIPTIVE ANALYTICS TOOLS

Prescriptive analytics tools help shape the future you want to have with insight and guided actions based on data, algorithms, and a clear vision for a desired outcome. This is in the upper right quadrant from Figure 4.1 because it is focused not just on predicting the future, but shaping it through action guided and driven by analytics.

Next we briefly explore a few classes of prescriptive tools.

Business Frameworks

You may not have thought about it this way, but you likely use low-level prescriptive tools frequently. There are many tools and frameworks that have proven useful in helping you make business decisions. They are generally not ironclad laws with deep data, but they are useful prescriptive tools, honed over years of study and application that have proven their worth by guiding our actions for a future decision, which is the definition of prescriptive analytics.

Common examples of these tools include simple calculation tools, such as net present value calculations, margin/asset analysis, asset valuation, or return on investment (ROI) estimates, to more conceptual frameworks, such as game theory, principal agent theory, or other strategic tools that help guide a firm's future actions.

Emerging tools based on more data can be more precise and scalable and offer additional insights, but it is worth remembering our prescriptive roots so we can better understand where new tools are likely to take us. Sometimes tools are improved by being able to code them into more precise, scalable, and granular models that can be applied at scale.

Dr. Rudi Pleines actually developed a framework for identifying leadership potential they used for hiring top talent at a consulting firm where Pleines previously worked. I had the good fortune of seeing this leadership assessment framework in action over several years while directing our university's MBA program.

Pleines was kind enough to travel from Europe to the United States and volunteer for a week to assess our students, providing coaching and feedback based on the results. He had developed a business simulation tool that engaged my students, or the job candidates for Pleines's firm, in various realistic business challenges. Although they did care about decision outcomes, what they cared about more was the candidates' ability to work with a large amount of data and derive meaningful conclusions, their ability to apply theoretical concepts such as accounting rules in real life, their general business sense, their ability to speak up, and, most important, their leadership skills and ability to effectively work together as a team.

Over time, Pleines has developed several useful metrics to assess leadership potential and has trained collaborators sit in on various team meetings, taking notes and scoring each person on several dimensions. At the end, we had data to assess how our program was doing on training our students in leadership, giving valuable feedback to improving our program, and, just as important, customizing feedback for every student to help them improve on the dimensions assessed in Pleines's standardized metrics.

Known Algorithms

The next class of prescriptive tools are known algorithms that can guide and optimize business decisions. Many of these algorithms come from the domain of operations research and have been focused on helping businesses run better and more efficiently.

These prescriptive tools usually take generic business problems with known approaches and algorithms useful in solving them and apply these algorithms to your particular situation. Examples include routing (traveling salesman problem), product/portfolio optimization, pricing, scheduling, and network modeling for supply chain management. They use optimization; linear, integer, mixed, and constraint programming; as well as other tools to find prescriptive solutions that maximize value for these types of problems.

Although most of these approaches have been around and used for a while, what is different today is the availability of more granular data and orders of magnitude more computing power. These differences are making what historically has been mostly an application of mathematical formulas into a tool that can ingest and process much more relevant data, allowing for continuous real-time optimization solutions such as adjusting the supply chain or routing ride-share taxis in real time (e.g., Uber, Lyft, Waymo) and layering on surge pricing to maximize profit.

Dr. Karl Kempf used a variety of known algorithms in the family of stochastic modeling over more than a decade at Intel to optimize for production and sales of thousands of products to thousands of customers, with documented savings of more than $55 billion, as mentioned previously.

Experimentation and Simulation

In addition to the established frameworks and known algorithms described here, there are a few techniques that are useful in generating prescriptive guidance. The first is based on mass experimentation, which generally focuses on gathering diagnostic information or brute force optimization, as discussed previously. However, when combined with important economic impact variables, it can be used as a tool for prescriptive analytics.

By looking at probabilities derived from prediction models and/or experimentation, and linking them to economic impact variables based on probable outcomes, you can develop objective maximizing solutions such as optimizing profit. Airlines have been doing something similar for decades by giving customized prices at different times to different seats trying to maximize revenue and profit based on demand forecasts. What is different now is that it can be done at the individual level with more focus and granularity in near real time.

Another technique in this area is simulation. By taking what is known about a problem and probable outcomes, a solution can be simulated thousands of times to find the most likely range of outcomes that will produce a described result based on available inputs. We see this technique used in climate modeling, for example.

A nice feature of this technique is that it lets you play with various ranges of inputs and do what if scenarios to better guide your decisions. As more computing power and data continue to become available, these types of tools will continue to grow in their application and usefulness.

Anthony Berghammer, now a data scientist at RTI International with stints at EY and other companies, shares an interesting story about working with the major league baseball team, the Astros. Popularized by the movie *Moneyball*, several baseball teams started using what they named *sabermetrics* to describe this type of sports analytics.

Berghammer's team was trying to optimize for pitcher fatigue. Different pitchers have different strengths and abilities, useful at different times and places in the games. However, like all of us, they get tired and their performance begins to suffer. Therefore the team manager could not just leave their star pitchers in the game but had to manage both the skills the pitcher needed and the ability of the pitcher to deliver them at that time, taking into account the fatigue that built up during the game.

Berghammer's team identified relevant and important variables and concepts, which they collected and then feature engineered to fit their models. They then ran thousands of simulations of likely inputs and outcomes for the games based on pitcher fatigue level and other important factors. The result is that they were able to optimize and prescribe the right pitcher to put in the game at the right time for both fatigue level and game needs, improving their team's performance on a variety of metrics, including wins.

Reinforcement Learning

Most machine learning tools are static in the sense that a model is built on a snapshot of data and applied to future applications. Certainly there are some adjustments made over time to maintain and improve the models, but inherently they are built on mostly static data.

Reinforcement learning is different. It is designed and built for continual learning and adaptation to new and dynamic circumstances. Reinforcement learning is like playing a game of hot and cold, where you get feedback for every action you take, with rewards (hot) and punishment (cold) based on the outcome. Reinforcement learning adds an important time dimension in that it acts, gets feedback from the outcome, then it reevaluates. In this way, it has the potential to be quite prescriptive in its effect.[7]

For these reasons, it is considered a new, third type of machine learning, in addition to supervised and unsupervised learning. It is best used where continual learning and automation are important. For example, this is one of the core technologies behind self-driving cars and winning ML video game applications, such as Alpha Go. It is the continual learning and adaptation-based feedback received in the terms of rewards and punishment that can make it useful in prescriptive analytics. Because it learns from the environment, it can quickly adapt to new situations and has potential in automation and optimization.

The integration with dynamic time, as opposed to the other one-shot categories of algorithms, has many advantages, but also has its challenges. One significant challenge is that it is often hard to know which action caused the desired impact, after thousands or millions of actions. Another is that in real life and business, you do not get many do-overs, so a mistake early on in reinforcement learning is difficult to overcome. Machines can do things very quickly, but generally lack judgment. For a video game,

Table 4.5 Prescriptive Tool Class Summary

Tool Class	Function/Job	Common Algorithms
Business frameworks	There are a number of proven business frameworks built on wisdom and experience that have been used for decades for various types of problems. Start with what is known, then adapt to suit your needs.	Balanced scorecard Porter's 5 forces SWOT analysis
Known algorithms	There are many known and proven algorithms that can apply to many business problems. Many are from the category of operations research and can be incredibly valuable.	Linear programming Simulated annealing Genetic algorithms
Experimentation	We distinguish two types of experimentation in this chapter. The first is aimed at understanding and the second is aimed at optimizing. Understanding often leads to optimizing, but it can be done with experimentation through trial and error alone. I do not recommend it, because these optimizations are often inefficient and shaky, but if you care only about short-term optimization, it might be worth it.	A/B testing at scale for optimization of outcomes
Simulation	Simulations look at probabilities, interrelationships, and likely interactions, then simulate an event happening thousands or millions of times. This repetition gives a better sense of the shape of likely outcomes for different scenarios.	Monte Carlo Discrete event System dynamics
Reinforcement learning	Most machine learning algorithms are considered one-shot learning—built and run. By contrast, in reinforcement learning, learning occurs continuously as new data comes in and constantly adapts to new environments and situations, often finding novel and useful solutions that were previously missed.	Q-learning Multi-armed bandits Deep Q networks

where there can be infinite attempts at resetting the game, this works well, but for business applications we usually just get one try, unlike video games.

Dr. Wayne Thompson loves reinforcement learning and is very bullish on its largely untapped potential to be used more widely in business analytics. It has applications in pricing, marketing, fraud detection, supply chain management, and even customer service. Reinforcement learning is the ability of these systems to continually learn and adopt, as opposed to one-shot learning, which makes them potentially so valuable to businesses. Table 4.5 presents classes of prescriptive tools, their functions, and common algorithms.

TOOL SYNERGIES

Each of the classes of tools described here can add significant value for a firm. Each has its own place in helping executives make better decisions and forms a vital part of an analytics portfolio. Yet, the tools are interdependent in many ways.

It all starts with descriptive information. Without the high-quality and relevant descriptive data you cannot do good diagnostic or predictive analytics, and many operations research models become difficult to accurately tailor to your situation. Gathering relevant, quality, and timely descriptive data facilitates quality and accurate diagnostic and predictive analytics. Better diagnostic and predictive analytics enables the building and use of better prescriptive models.

Although there are a few prescriptive frameworks and tools that have been developed and built on prior evidence that can then be used right away, the most powerful and customized ones are based on your data and customized to your situation. They are informed by insights and feedback from diagnostics and predictive work that will help you build better models and generate more stable generalizable knowledge for the world.

Descriptive analytics tells you what is. Predictive analytics tells you what will be, but diagnostic analytics tells you why. Knowing why something is or will be creates more stability and insight than just knowing it. Predictive analytics lets you generalize to new situations and builds your capacity for more and better work. Both diagnostic and predictive analytics can inform and improve prescriptive analytics. However, building on diagnostic analytics is more stable and also informs prediction.

Yes, prediction can also give you insights for things to investigate with diagnostic and prescriptive analytics, but without eventually getting to the root cause, identifying and showing it, there is always a question about its stability and limits of its applicability over time and to new situations.

For this reason, Figure 4.4 shows a solid line from descriptive analytics passing through diagnostic analytics and on to prescriptive analytics, and another solid line from diagnostic to prescriptive analytics. This is also why it shows a dotted line from descriptive going through predictive analytics to prescriptive analytics and from predictive to diagnostic. You can get there, but the ground is often shakier.

In addition to the business risk of skipping diagnostic analytics, there are also many ethical concerns emerging in analytics. If you do not take time to investigate and understand, you may still be able to develop a predictive or prescriptive model that makes money. However, if you do not invest in understanding the underlying phenomena, it is hard to know if the model is ethical and appropriate to use.

Your algorithm may be picking up a signal that is illegal or unethical to use, that you may not even realize is a problem until it is too late. For example, analysts found that certain types of music preferences were associated with different loan repayment rates. However, it turns out the signal was another type of racial profiling in disguise. Different ethnic groups tend to have similar tastes in music, so the hidden element was not the music, but the race behind it, which is illegal to use in many jurisdictions.

All types of analytics are helpful and useful. Knowing why makes them more trustworthy and reliable over time and to new situations for both predictive and prescriptive analytics. It also better informs the most relevant and useful types of descriptive data that should be collected. It is worth the time to include diagnostic analytics in your portfolio. Sadly, too many analysts jump straight to prediction without taking time to diagnose and understand, which is a treacherous and risky path.

The good news is that prescriptive analytics is a type of analytics that is growing fast and has the most opportunity for growth and value as we go forward. We are really only beginning to tap into the potential of this category of analytics. Figure 4.4 shows how the various analytics tools, classes, and approaches can be used to create synergies.

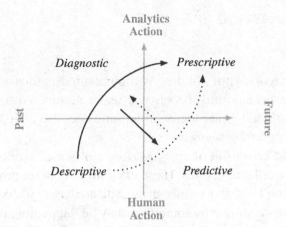

Figure 4.4 Tool Synergies

LIMITS OF ANALYTICS TOOLS

There are many analytics tools with real-world applications to help solve business problems, but they have, and likely always will have, their limits. For example, the US Geological Survey says no one can predict earthquakes.[8] Although we can identify high-risk areas, we do not have the right data, understanding, and systems in place to predict them, and likely never will. They are rare "black swan" style events that are thankfully rare.

Prediction is based on data from the past. When the data from the past is sparse, it is difficult to properly diagnose and understand it to the point of being able to make precise (useful) predictions. Even more so, one might imagine that to predict earthquakes, sensors would be needed deep in the earth with very granular and relevant data, which would be difficult to accomplish. Moreover, due to the sparseness of that data, even if you had it, developing accurate algorithms would still be challenging. More likely, the best we could do is get an earlier warning for when an earthquake is about to happen.

Similar to earthquakes, there are many types of events with low frequency and probability that, if they happened, could have a dramatic impact on the world, for example, the COVID pandemic. Scientists knew an event along these lines could happen, but predicting exactly when, where, and to what intensity is beyond our capabilities, and perhaps always will be.

There are too many random elements that are nearly impossible to predict. It may be that the best we will ever be able to do is a risk assessment for these types of events, along with impact modeling and simulations that can help us prepare for these events appropriately. This risk assessment is still very helpful, but not the same as knowing the future. It is important to realize that the data is only as useful in as much as the future is similar to the past. In a changing world, there will always be limits to what analytics can do. We should use these tools but understand what they can and cannot do well, so we can manage them appropriately.

CHAPTER SUMMARY AND EXERCISES

Task 4: Summary

The most important tool is your mindset. Without a mindset focused on making better decisions with data, no amount of tools will really matter. With the right mindset, executives can and should guide tool selection and use it to align with the organization's needs, with integration being a key factor.

There are several categories of analytics, many of which require specialized tools for each, and some overlapping ones. These categories are descriptive analytics, which focuses on identifying facts and trends; diagnostic analytics, which focuses on building theory and understanding why something may be happening; predictive analytics, which focuses on identifying what will likely happen in the future; and prescriptive analytics, which focuses on shaping your optimal future. There are various classes of algorithms that can do various tasks within each category. These tool categories should work together synergistically.

Within each category of analytics (descriptive, diagnostic, predictive, and prescriptive), there are many tools that can be used in which you can better understand and draw insights from your data. Though there is some overlap, by focusing on the primary job you want done, these algorithms and methods can be grouped into the following categories, making it easier to navigate the ever-expanding world of algorithms. Summaries of each tool can be found in Tables 4.1, 4.2, 4.3, 4.4, and 4.5 and should be carefully reviewed and understood.

Taks 4: Exercises

1. Describe the executive team's role in tools selection and use and why it is important they engage in this process.

2. List and describe each of the primary categories of analytics (descriptive, diagnostic, predictive, and prescribe) and give your own real or hypothetical example of each one in use.

3. Out of all the tools described in this chapter, or others in which you may have become familiar, list and describe three that seem particularly relevant to you and your current or intended career. Include a short description on what the tool does, that is its job, as described in the discussion on milkshake marketing, an example of how each one could be used to help you as you travel further down your intended path.

4. Consider the concept of tool synergies. Briefly discuss why considering tool synergies is important, give an example of synergies, and describe what you can do to take advantage of potential synergies.

5. There are some things that no tool, however powerful, will be able to accurately predict or prescribe. Discuss what some of these limits might be, why we have them, and what their implications are for business and analytics leaders.

NOTES

1. https://www.linkedin.com/pulse/4-stages-data-analytics-maturity-challenging-gartners-taras-kaduk/
2. https://ifvp.org/content/why-our-brain-loves-pictures#
3. Foster Provost and Tom Fawcett, *Data Science for Business* (Beijing: O'Reilly, 2013).
4. D. L. Dickinson, J. A. Cazier, and T. G. Cech, "A Practical Validation Study of a Commercial Accelerometer Using Good and Poor Sleepers," *Health Psychology Open* (July–December 2016): 1–10.
5. Antonio Rafael Braga, Danielo G. Gomes, Breno M. Freitas, and Joseph A. Cazier, "A Cluster-Classification Method for Accurate Mining of Seasonal Honeybees Patterns," *Ecological Informatics* 59 (2020). https://doi.org/10.1016/j.ecoinf.2020.101107.
6. E. Hassler, P. MacDonald, J. Cazier, and J. Wilkes, "The Sting of Adoption: The Technology Acceptance Model (TAM) with Actual Usage in a Hazardous Environment," *Journal of Information Systems Applied Research* 14, no. 4 (2021): 13–20. https://jisar.org/2021-14/n4/JISARv14n4p13.html.
7. Brian Christian, *The Alignment Problem: Machine Learning and Human Values* (New York: W. W. Norton, 2020).
8. https://www.npr.org/2023/02/07/1154893886/earthquake-prediction-turkey-usgs

Execution

EXECUTE = ACTION

The word *execute* can be defined as to "put into effect," a synonym for making change and taking action. Execution, the fifth manageable task in analytics, is the task that harvests value by ensuring that beneficial action is taken. Although there must be sustained action in the end for value to be realized, the process of ensuring that appropriate action is taken starts early and continues long after the project has concluded.

To succeed, executives responsible for putting analytics into effect must manage change, which includes making sure it is the right change for the organization and that it is accepted and implemented in the organization in a sustainable way and that it also can be built on in future initiatives. If this task is not done well, not only will this project fail but also it will very likely create distrust in analytics and doom future projects before they even start. Thus, proper execution may be the most important task in using analytics to add value to the firm. No matter how deep the insights, with no action, little is accomplished.

Executives must manage change by ensuring the right analytics actions are put into effect at the right time in the way that most benefits the organization. This means managing the analytics process, which means managing the people championing, creating, using, and affected by the analytics as well as addressing problems that arise along the way.

Yet, this chapter is centered on more than managing the process, people, and problems. As Steve Stone, a seasoned CIO, told me, "sometimes analytics is about taking a leap of faith." Change is hard, and without change execution will fail. For people to change, they first need hope: hope for a better way of doing things, hope for some benefit from the analytics, and hope that it will make their lives easier, better in some tangible, meaningful way, a way that is important to them, not just some CEO.

To execute well, executives and analytics professionals alike must first feed hope, sharing a vision for a better life, a better way of doing things, a better outcome for the intended analytics that the adopters desire. Once hope has taken hold, then comes faith, faith that the project will deliver on the promise of hope. At this stage, the executives' and analysts' objective must be to build and bolster faith, especially with the business process owners, that the hoped-for outcome will be achieved by following a trustworthy development process full of best practices throughout the analytics life cycle and ensuring that people throughout the organization receive the desired benefits in implementation.

This chapter focuses on how business leaders, including executive champions and business process owners, can help with the analytics process, followed by advice for the analytics team to help them better work with the people they are working for and affecting, most prominently the executive champions and business process owners, and concludes with advice for addressing problems that often arise associated with executing well on an analytics project.

PROCESS

Executives, with help from business process owners and other stakeholders, need to understand the analytics process in order to manage it effectively. For this purpose, it can be helpful to think of analytics in three phases: preparation, discovery, and resulting action (see Figure 5.1). At each phase, executives can be supportive in different ways. Here we give an overview of the process, then share best practices executives should follow to help analytics succeed.

The first stage is preparation. Here you identify relevant data, extract it from your system or related sources, transform it into a starting format that can eventually be cleaned and modeled, and load it into your analytical tools for analysis. This critical stage takes a great deal of planning, including identifying the problem, finding relevant data, and making the data accessible.

The discovery phase is the one that most people think about when they imagine analytics. Here, you clean the data, develop features by transforming the data into something more predictive, perform the actual analysis, assess the model's validity, and measure its likely impact.

When the discovery phase yields something believed to be useful to the organization, the next stage is putting it into action. Implementing the findings could mean changing an offline process or, more commonly, an online one with an analytical product or tool. Both need to be integrated into the business process for change or action to occur. Machine learning operations or development operations are increasingly popular ways to integrate analytics into current business processes to ensure action is taken.

Preparation

Executives are critical to success in the preparation stage. First and foremost, they need to guide the analytics team to the right problem, one that is valuable, amenable to a solution, and would be adopted. The problem must be one that has or can garner strong executive support that will carry through to adoption and continual use, as discussed previously. It is also important to assemble and effectively manage the team, keeping them focused on adding value, aligning their analytics orientation with project goals, and having the right talent mix, as discussed in Task 2: The Team. The analytics team, executives, and business process owners all need to have the right mindset and tools, as discussed in Task 4: The Tools. All of these elements are critical.

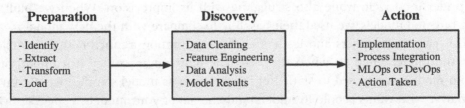

Figure 5.1 The Analytics Process

Yet, at this stage in the process, those elements should have already been set up and put into place. Yes, some of them, especially the business problem, will need to be modified and adapted as you move between data and analysis and problem, and then back again. But executives need to ask key questions about the data in the preparation stage to make sure the analytics results are sound. You may not need to know all the answers, but should be satisfied that someone does. To this end, you need to ask critical questions and make sure the analytics team has credible answers for each. Here are a few points to consider.

Prioritization

Prioritization was discussed at length in Task 1: The Problem, but it should be revisited here, at least briefly, because priorities change in dynamic environments. Leaders should check to make sure the analytics solve an actionable, high-value problem that has strong executive support, has a high impact for effort, has an appropriate time to value, and ensures implementation and action are likely to result.

Well-Defined Problem

Likewise, it is worth checking that the problem statement is crystal clear. Cecil John, an enterprise cloud architect, said in an interview that if you cannot explain it to a child, you are not focused enough. In decision-centric analytics, the problem statement defines the project goals and is essential to getting the analytics right and focused. Leaders should make sure the goals are clear, the hypotheses are testable, there are relevant business metrics, and success is defined, agreed to, and verifiable.

Baseline

Executives should always try to find a baseline in which to compare the analytics to know the data is effecting the desired change. Many times this will be a comparison of human versus algorithmic performance, but it can be other metrics, too. However, having a baseline lets you more accurately measure the value and impact of your analytics. The most common baseline is your current decision process, but other metrics can be used, especially for new areas.

For example, when my team and I were modeling energy demand, we learned that previously the organization had used the temperature in the largest metro area in the service district to estimate demand, because HVAC systems had a significant impact on electricity consumption. This was a process that the organization had used for years and understood well, while also struggling with its imprecision. When we built our more targeted models, we used their baseline to compare with the new models.

This gave the workers and leaders in the organization a much better example of what the model could do when they saw the improved accuracy in comparison to the old model, as opposed to statistical metrics such as model significance. If you are an analyst who wants people to understand and adopt your models, I suggest always finding an acceptable baseline that potential adopters already understand, and comparing your model performance to that baseline. A meaningful comparison is so much more effective than saying something like "this has a p-value of .0002 and . . . ."

Stakeholder Engagement

Stakeholder engagement, in most cases, needs to begin early and include frequent follow-up. If the analytics team is not taking stakeholders along with them on the journey, it is not going to go well, says Dr. Hina Arora, associate clinical professor at ASU and former analytics manager at Microsoft. The earlier and better you engage, the more likely you are to have stakeholders' support when it comes time for adoption, which is when you realize value, and the more likely the project will be what they need.

Stephen Kimel, now a data scientist at Red Hat, talks about having "unicorn" analytics leaders who can straddle both the technical and business worlds, similar to analytics translators. Bill Franks also has a book that can help, *Winning the Room*,[1] which is aimed at teaching analytics professionals how to work with and better communicate with those on the business side. I highly recommend it as required reading before leaders send a "nerd" to present to executives.

Manage Biases

Dr. Joseph Byrum, CTO at Consilience AI who is also a quantitative geneticist, accomplished data scientist, and an INFORMS Edelman Prize winner for some of the very entrepreneurial analytics initiatives Byrum led at Syngenta, talked about bias. Byrum wisely believes that every analytics professional should study their biases, understand them, put realistic plans in place to mitigate their impact, and then follow through. Here are a few common biases of which to be mindful:

- **Confirmation bias.** When we see something we already believe, or wish to believe, we often accept it without thinking about it critically. At the same time, we tend to reject things we do not believe, despite evidence to the contrary. As analysts or anyone who wishes to really make better decisions, we must always maintain an open mind and follow the evidence. Otherwise, why are we doing analytics if we only believe it when it says something we already think we know?
- **Group think.** It is easy to try to fit in the group, not think critically on our own, and follow along with what others are saying, especially the leaders. However, this approach seldom adds value by fostering better decisions. Of course, there is a time to follow orders and directions. But when you are problem-solving, it is important to also seek the truth and look for the best practical answer.
- **Time-based biases.** Most people tend to have several time-based biases. We often look at the past—hindsight bias—and naturally believe the future will be similar. Sometimes it is, but often it is also very different, so care should be taken. We also tend to favor recency and the status quo, compressing this time bias even further and often missing an important opportunity in times of change.

- **Data availability bias.** All of us can fall prey to the trap of data availability bias. This is when we value the data we already have more than the data we do not have. This is a special case of a more general bias known as the endowment effect, which means we also place more value on items we already own over others that are of equal value or even potentially more valuable.

- **Survivorship bias.** Our data is biased. Even if it is high quality and perfectly represents what happened, which is rare, it is still subject to survivorship bias. Data is in your system and available to you to analyze because someone used your product or service, enabling you to collect their data as part of doing business with them. What you are likely missing is data of those who might have done business with you, but did not. This data can actually be quite important and worth gathering as you make decisions, especially if you want to grow beyond your current base of business.

- **Historical data bias.** There are many wonderful records in data from our past, but there are also some terrible ones. Data from the past frequently has bias. We could not, did not, measure everything perfectly, and even if we had, we want our future to be better than the past, not the same or worse. We should be mindful and adjust for historical biases in our data and focus on data that will help us build the world we want to live in.

- **Cultural bias.** Different cultures often have different values and beliefs, even within the same country. Assuming that data from different cultures is a monolith, even if it appears to be the same data, can lead to significant errors. It is worth taking time to understand and test for differences in data collected from different cultures and subcultures.

Quality Data

Without quality data to address the problem and manage the biases, success will be limited. Here are a few attributes of quality data that executives and business process owners should check and verify at this stage of the process, some of which are essential to address the biases just discussed:

- **Quantity.** The more complex the algorithm, the more data it requires to work well. Most analysts will check this, but it can be helpful for leaders to benchmark and make sure it is appropriate for the task.

- **Balanced.** For some types of predictive models, it can be very important to have, or create, a balanced dataset with a large enough proportion of what you are looking for to build a useful stable model. For example, if 95% of the data is negative, such as in a direct marketing campaign, the algorithm can be very accurate saying everything is negative, which adds no value. Creating a more balanced dataset, then adjusting it, enables more insights into the positives you are seeking.

- **Coverage.** Even with a high volume of data, there are likely pockets of data that are quite sparse, making predictions of similar categories to them difficult.

For instance, we see many concerns expressed about algorithms that do okay on white males for facial recognition, but then have a high error rate on other groups such as minority females, raising both performance and ethical concerns. Executives should be mindful of the coverage of their data and be cautious of uses that go beyond the base data that trained the model.

- **Representative.** Executives should evaluate the degree to which the data you have is likely to represent the future you expect. Consider whether the environment has changed and, if so, to what extent before deciding how much to rely on its predictions.

- **Validity.** Executives should ask if the data measures what you think it is measuring. Most available data was collected to support business operations, not necessarily analysis. You can still learn from it, but take time to understand what it is really measuring.

Automation

There is a lot of drudgery in data science, especially when it comes to gathering and cleaning poor quality data. Patrick Getzen, retired chief analytics officer for Blue Cross Blue Shield of North Carolina, shared how important it was to use automation to manage that drudgery and free up the analytics professionals' time to focus on solving problems. Strategic automation that tests and manages data quality and makes it available performs key tasks that will make your analytics team much more efficient and engaged. Giving the analytics team the proper tools improves the likelihood of actually being able to solve a problem.

Discovery

Most of the discovery process will be managed by the analytics team. Most of them will be very thorough in their work. Yet, it can still be helpful for executives to check on a few common traps in discovery by asking a few relevant questions to gently remind the analytics team of their importance and making sure those traps have been addressed. But the first step for executives is to understand the difference between production and discovery.

Discovery Versus Production

Analytics starts with discovery and should conclude with production. These are two very different phases, with different mindsets and skills required for each one. The data scientist is trained to think about discovery and naturally gravitates to finding answers to questions. This skill is indispensable to a project and gives business leaders insights to work with. That said, data scientists are generally not trained to think about production. Yet, it is also an essential step to achieving value for the firm. Failure to manage both the discovery and production processes is a key reason many analytics projects fail. Here are a few best practices for executive champions, business process owners, and the analytics team:

- **Begin with the end in mind.** Polly Mitchell-Guthrie, VP of industry outreach and thought leadership at Kinaxis; Bill Franks, director of the Center for Data Science and Analytics within the School of Data Science and Analytics at Kennesaw State University; and a few others emphasized the critical importance of beginning with the end in mind, that is thinking about production from the very first day. This way of thinking is generally not natural for data scientists who are trained to and prefer to focus on the discovery part of analytics. But someone needs to be thinking about, and planning for, production from the very beginning.

- **Dance with the problem.** Discovery requires iteration to get it right. Because discovery is about looking for something that is not known, it is rarely right on the first try. You have to discover what works by dancing with the problem, meaning going back and forth among data, analysis, and the problem to discover possible solutions. This process cannot be rushed; science takes time. Feedback, iteration, and experimentation are key to discovery. Once the solution is known, business process owners can start shifting more of their focus to production. Of course, as stated previously, someone should be thinking about production from the first day.

- **Fail fast.** Executives can improve efficiency by setting up clear criteria for success, with metrics for measuring it, and then encouraging rapid experimentation to reach those objectives. This approach can help balance the need for discovery and production by letting the analytics team more easily experiment and iterate, and then jump to other possible solutions with clear criteria for failing fast and moving on. Care should be taken to balance exploration time and failure criteria to best manage the tension between discovery and production.

- **Uninterrupted time.** Chris Pitts, an information security manager for TIAA, shared how critical it is to ensure technical teams have time to focus on tasks. Much of the deep technical work requires deep focus, and a five-minute interruption can derail an entire train of thought for hours, destroying productivity, frustrating team members, and reducing quality. Many executives and business process owners find uninterrupted time very hard to understand, because management requires paying attention to many tasks at once, so it is natural for them to assume others operate the same way. Natural, yes, but it is a big mistake that saps productivity and batters quality.

Understand Error Types

In addition to biases that can occur in data collection, and quality issues with data, there are three common errors in analysis. Statisticians like to talk about the first two;

business people usually love the third. Yet, these errors are all important and should be understood and avoided.

- **Type I error.** The biggest taboo for a scientist is to say something is true, when it is in fact not true. Most of science and statistics are set up to avoid this taboo most of the time, which is why we traditionally use a p-value, or probable value, of .05; this means that 95% of the time you should get it right, which was considered an acceptable trade-off in the early days of science. I explain to my students that a type I error is akin to telling a lie, however accidentally, and is the most serious error for a truth-seeking scientist.

- **Type II error.** This is the opposite of a type I error, which is failing to find and report something that is true. This is undesirable, but preferable to reporting something that is not true as true. The consequence is not pointing other scientists in the right direction, and wasting effort, rather than type I, which points them in the wrong direction.

- **Type III error.** This type was mentioned in Task 1: The Problem, which was solving the wrong problem. It is generally much more important to businesspeople with production goals to reach than for scientists focused on discovery and fueled, in part, by curiosity. However, for analytics to succeed and scale across an organization, it must add value, or it will be refined as a failure.

All of these errors are unfortunate and can be avoided by following a rigorous analytics methodology.

Experimental Design

Dr. Joseph Byrum emphasized the importance of good principles of experimental design in analytics. This is a foundational principle of a science that increases the quality of, and our confidence in, our findings. By taking time to think about cause and effect, how to avoid biases, how to build on established knowledge and theories, and how to set up falsifiable hypotheses to build new knowledge, we improve the quality and reliability of our models now and in the future. It is especially true if we also document and consider publishing our findings, when appropriate, to add back to the store of knowledge and build a cumulative tradition.

Executives can help this process by asking questions about the design and encouraging knowledge sharing, at least internally and where competitive pressures allow.

Develop Feature Stores

Dr. Wayne Thompson, formerly chief data scientist at SAS and currently executive director at JP Morgan, talks about the importance of having feature stores. Features are transformations and derivatives of your data that have often proved useful in prior modeling efforts. Having the best features precomputed and available for easy inclusion in future models can save time and improve quality by building on prior successes. This is a critical and time-saving process that increases model building efficiency and quality by building our cumulative knowledge.

This process is commonly referred to as feature engineering and usually requires business domain knowledge to know what to build and where to integrate features. Many executives and business process owners may not realize that most data is not particularly useful in its raw form and needs to be processed and prepared into these features that can be modeled into an equation. More important, they may not realize the role that they can play, as business leaders, in pointing the feature development in more relevant and useful directions.

For example, consider managing loan repayments. The raw data will have information about the date of the loan, the loan amount, the interest rate, and a history of payments received with dates and amounts. This data is not in a state that can be easily or effectively modeled directly. It needs to be engineered to highlight aspects of it that are important to the business and are likely to be useful in a model. In this case, if a standard definition of default were defined as "90 days late after last payment due," calculations would need to be made on the raw data, along with any other features of interest, to determine if that was the case, and those would need to be stored with, or in place of, the data where they could be analyzed.

Still, there is often additional transformation that may be made to features to better represent those features in a model, often including statistical transformation that better aligns with statistical assumptions or provides more predictive power. But a feature store is essential in making intermediate data useful to the business accessible quickly and easily.

Overfitting

With the abundance of data we have today, coupled with the exponential growth in computing power to process it, it is easy to find random patterns in our data that are, well, just random. With enough data, rare and seemingly impossible events will occur. They are usually real findings that happened, but it does not mean they are indicative of future events.

This problem of being fooled by randomness is related to one of the biggest challenges in machine learning today, which is the concept of overfitting. We want our models to pick up the real patterns in the data that are indicative of future events, while avoiding the random ones. Overfitting means our model is too flexible and is built on random, as opposed to real, patterns in our data, leading to false conclusions and recommendations.

There are a number of techniques to address overfitting. The most common one is splitting your data into three parts: one for building (training data), another for trimming random findings (validation), and a third for testing the final result to estimate impact. Sometimes testing is done in production to save time, but without these controls it is easy to be fooled by randomness, leading to false conclusions and unfruitful actions.

When predictive models are developed, executives should ask about how the analytics team controlled for overfitting and make sure there is a known, established process for them to check out this possibility. This process is highly emphasized in nearly every analytics program, so most experienced analysts will do it naturally.

Target Leakage

Target leakage can be sneakier and harder to detect than overfitting, but it is still a problem. Target leaking occurs when data from the future, or your target, leaks into or finds a way into the model. Of course, the data is not really from the future, but because your data is historical data, the event you are looking for has already happened in your data from the past.

Target leakage usually happens when starting a modeling project because analysts naturally pull all data associated with a desired event they are trying to predict, which is usually the end result. But when that data comes, many intermediate signals before the prediction event, data that will not be available at the time a decision is made. This is because the data you are given to model has often already had whatever you are looking for happen to it, and sometimes hints from that future event are present in the source data, but won't before new data.

Having data from the future in your model is like having tomorrow's newspaper and will make your predictions appear far more accurate than they really are. The problem is that you will not have that newspaper to help you when it is time to go into production, and it will fail to deliver results.

For instance, if you are modeling loan defaults, the file will likely also have data on late payments, which are highly associated with default rates, but are unknown at the time a loan is given. Data from the future will have leaked into the model if future data elements are not carefully removed.

A key principle of building useful analytics models is that data from the future, meaning data you will not have in the system after launch, should never be in a predictive model. However, this scenario is easier to let happen to analytics team members than most would guess, and usually occurs for these reasons:

- **Performance pressure.** Performance pressure results from the rush to deliver results without stopping to understand all the potential variables in the model. We all make mistakes when we do not have time or take time to stop and think carefully. When we do not budget adequate time for analysis, mistakes happen.

- **Technical versus scientific training.** Data science requires a mix of technological and scientific backgrounds. Because technology is so powerful and changing so rapidly, many analysts focus more on the technical and are often not aware of, or do not prioritize, the scientific best practices needed to avoid these types of errors.

- **More data.** We have more data than ever before, not just in volume but also in variety, not just in the source data but many transformations and combinations that are done to improve predictive power. It is not uncommon to have hundreds of predictive candidate variables, many of which are complex, derived, or combined variables not readily understood, that could be used in a model. This abundance of data makes it harder to identify leaked data or variables.

- **Limited domain knowledge.** Analysts are trained in data science and technology. Domain knowledge requires time in the industry and business training to understand. Without domain knowledge of the data in use, it is harder to detect data that does not belong in the predictive model.

These issues have inadvertently led to a lack of intellectual rigor in many models, with time-pressured, narrowly trained, and inexperienced analysts sometimes ending up on a fishing expedition where everything is thrown at a powerful machine learning algorithm, even when it should not happen.

If the results seem too good to be true, it is often from target leakage and should be investigated by the analytics team. To increase model quality and avoid these problems, executives should consider these factors:

- **Business knowledge.** Ensure the executive champions and business process owners are not only represented but also carefully participate in the variable selection process by helping to ensure the data for each candidate variable is well documented, communicated, and understood by the analyst. These business leaders should also ask thoughtful questions about nonintuitive variables included in the model. Anything that can be done to improve an analyst's domain knowledge is also helpful.

- **Scientific rigor.** Introduce, maybe even require, more scientific rigor where cause and effect and likely candidate variables been vetted and justified in advance to improve the quality and stability of models. But note there is a cost in that nonobvious, or currently unknown but real patterns, may be missed and not discovered. It is important to have a balanced approach that avoids errors while allowing for exploration.

- **Performance testing.** Follow rigorous performance testing between discovery and production as a best practice that can help detect overfitting. Target leakage can easily be missed if live or carefully screened data that mimics new incoming data (only) is not part of the testing process. Performance testing needs to be done on the type of data the model will receive in production.

Concept Drift

Learning from historical data assumes that the future is similar to the past. Fortunately, this idea is often true enough to make analytics useful. However, we all know that things change and, when things change, the data from the past may not always apply. This is known as *concept drift*, meaning the concept we are trying to model has evolved and has drifted away from the concept in our historical data. When it does, models on historical data no longer apply and performance degrades.

Performance monitoring should be put into place to catch concept drift and update the models. Often model building is done with recent data that may be more like the future. However, this approach necessitates a time delay between a concept drift occurring and the response of a new model, which can result in missed opportunities, or worse, poor decisions.

An advanced practice for the most important and time-sensitive problems is to not only monitor performance but also to monitor the shape of new data, known as *data visibility*, by looking at the input to the model and detecting when the data is changing, before the model degrades. An even more advanced practice is to analyze historical data, going back as far as possible to identify the shape of the data at various times under changing market conditions, and to segment that data into similar shape patterns for deeper analysis. The deeper analysis would focus on understanding the conditions that lead to the different shape, perhaps including macroeconomic conditions or other business environmental changes, and seeing how it drives change in the data.

This deeper analysis can then be used to monitor and predict market changes, with an early warning system, to look back at the historical shapes of data that are most similar, and to more quickly adapt the model based on shape similarity, leading to faster and more accurate responses. A simple example is how Walmart has analyzed retail sales during hurricanes and used their results to prepare for similar future events. Of course, the potential of data-shape analysis over time is much greater and is just beginning to be used and understood. It is time-consuming and expensive, but for mission-critical functions, it can be a valuable approach to use.

Model Assumptions

Every statistical model has assumptions built into it. Executives do not need to know what they are, but they do need to know they have been addressed. For example, they could say this: "Tell me what assumptions your model is built on and how you made sure they were valid." Most analysts are rigorous about model assumptions and will have a ready response. But showing they have thought it through and having this ready response can build trust and confidence in the result. This list suggest some actions executives can do to help ensure a higher-quality analytics process:

- **Implementation.** Change and implementation are hard. Part of your change strategy should be to make the system as easy to use as possible, with clear quantifiable benefits. Building world-class interfaces increases the chances of adoption.
- **Relevant high-quality data.** Data is the oil that fuels the analytics engine. Without high-quality, relevant data available in the right level of granularity to address your business problem, the rest does not even matter. Your data must be governed well, available, and related to the problem you are trying to solve.
- **Balanced team.** A well-balanced and diverse analytics team with different viewpoints and perspectives will make your solution more robust. Having a unicorn (one of those brilliant, high-dollar data scientists with broad expertise) lead your team can help keep the solution relevant.
- **Methodology.** Following an approved data analytics methodology will increase your chances of success. INFORMs offers a good model that is linked to their vendor-neutral Certified Analytics Professional (CAP) designation. I highly recommend using this model to ensure quality and effectiveness.

■ **Iterative.** When searching for business value using advanced analytics, you are exploring an unknown space using data, math, technology, and business acumen. Just as with any exploration, this is an iterative process. That means you will need time to look around and explore before you can find the best solution. Be patient with this process and be prepared to adjust as you learn more about the space you are exploring. Only then can you maximize business value creation.

Action

As stated many times in this book, the only way to realize value, and hence have successful analytics, is to ensure action is taken as a result of your analytics efforts. Here are a few challenges executive champions, business process owners, and the analytics team collectively need to overcome to take action.

Statistical Versus Business Significance

Mathematics is focused on finding statistical significance. Very often the analytics team can find statistical significance that does not translate into value for the firm, meaning that it is not operationally significant or does not translate into tangible value for the firm. Occasionally, there may be a finding that does not rise to statistical significance, but could nonetheless be meaningful enough to have business value even if there are only slight improvements in performance, but spread out over millions of records.

Statistical rules give guidelines that introduce quality and trust into modeling. However, the results should be tested and measured not only for statistical significance but also for business significance. This process can be helped by focusing on business metrics, often in the form of KPIs, and measuring their impact there as much as the statistical significance.

Tha analytics team should take care to focus on what can be controlled and influenced, and control for as many influential factors as possible. Good experimental design, as discussed previously, is key. I have had many naive graduate students and more than a few employees say our objective is to increase profit—that is our KPI. Sure, that is true to an extent. But many thousands of variables, most of them out of your control, will affect KPI. You also need to control for other factors, or how will you know if what you are doing is right? Data science can learn from basic science here, where incredibly careful thought is put into place to control for all the factors that can affect what you are trying to change or measure. You then know what you know and will not be fooled by random noise with sloppy analytics problem framing, as outlined in Step 2 of the INFORMS Analytics Methodology.

Changing Environment

The markets and indeed our whole world is evolving and changing constantly and rapidly. This evolution is even more true with technology than most other fields. In this dynamic environment. executives always need to be on the lookout not just for what their firm needs today, but what it will (likely) need tomorrow. Executives should anticipate and not just react to the changing environment. This awareness is challenging to achieve because it is hard to predict and build support for market and technological changes. Making this situation even more challenging is the notoriously short tenure of many CIOs and analytic leaders, which is usually less than three years. But the reward for visionaries who get it right can be quite significant.

Organizational Change

As discussed throughout this book, organizational change is critical to action. Without it, the project will likely fail. Many obstacles can stop or delay organizational change, including politics. Organizational change means business processes will have to change, which is hard, especially when people are involved. This change will need to be managed carefully. Executives should be mindful of the operational processes listed here:

- **Administrative burden.** Sometimes the administrative burden, or overhead, is higher than it is worth. One of our experts shared a story about how a firm built a wonderful model that improved sales in the organization. However, it required the sales staff members to spend about 40% of their time entering in data, rather than making sales calls. Not only did this irritate the sales staff members, overall sales dropped even as efficiency went up, leading to a loss of revenue. This burden should be carefully considered during and leading up to the action phase to make sure the payoff is enough to justify it.

- **Complexity.** Complex models are harder to operationalize. A classic example is the Netflix prize, where Netflix paid a winning team to develop a better movie recommendation system. They did, and it was better. However, it was also so complex that Netflix was not able to make it work efficiently enough to be worth the extra benefit and they had to go with a simpler, not better, model.

- **Model interpretability.** No one adopts a model they do not understand, especially if humans are in the loop. Make sure the model is understandable because it will increase adoption and reduce compliance and regulatory risks.

- **Impact documentation.** To help future projects succeed, it is important to actively document success in business terms. This is also true with current projects as you seek to expand them across the organization. Early success from pilot studies or from early adopters should be documented and shared to build momentum. Building a responsible data and analytics culture is covered more extensively with Task 7: Responsible Analytics.

- **Manage relevant stakeholders.** Depending on the project and initiatives, there can be other important stakeholders to consider. They may be customers, suppliers, important shareholders, and others. The power dynamics may be a bit different, but the principles are similar. Seek to understand issues and motivations, build relationships, maintain your integrity, and avoid stepping afoul of issues by steering to projects you can ethically do.

- **Maintain congruent communication.** Diego Lopez Yse, VP of operations leading data science projects for Moody's, shared how important it is to match the communication style and frequency to the needs of the intended audience, with the focus on them, not the analytics team, to help drive adoption and action.

- **Learn from past projects.** Pay attention to what goes well and what goes wrong at every stage in every project. Then, bring your best practices to future projects, sharing them with the entire organization. Bonus: pay attention to best practices from others in and outside of your organization. Always stay up-to-date with what works well and what does not.

- **Conduct early legal and ethical review.** Legal and ethical issues can quickly kill an otherwise "good" project and should be actively explored and given thought in advance. Bad publicity, which can happen even for legal and ethical projects, could also kill a good project. These issues will be discussed at length in Task 7: Responsible Analytics.

- **Contingency plan.** Always have a contingency plan. Assume something will go wrong and that you just will not know what it is until it happens. So you need to be prepared for everything.

- **Manage organizational bandwidth.** There are many initiatives going on in an organization at any given time. Only a few of them are related to analytics. If there is too much noise from too many initiatives, your project will get lost in the noise and fail to be adopted, even if it is a great project. There will just be too many other things vying for the organization's attention. The bandwidth for organizational change is limited. Where and how your project fits into that dynamic should be carefully managed in relation to everything else and timing should be prioritized for success.

Table 5.1 summarizes the roles and responsibilities of business leaders, including executive champions, business process owners, and analytics team leaders in the analytics process.

Table 5.1 Business Leader Roles at Each Phase of the Analytics Process

Preparation	Discovery	Action
• Manage data availability bias. • Consider survivorship bias. • Optimize data attributes for better analysis. • Develop feature stores for better availability of key concepts.	• Ensure good experimental design. • Manage overfitting. • Avoid target leakage. • Prepare for concept drift. • Test for concept drift. • Verify model assumptions are met.	• Evaluate business significance, not just statistical significance. • Prepare for a changing environment. • Drive organizational change. • Weigh legal and ethical issues. • Document and share successes.

PEOPLE

There are several groups of people important to the analytics process, particularly when it comes to ensuring sustainable analytics actions are implemented. These people include executives, adopters, development partners, and a few other relevant stakeholders. We discuss each in the following sections.

Executives

There was universal agreement among the panel of experts interviewed for this book that executive support was one of the most important factors of success. Dr. Karl Kempf shared that one of the most critical parts of his role at Intel is focused on finding, building, and maintaining executive support for the team's analytics project. Nearly everyone talked about the importance of maintaining executive support throughout the project. It is probably *the single most important task* for anyone working in analytics to do.

Although analytics projects can and do still fail, even with executive support, without it there is a dead stop. Moreover, executives heavily influence all other groups involved in the analytics process, including the business process owners who need to change for analytics to work. You do not just want their passive support or acquiescence, but their enthusiastic support and their willingness to put in efforts to ensure adoption. If other groups sense reluctance or hesitancy on behalf of the executives, they will often adopt a similar attitude and see an opening to resist change if the business process owners are not already strong supporters of the project.

Here are a few best practices our experts use to build and maintain support with executive champions and business process owners before, during, and after the project.

Listen to and Understand Their Goals and Strategy

It is good to have good ideas. Most analytics professionals are very curious and often creative, too. Consequently, they can often think of a hundred ways that analytics can be used to help the organization. However, only a few of their ideas will have the potential for long-term executive support. Suggesting too many ideas too quickly is a recipe for failure and causes a loss of support as executives get confused by what is possible and face the back-and-forth of too many ideas that may or may not match their goals. This is especially true in the early stages of analytics maturity before trust is built.

The analyst needs to stop and focus on the most important problems and gauge the appropriate time to share other ideas when they are relevant and helpful. A better strategy is to use one of Steven Covey's *7 Habits of Highly Effective People:*[2] seek first to understand, then to be understood. Be humble, listen first to the executive's goals and strategy, and identify pain points and problem areas where analytics can help. Once you understand, you can prioritize and address the most important ones first.

Once executives and business process owners see you as a helpful ally who delivers relevant results important to them, they will be much more open to listening to new ideas that you may have, as long as you focus and filter them carefully to make sure those ideas continue to support and accelerate the executive's goals.

Use Business Language

In addition to understanding and being guided by the executive's goals and strategy, it is critical to communicate with them in their language—the language of business. Any technical jargon, even if understood, will be inefficient and detract from their core issues, which are critical for maintaining support.

You must not only become fluent in translating analytics processes into the business terms executives use every day but also translate that way of speaking into the impact of doing, or not doing, a particular analytics project and how it will affect the executive's goals and objectives. This approach applies to the current project and other downstream analytics projects that can build and expand on the current one as you move toward analytics maturity. Using and engaging analytics translators, as discussed in Task 2: The Team, can be a critical part of ensuring that this communication is done effectively. Analytics translators can also educate your analytics team on key goals and business terms common in your industry and firm.

Dr. Wayne Thompson strongly emphasized the importance of also including business metrics, not just statistical metrics, in nearly every model built. By factoring in business metrics and impacts from the very start of a project, communicating in business language will become more natural and keep the focus properly centered while building and maintaining executive support.

Use Process-Based Trust

Executives will not support, adopt, and, crucially, fight for analytics they do not trust. For projects to succeed, they not only need to be good, they need tenacious executive support to carry them through. Executives will only support a project tenaciously if they see that it (1) benefits goals and objectives they care about and (2) is very likely to deliver that result. We talked about the first in the prior section. The second one requires trust.

There are several types of trust and different ways to create it. For executives, two types of trust are the most critical. The first is interpersonal trust, or trust between individuals. This type of trust is important for most relationships and can be enough for you to start experimenting with a few small analytics projects. However, as important as interpersonal trust is, it is not scalable across the organization, which will limit an organization's long-term success with analytics. To build broad support and the type of tenacious support that leads to resilient projects and more adoption, you also need process-based trust.

INFORMS, one of the oldest and most prestigious organization for analytics professionals, has outlined a mature process for analytics professionals to follow, one that builds process-based trust and also increases the likelihood of success. Outlined in the CAP program, they offer a way to build trust in analytics and to certify that CAP holders, like me, know and pledge to follow a proven analytics process.

Sure, there are a few other methodologies available. I have used several of them, and although they all have trade-offs, I have found the one developed by INFORMS to be the most focused on business success and well suited to decision-centric analytics. Here are a few reasons why this is my favorite decision-centric analytics methodology:

- **Problem-focused.** The methodology always starts with the decision to be made or the problem to be solved. It does not advance to the next level until this is clearly identified and agreed to by all sponsors and stakeholders, virtually ensuring executive support while giving a clear direction for where to focus their efforts.

- **Stakeholder management.** Stakeholder engagement and management is required throughout the process. This requirement includes the analytics problem framing portion that converts the problem statement into an action plan for analytics, and requires the stakeholders to define success and agree to the plan, in writing, up front, which is crucial to ultimate adoption.

- **Business focus.** At every stage of the process, the likely business impact is assessed and the project adjusted as needed, making it more likely to reach its business objectives, not just the modeling ones.

- **Deployment.** This process requires thinking about deployment early and assessing where and how the project could and should be deployed across the organization. It also requires after deployment monitoring to measure and adjust the model even after the project is complete in case there is concept drift.

- **Vendor-neutral.** The process is vendor-neutral and tool-agnostic. This vendor- and tool-neutral process keeps you focused on what matters, not how to get there. It also gives this analytics methodology greater longevity and durability, enabling it to withstand and thrive in an environment where tools and techniques, and those that provide them, are changing rapidly.

- **Leadership and ethics.** INFORMS requires that CAP holders be evaluated on their leadership skills before becoming certified, and all of them must pledge to uphold clear ethical guidelines, which are discussed in Task 7: Responsible Analytics.

- **Proven.** The best reason to follow the INFORMS methodology outlined in the CAP is that it is a proven methodology, used and understood by thousands of INFORMS members, and built on their wisdom and experience.

Following this methodology is one of the most effective ways I know to make immediate gains in the battle to conquer the last mile of analytics in overcoming barriers to adoption. It is not the only factor, but it can go a long way in getting you over that last mile.

Please note, however, that the INFORMS CAP methodology intentionally focuses on decision-centric analytics, which is both a strength and a weakness. Its decision-centric focus makes it much easier to align with business objectives and hence to maintain executive support for implementing successful analytics. However, the price of this focus also tends to limit the exploration of data-centric and action-centric analytics.

Even so, the trade-offs are generally well worth it in the early stages of analytics when building process-based trust is essential to success. Once trust is well established, it allows for the eventual expansion into these other important centricities, as analytics acceptance grows across your organization.

Use Social Proof

Executives collaborate. They know loners fail and leaders need friends and allies to survive and thrive in any organization. They likely got to where they are by being smart, well connected, goals focused, and hard working. They are willing to take bets that advance their goals, but only when there is a high chance of success. They know failure is often punished more than success is rewarded, unless you own the company and are very secure in your position.

Yet, there is safety in social proof. If others in their network, and the network of other executives' peers, are thinking and doing similar things, it lowers the perceived risk of analytics adoption and, yes, even failure. If others are doing it and it seems like the right thing to do generally in their circle, the social and political cost of failure is lower and more acceptable, making it easier for them to adopt.

Today, analytics is pervasive enough in executive circles that most will be aware of its potential benefits and how other organizations are using it. They will also have heard many sales pitches from vendors offering to solve all their problems with the click of a button. This scenario might make it difficult to separate the myth from the reality, leading to either over-enthusiasm or undue skepticism and hesitancy.

Social proof can help. Make sure your executives are aware of similar applications to the ones you think can help address their problems. Bring to their attention successful use cases and even failures or overly optimistic analytics attempts at companies they recognize and respect. The closer you can match analytics applications in their social circle, the more likely they are to listen.

Social proof is an important tool for educating and building trust in analytics as well as spurring action by lowering the risk. It can also be used to avoid over-hyped technologies likely to fail, if done prudently.

Be Politically Aware

Where there are people there is politics, and if you are not cognizant of that fact, you, your projects, and those you care about can be burned by it. Analytics professionals are often baffled and frustrated by political situations that benefit the person while hurting the organization as a whole. Most analytics professionals find this type of politics distasteful due to their personal and professional commitment to abide by ethical decisions focused on using data to drive the best outcomes. Although we all know that much of politics can be offensive, it is a fact of life that we need to be aware of to manage successfully.

As analytics professionals, it is our professional and ethical duty to provide unbiased advice, based on data and appropriate analysis, to help our organizations achieve their goals. Therefore, I do not advise engaging in political games because it erodes trust in our integrity and stains our profession in a way that will hamper long-term success, even if there are a few short-term gains. Most important, avoiding political games is just the right thing to do.

Here are a few tips to help analytics professionals survive organizational politics while maintaining professional integrity and commitment to ethical actions:

- **Awareness.** Keep your eyes and ears open to the politics of your organization. You do not have to contribute to it to be aware of it. By being aware, you are more likely to be able to avoid being harmed by it.

- **Relationships.** The farther I travel in my career, the more I realize the value of relationships. I hope you learned this sooner than I did, but if not, know that strong relationships are essential to long-term success and can help you navigate politically tenuous situations, as long as you do not contribute to the political mess.

- **Values.** Know your values. My friend Dr. Beverly Wright, head of data science for Burtch Works, is quite passionate about this, to the point of writing them down and reviewing them frequently. Wright knows that those values include being a truth seeker and can define who we are and what we do. Knowing our values is the first step to staying true to them and can help you better navigate thorny political issues more successfully.

- **Communication.** The last thing you want to have happen in a politically charged environment is to be misunderstood or have someone take advantage of you. If your words, even unintended words, can be twisted, they can be turned into a liability that could have been avoided. Learning to communicate clearly and precisely with forethought not only helps avoid political fallout but also makes you a more effective analytics professional.

- **Reputation.** Our reputations matter much more than we often realize. This is even more true for analytics professionals than for many other professions. Integrity is key to trust, and trust is key to action and adoption, which is the key to creating value. Unfortunately, we also live in a world where some people value personal gain over integrity and will play dirty politics, perhaps spreading sheer lies and falsehoods, to tarnish your reputation for some small advantage. Many analysts assume that because they have integrity, their reputations will be protected. This is a false assumption because reputations also have to be managed. Maintaining your reputation is not automatic, even when you are worthy of it.

Business Process Owners

Those who use the systems and tools built as part of the analytics process are another group critical to analytics adoption. Sometimes they are executives, but more often they are those being managed. Executives hold a lot of influence and control over those whom they manage, but there are limits. Even with strong executive support, business process owners should plan for and cultivate adoption using the principles outlined here. When executives are the primary users, it is even more important to follow these principles.

Acceptance Versus Enthusiasm

For analytics adoption to be successful over the long term, you want not just acceptance and acquiescence to executive orders, but enthusiasm. This should be the main focus and goal for high value and high touch projects that require many people to use and adopt over time. This is true for employees, channel partners, and even customers.

If the analyst's mentality is to just get the project done, as opposed to pursuing excellence and acceptance, the project may be adopted, but not with the enthusiasm that leads to long-term impact and support for many future projects that build analytics maturity. To build enthusiasm, business process owners need to improve the existing process, anticipate unintended consequences, keep it simple, and make it useful and easy to use while steering clear of political land mines.

Solve the Real Problem

An experienced analyst knows that the first problem people come to them with is seldom, if ever, the real one. My friend Dr. Beverly Wright likes to say you have to get to the "why-why," which is the real reason they are asking for help. This idea is similar to the concept of the five whys discussed previously. Adopters often see symptoms but may not be aware of or be able to clearly communicate the cause. Business process owners need to make sure the analytics team is focused on the real problem and help them solve it. Once they do, adopters are much more likely to use the solution.

Integrate Versus Replace

Change is hard, especially when people are involved. It is a much easier lift to integrate analytics into the current process than to replace it with an entirely new solution. This truism has the benefit of making it more likely that people will begin to use and adopt analytics now and in the future if you build trust and ease them into change.

However, there is also a downside to building on the current process. Sometimes the old systems and processes are ineffective and inefficient and fail to take advantage of new approaches that the technology can provide. In these cases, executives need to help guide adoption of a new approach and replace the old process. At the early stages of analytics maturity, integration is generally better than replacement. As trust builds, there will be more opportunities for additional changes to support the business.

Whether the analytics solution goes into the old process or a new one, it must be integrated into a business process that is enforced and managed by executives, according to Dr. Rudi Pleines, head of business transformation at ABB Robotics. Otherwise, the analytics are unlikely to be used. Pleines went on to share a personal story of an organization Pleines once worked with. In this case, the analytics team had rolled out an application to every computer in the company by putting it in the configuration file for all computers so it was accessible on every single device. They then went on to claim that they had 100% adoption of their project's outcome, expecting to be praised for their efforts.

However, when they looked deeper, they saw that although it was on every computer, it had very little use, because it had not been integrated into core business processes and there was no enforcement mechanism for anyone to use it. Because use had little impact on people's careers, and change is hard, most did not use it, even though all of them had it easily available on their devices. Availability is necessary, but not sufficient for adoption and use. The application must be integrated into business processes to have widespread effective adoption, no matter how good it is.

Partnerships

Integrating into and improving on current solutions, as mentioned previously, builds partners versus adversaries. It also builds trust and facilitates adoption of technologies. Executives and adopters both need trust to adopt but, crucially, the type of trust they need is different. Executives need to know that the process of doing the analytics is reliable and will likely yield value. They need to understand and be able to interpret it and see how it furthers their business goals.

Crucially, according to Harvard[3] research, adopters, however, sometimes do worse when they think they fully understand the model and analytics. In this case, they often start to second-guess the model, thinking they know better, and override its recommendation. This scenario leads to model rejection and poor outcomes.

A better approach is to build trust through a transparent collaborative process by working with the business process owners and other stakeholders from the very beginning. These Harvard researchers found that when adopters believed that well-respected colleagues had a role in the analytics creation process, they were much more likely to trust, accept, and use the model

A best practice is to partner with the people who want you to build the analytics, showing mockups and prototypes while codesigning with them, or at least the most trusted among them, to make sure it really solves their problem, can integrate into their process, and is easy to use. If adopters feel like they helped design the solution, that is a powerful force for driving adoption and use, not to mention just increasing the odds of getting the solution right.

Embrace Simplicity

One of the oldest and most studied theories in the field of information systems is the technology acceptance model (TAM).[4] Although TAM has been extended in several ways, including by me, the core tenants have been validated more than a thousand times in peer-reviewed research studies. The essence of the model is that two things matter most: ease of use and usefulness.

Although executives usually care most about analytics usefulness, those using it care most about ease of use. Ease of use has grown in importance over time as adopters have been exposed to world-class applications on their smartphones and, now that they know what is possible, they expect a much more enjoyable experience with applications than in the past. The analytics needs to provide a useful solution in order for executives to adopt and sustain their support, but it needs to be easy to use, maybe even enjoyable for adopters, to sustain and spread its adoption over the long term.

Ahmer Inam, chief data and artificial intelligence officer at Relanto, shared how important it is to build a "minimally lovable product", a turn on the popular minimally viable product entrepreneurs often promote. If potential analytics users love it, they are more likely to adopt it. It may also turn them into analytics promoters, helping drive more analytics maturity across the organization.

Lindsay Marshall, director of data and analytics at Gilbane Building Company, shared how it is much easier and more effective to go on an analytics roadshow with a very simple, understandable, and easy-to-use model. When people see and understand it, they are more likely to use it. Roadshows sharing those features can help break down some of those barriers to adoption.

Consider International Culture

If you are in an international organization, or even a forward-looking company with a diverse workforce where you are located, different cultures, specifically international ones, can have a dramatic impact on acceptance and use, and what is or is not legal. David Houser, chief revenue officer at ReverseLogix who has had many prior business and technology roles elsewhere, is passionate about knowing and understanding the culture in which you are or will be working.

Houser shared how very often a given technology or application works very well in one place and not in another. Different approaches work in different places with different cultures. It is important to look at those from diverse cultures and with diverse pockets within the firm and consider their input independently, and test the model for effectiveness, adapting where needed. If ignored, this factor can become a blind spot that can shut down or limit your project.

Manage Unintended Consequences

Many actions we take have unintended consequences. The more complex they are, the more likely there are to be unintended consequences. Occasionally, good unintended consequences happen and we get lucky. Most of the time, these unintended consequences are a cause for concern and require preparation. Some of these consequences can be ethical in nature; others are more directly related to execution. This chapter focuses on the ones related to execution.

For example, one of my former students encountered deep resistance from the staff members who were supposed to be adopting the analytics. As the student dug into it, it became clear the staff members were worried about losing their jobs and the autonomy they felt they needed to adjust to changing conditions. It also became clear that the way the student and the team thought that part of the business worked, based on documentation, was not how it worked in reality.

It turns out the automation and analytics the student and the team were building changed the way the business process owner's team would have had to do business in a way they did not understand, and would have had negative unintended consequences for the firm. By listening to and learning the real business process, not just the one on paper, they were able to see the consequences more clearly, adjust their approach, and avoid the unintended consequences.

We dive into the importance of considering ethical, unintended consequences in Task 7: Responsible Analytics.

Politics

Friendships, political capital, loyalty, and connections matter to people who work in and run organizations. It is important to build and maintain good relationships and integrate yourself well into the organization while maintaining integrity and providing honest advice. The politics are a little different with nonexecutive employees, but they can still have an impact, so it is important to be mindful and plan accordingly.

External Developers

Sometimes it is important for executives to outsource roles to save time and execute faster as many of our experts shared. This time to value is often critical to success in a fast-changing, global environment. Sometimes, to do something we have never done before, we need help we never had before to succeed. Other times, we need additional hands on deck to reach our goals quickly, especially in very competitive markets where first-move advantage comes into play. In these cases, bringing in outside help with the needed talent and expertise is often essential.

Development partners service many organizations and often have deep expertise in their area. They can often scale quickly and even elevate the skills of your current team by challenging the status quo with new ideas and enlarging current employees' picture of what is possible. They can help you stay focused on your core competencies while they help with needed supporting areas, freeing up your team's time to focus on what is most important to you and your organization.

If you do need to bring in outside talent to implement and scale your analytics initiatives, consider following Pleines's rules for external use of vendors, adapted from an interview with Dr. Rudi Pleines.

Pleines's Rules for External Engagement

- **Own the strategy.** It is your firm, and needs to be your strategy. They can advise and share ideas and best practices, but you have to own it and drive it. Make sure the strategy is best for your firm and the direction you need to go. If there is not strong alignment with your strategy, even if they build something great, it will likely fail to do what you need.

- **Align incentives.** Think carefully about your incentives and theirs. The incentives are seldom identical, but they should line up so that when you win, they win. An incentive mismatch can lead to failure and often unintended outcomes.

- **Set clear expectations.** It is important for both sides to have clear expectations of outcomes. They should be written down, in clear and understandable language, and referred to often while preserving some ability for adaptability as the situation becomes more clear and circumstances change. Starting with clear expectations increases the odds of success.

- **Ensure the internal team leads.** To benefit your company, your internal team needs to lead. Outside firms and experts can help, but they are, fundamentally, outsiders. If the analytics is to take hold in the firm, it needs to be guided, nurtured, and led by someone in the organization who can do it effectively. No matter how skilled the outsider is, an insider is essential to success.

- **Give internal team resources.** For the internal team to lead effectively, they must be given sufficient resources. Without these resources, the project will fail, even if they lead. This may mean sufficient time reallocation, funding, and political support.

- **Enable internal takeover.** In the end, the internal team must be able to take over the project. If not, there will always be a dependency on the outside firm and misaligned incentives. In reality, even though the long-term revenue of supporting the project may be enticing to the outside firm, both are better off when the internal team takes over. This means clear documentation and involvement in the process at every step in the process is necessary.

- **Be attuned to politics.** Many political considerations may come into play when outsourcing. Be aware and mindful of the risks and rewards.

Pleines notes that this is also very frustrating for the consulting team and not in their best interest for the long term. One might think they would be happy because they were paid, but the reality is that they, like the rest of us, like for their work to have a real impact and to see value from it. Even if it were the case if all they cared about was revenue, it is still not helpful to them over the long term, because non-adoption builds the perception that the project failed, which damages their firm's reputation even if they had done their part well and reduces future work and opportunities. The best approach for both the external partners and the sponsoring organization is to work together to ensure these conditions for adoption are met.

PROBLEMS

Data scientists are highly curious and love to build things. They need freedom and support from executive champions to explore and innovate. The data scientist's value is in using their expertise to find and create value for the organization. They tend to get bored implementing projects, preferring to move on to other challenges once they solve a puzzle. Businesses need them to explore, but then need others to support and execute. Because of their ability to see and seize new opportunities, data scientists are often some of the highest paid professionals in an organization.

These same characteristics that make them so valuable can also make them a challenge to manage during execution. This section reviews some of these characteristics in more detail and compares them to the similar high-demand field of data engineers, with whom data scientists sometimes struggle to work effectively. Then it offers detailed advice from two of our experts on managing them well. First, Joshua Cazier of Qualtrics focuses on giving broad advice for running analytics teams. Then, Dr. Rudi Pleines gives very complementary advice for executing on a particular project.

Data Scientists Versus Data Engineers

Data scientists focus on discovery whereas engineers produce. An executive could be forgiven for confusing data scientists and data or production engineers. They both work with technology and do many similar tasks for the organization. However, their mindsets and focus are generally very different, even though they use very similar tools. Therefore, data scientists need to be managed differently.

Dr. Wayne Thompson talks about the many challenges in blending these two mindsets to get the project out of the lab and into production. Many projects require up to three times as many data engineers[5] working with the data scientist to get the data needed for the project ready so the analytics team can analyze it, and then again at the end of the project so they can put it into production and realize the anticipated value for the organization. Although data engineers generally fit well in the usual corporate structure, which often has a long history of productionizing goods and services, managing a data scientist is much more akin to managing a classic scientist who is intent on following their curiosity and interest, coupled with the knowledge that data scientists are in very high demand and can leave at any time.

A now famous *Harvard Business Review* article titled "The Sexiest Job of the 21st Century"[6] described not only the demand for data scientists but also some of their key characteristics that take a little extra thought and care to manage effectively. I will share a few of the article's insights here:

- **Puzzle solvers.** They tend to be "big-picture" thinkers who love to solve puzzles. That is good because the puzzles they face include not just challenging analytics projects but also strategies to incorporate analytics into their organization.

- **Intense curiosity.** Curiosity is a near-universal and intense trait that nearly all of the best data scientists hold. Indeed, it is one of the most easily identified characteristics of a grade A data scientist, and leaders should give them some room to explore their curiosity if they want to keep them around.

- **Freedom to explore.** Data scientists cannot excel on a short leash. They should have the freedom to experiment and explore possibilities. That said, they need close relationships with the rest of the business. The most important ties for them to forge are with executives in charge of products and services rather than with people overseeing business functions.

- **Impact.** Data scientists want to have an impact. They are often compared to Mr. Spock on the 1960s TV show *Star Trek*. They are there to advise the captain and save the day with data and analysis.

- **Relevance.** Data scientists need a close relationship with the business, not just with the executive champions but also with the business process owners and regular employees and partners. They can model solutions effectively only if they understand the process well enough to do so.

Joshua Cazier on Leading Analytics Teams

Joshua Cazier focused on how to manage teams to ensure action is taken:

- **Vision + energy.** Make sure that you have a clear vision with written goals and initiatives, including the mechanisms and energy behind them, so everyone knows what you are trying to achieve.

- **Empowerment.** Empower those who can have an impact to do so. Delegate the authority and train them on how to contribute to achieving the goal.

- **Accountability.** Hold your organization accountable, making sure they appropriately and effectively act on the information they are given.

- **Measurement.** Measure what worked and improve from there by building your findings back into your process. In essence, practice continual learning and growth.

By using this framework, you too can help ensure action is taken. Insight is interesting; action is profitable.

Dr. Rudi Pleines on Leading Analytics Projects

Pleines shared his wisdom for helping projects succeed, which is summarized here:

- **Know what is going on.** Always make sure you know what is going on in the projects you supervise. The points here help achieve this goal.

- **Adopt a no-surprise policy.** Adopt a no-surprise policy in which you insist that you always know what is happening. Only then can you intervene to ensure the projects go in the right direction. Keeping everything transparent increases the odds of success. And it provides the ability to pivot by detecting problems early. The no-surprise policy is not only critical for the person leading a project. As a project leader you also have to make sure there are no surprises for key stakeholders if you want the project to run smoothly. This means sufficient information and alignment before every critical decision point in a project is essential.

- **Maintain good governance mechanisms.** Have well-defined deliverables and project milestones you can use to gauge progress at regular meetings and in reports.

- **Keep deliverables clear and simple.** Keep project milestones and deliverables simple and not overly burdensome to administer. They must also be clear and well defined. This is your measuring rod to make sure you are on the right track.

- **Conduct regular risk assessment.** Do regular risk assessment with your team to evaluate the level of risk for each deliverable. Use established milestones to make sure you are on track.

As an executive, your primary focus should be on execution, and the best practices in this chapter are designed to help.

CHAPTER SUMMARY AND EXERCISES

Task 5: Summary

One of the key factors for successful execution is a relentless drive toward action. Without action taken based on the result, little value will be created. But it is also important that the action is the right action or at least one that adds value. Therefore, it becomes very important to prioritize high-value analysis and to follow an end-to-end, proven methodology that helps ensure quality, such as the one developed by INFORMS for the CAP credential.

During execution, it is important to manage processes, people, and problems. A methodology helps manage the process; people take a combination of good management and leadership, such as understanding different approaches to engineers versus data scientists and the leadership techniques presented by Dr. Pleines and Joshua Cazier. Problems take awareness and active management to look for biases or technical errors in the data and analytics process.

Task 5: Exercises

1. Discuss the analytics process by listing and describing each of the three major steps in that process, namely, preparation, discovery, and action. Conclude with a discussion of why it is important for business leaders to understand this process and what these leaders' roles are at each step.

2. Similar to question 1, discuss why it is important for business process owners to understand this process and what these processes owners' roles are in each step in the analytics process.

3. Discuss the important roles and responsibilities of analytics professionals at each stage in this process and what key things they should watch out for and do to ensure quality analytics.

4. Consider that throughout this book we have referenced the technical and analytics teams' roles in the analytics process. Although it often appears as one technical team to outsiders, and there is obvious overlap, we can simplify the

definition to say that the technical team is mostly focused on production and operation and the analytics team is mostly focused on discovery. Discuss the key similarities and differences between the production staff members, such as data engineers, and discovery staff members, such as data scientists. Identify which one best defines you and how this might affect you going forward.

5. Review the sections on managing external partners and leading internal teams by Dr. Pleines, as well as the section on leading analytics initiatives by Joshua Cazier. Identify three principles that stand out as important to you and to your intended career path. List and describe them and share why they stood out to you and how you plan to use them.

NOTES

1. https://bill-franks.com/winning-the-room.html
2. Steven R. Covey, *The Seven Habits of Highly Effective People: Restoring the Character Ethic* (New York: Fireside Book, 1990).
3. Rachel Layne, "What Makes Employees Trust (Versus Second-Guess) AI?" Harvard Business School (January 19, 2023). https://hbswk.hbs.edu/item/what-makes-employees-trust-vs-second-guess-ai.
4. E. Hassler, P. MacDonald, J. Cazier, and J. Wilkes, "The Sting of Adoption: The Technology Acceptance Model (TAM) with Actual Usage in a Hazardous Environment," *Journal of Information Systems Applied Research* 14, no. 4 (2021): 13–20. https://jisar.org/2021–14/n4/JISARv14n4p13.html.
5. https://www.mihaileric.com/posts/we-need-data-engineers-not-data-scientists
6. Thomas H. Davenport and D. J. Patil, "Data Scientist: The Sexiest Job of the 21st Century," *Harvard Business Review* 90, no. 10 (October 2012): 70–76.

TASK **6**

Analytics Maturity

DEFINING ANALYTICS MATURITY

Most of this book focuses on how executives can help their particular analytics projects succeed. Successful analytics projects create value. The next task is to go from helping individual projects succeed to creating a process and culture of analytics decision-making that takes a stream of individual projects and turns them into a river of projects working together that creates synergies and builds a mature analytics organization. This dynamic and synergistic environment is where the greatest value is derived from analytics.

This chapter is about developing a process and culture that supports analytics, not just for individual projects, but as a way of doing business that is focused on making better decisions with analytics. It is an organization with a mindset and culture that first turns to data and objectively evaluates the options to make better decisions and take better actions. It is an organization with mature processes in place that ensure quality analytics, acceptance, and support across the organization.

Many times I have had people ask something along these lines: "But what is analytics maturity? What does it even mean or look like?" Some would say it is going full speed ahead, using the most advanced analytics you possibly can, taking advantage of the latest and greatest technologies and methods to achieve success. Certainly that is one way to think about it. This approach could also be fun to do, as many of us analysts love playing with new tools and technologies. This approach would also be a costly mistake.

From my perspective, analytics maturity is not about maxing out every tool and algorithm to achieve dominance or show your competitors you have the fanciest toys to play with. Maybe that could be a viable strategy for a few digital-native organizations whose business models depend on them being at the cutting edge, where pushing the frontier of analytics in an ever-increasing arms race to digital supremacy and beating other digital-native companies is key to business viability, maybe even survival, in the winner-take-all games of Silicon Valley–style capitalism.

Yet, as fast as data is proliferating, technology is advancing, and knowledge is growing, this type of winner-take-all competition may be a never-ending race. It may also be one that is never truly won because rapid change in technologies and their application can cause rapid change in market conditions. I am glad these innovators are there because we can learn much from them and their investments, which can be applied in other places.

For traditional organizations whose life and viability depend on physical goods, however, they may be better off using analytics to improve the use of those assets, rather than doing analytics for analytics sake. Those with real traditional assets and a life outside the technosphere, with a mission in manufacturing, retail, engineering, education, government, public service, or other fields, it is not about the technology. For them, it is about what you do with it.

Maturity is not about maxing out everything to the fullest extent possible. It is about wisely and thoughtfully managing trade-offs among various options. You cannot, and should not, optimize for everything at the same time. You need to pick a few analytics priorities that align well with your strategy, or set your strategy in a way that aligns with those priorities, and optimize for doing what you do, or intend to do, better.

For me, analytics maturity is about using the right analytics, in the right place, at the right time, for the right purpose. It is about matching the function of the analytics with the ability to do it well, analytics that fulfills the needs and goals of the organization. My one-time student and former employee, Thomas Cech, who is now a senior data scientist at NCCEP, published a paper on this topic a few years ago. In it, Cech and coauthors developed a data competence maturity model,[1] illustrated in Figure 6.1.

The thing I love about Cech's model is that it illustrates the right balance to take with analytics and it provides a guide to finding the right size for analytics based on your maturity level. It shows the categories of analytics discussed in Task 4: Tools, namely, descriptive, diagnostic, predictive, and prescriptive, on the vertical y-axis and then matches them up with various levels of maturity in controlled data quality on the horizontal x-axis. They are nonempirical or gut-based methods, summary reporting, a collection of rich enough data to do correlational analysis and controlled studies suitable for causal testing and inference.

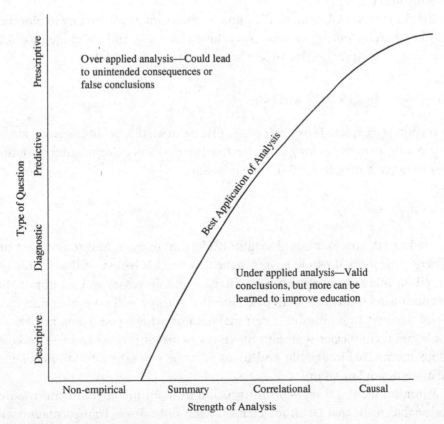

Figure 6.1 Data Competence Maturity Model

To me, maturity is being on the curved line in the middle, where you balance the state of analytics with the resources available to do them and aim them to where you need to go. The core idea is that you can both overuse and underuse analytics depending on your level of maturity with tools and data. Though not represented in Figure 6.1, you can also overuse or underuse analytics depending on your level of organizational engagement and receptiveness to analytics. It is important to right-size your analytics to match the state of your data and analytics and the state of the company, its market strategy, and its market conditions, and to not run blindly forward with every analytics trend or tool without thinking about your overall situation. Analytics is a tool, and an important one, but it is a tool whose use should vary based on where you are and where you want to go.

Analytics maturity is, first and foremost, a culture of data-driven decision-making with a solid commitment to making the best decision for the organization based on logic, analysis, and especially data. It requires mature processes and approaches for doing that at scale. It involves engagement with the analytics team, executive champions, business process owners, and many others in supporting positions in the organization. It involves many in the business, outside the analytics team, making decisions based on data and some doing citizen data science by touching the data directly. Analytically mature firms also invest in and use mature analytics technology and enmesh themselves with the broader ecosystems and technologies of their analytics partners outside their organization.

In this chapter, we take a deep dive into analytics maturity, first by exploring what it looks like, then by looking at how to get there culturally, and conclude by discussing the tools and techniques needed by a mature analytics organization.

VISUALIZING ANALYTICS MATURITY

In this section we explore how leadership, diverse analytics, an industrial scale, use of a proven analytics methodology, and effective internal and external engagement come together to make a mature analytics organization.

Leadership

It takes dedicated, consistent, and skillful leadership to build and maintain a mature analytics organization. It would be a mistake to assume it is easy or that it only goes in one direction. Maturity levels can both increase and decrease, and without sustained energy committed to mature analytics, analytics entropy will take over and maturity levels will descend into disorder. Even maintaining where you are is not enough as new tools and technologies will soon make your current process obsolete as competitors adopt them. This leadership and focus must be eternal to build and maintain a mature analytics organization.

At a minimum, this leadership must come from all members of the triad of the minimal viable team that Dr. Rudi Pleines, head of business transformation at ABB

Robotics, identified and we discussed in previous sections of this book. Sometimes more is needed from other groups, but influential representatives from all three member groups of the Pleines's minimal viable team need to skillfully and continuously work together to achieve and maintain analytics maturity. Without the full support and engagement of even one of these groups, full analytics maturity will not be achieved or maintained.

For this reason, Task 0: Analytics Leadership, is the foundation of this book and a prerequisite for all the other tasks, as it is only the leadership from the Pleines's minimal viable team triad that can manage these tasks consistently at scale. Yes, each alone can make some progress and achieve some success, but for it to become a sustainable competitive advantage, they all must work together.

Let us look a little deeper at the role of each Pleines's minimal viable team member and other supporters needed in building maturity.

Executive Champions

Executive champions are the ones most likely to be able to facilitate the Pleines's minimal viable team working together effectively for a common purpose. The other members, that is, business process owners and the analytics team members, can, and should, use their influence to encourage collaboration. But executive champions have more power to see that the analytics are acted on and executed well across the organization. For this reason, the subtitle of the book is *The Seven Critical Tasks for Executives to Master in the Age of Big Data*. That said, all members of the Pleines's minimal viable team have an important role to play.

Here is a summary of the important roles for executive champions to play in building analytics maturity:

- **Understand the what and where of analytics.** Executive champions may not need to know how to do analytics, but their position of responsibility in the organization, coupled with the rising role of analytics in a competitive landscape, gives them a duty to study and understand it, particularly in the matter of knowing what it can do to better guide where to use it to meet business objectives.
- **Use analytics.** First and foremost, executive champions must use analytics themselves, says former CIO Steve Stone. If executive champions do not use analytics to make their decisions, no one else will either.
- **Manage data relevance.** With their macro view, executive champions are in a unique position to help guide data relevance within the organization. This task requires some understanding of analytics, including knowing the inputs needed for the process and carefully aligning them with business goals. Executive champions also have a role in setting quality standards. But the first goal is to capture or acquire data that is relevant to their business because you cannot clean or analyze what you do not have.

- **Match analytics technologies to needs.** The analytics and technical teams can recommend and perform a due diligence assessment on tools and technologies, but executive champions need to ensure they are matched to the needs of the organization and to their current and desired level of analytics maturity. Dr. Pleines emphasized this need to get the right level is critical, as was illustrated in Figure 6.1.

- **Industrial scale.** For optimal value, executive champions should support and guide growing analytics from craft projects to industrial-level processes, as is discussed later in this chapter.

- **Ensure use of mature analytics process.** There is a process, a methodology, for doing quality analytics, and executive champions should ensure and verify that a mature analytics process is being followed. We discuss my favorite analytics methodology, developed by INFORMS, later in this chapter.

- **Champion change.** The executive champion's most important role may be to bring people together to guide, direct, facilitate, and enforce change. If not them, then who will?

- **Share successes.** Employees pay attention and listen to executives more broadly than any other group. They may not always trust them, but they do watch them. This visibility gives executives a key role in ensuring that analytics success stories and lessons learned are shared broadly in an effort to build and sustain analytics maturity.

- **Evolve from political to data-driven decisions.** Executive champions know that politics is real and likely understand and know how to navigate the political environment better than most. They should use this skill honestly to champion better and less politically driven decision-making through a process that is based on data and its analysis. Only within a real culture where key players are focused on making the best decision, through analysis, not just politics, will analytics maturity be fully realized.

Business Process Owner

If executives chart the course for the organization to travel, business process owners hold the keys for getting there. This group owns the critical processes within the organization that make it function, including finance, IT, marketing, sales, manufacturing, and supply chains. They are responsible for running these processes efficiently and effectively and ensuring established policies and procedures are followed or that there is accountability if they are not.

This group knows the business inside and out, not just the big picture like the executives champions, but the micro-level details in their domain, details that are important to understand so they can be modeled in the analytics effectively. Because this group is held accountable when there are problems with these important functions, they tend to be, of necessity, risk averse. Although there are some rewards for process improvements, the penalty for a problem or botched process is much higher. Although most executives want to grow and expand, business process owners are incentivized to avoid problems, creating a natural and healthy tension to implementing analytics.

Because business process owners own and manage so many of the core functions of the business, almost nothing changes without their participation. Executive champions also have significant influence on this group. But even executive champions who want to grow do not want to risk process problems that will hamper their core business and slow it down or cause them to abandon an analytics project if the business process owners convince them it will not work. There are many more business process owners in an organization than analytics professionals and executive champions, and they are some of the most important, 10-to-1 enablers of analytics.

Here are a few tasks for business process owners to do to keep things moving in the right direction:

- **Ensure data quality.** One of the first and most important priorities for business process owners is to ensure data quality for the relevant data the firm needs to do analytics. Without business process owners working to deliver this quality, the analytics of many areas, including in and beyond a given process, will suffer. Ahmer Inam, chief data and artificial intelligence officer at Relanto, and other experts stressed that quality begins at the source of the data, which is largely controlled by the business process owners.

- **Create analytics awareness.** Business process owners and their staff members should make an effort to know how analytics is being and could be used by others with similar processes and pay attention to what has generally worked to help identify opportunities in their areas.

- **Identify pain points.** Business process owners should clearly identify and prioritize pain points that analytics may be able to improve and bring them to the attention of executives and/or technical teams for exploration.

- **Ensure process explanations.** It is quite common for written documentation of processes to be out-of-date and to not accurately represent how processes are applied in practice. These differences need to be understood so the analytics team can model or automate the real process, not just the paper one. This process should be explained to the analysts in a way they can understand and model, with the appropriate level of detail. Even better is if an analytics team member goes on what Polly Mitchell-Guthrie, VP of industry outreach and thought leadership at Kinaxis, calls an *empathy walk* and does or participates in the work and follows the process with the business process owners team long enough to really understand it.

- **Experiment and validate.** Business process owners should work with the technical and analytics teams to experiment with approaches to improve their process and validate the results, while carefully managing any potential risks or disruptions to the process.

▪ **Incentivize improvements.** Business process owners often want to improve their processes, do their jobs better, and make their lives easier, if they can avoid risks of disruptions to their work. It usually takes a little more inducement for their staff members to become engaged. Change is hard and there is often fear that automation or analytics may replace them. Business process rewards can help by incentivizing their staff members to change with tangible rewards and building trust with assurances about their future, as long as leadership keeps their promises.

▪ **Be open-minded.** It is easy to focus on one's daily tasks and not seek ways to improve, especially in areas outside of the business process owner's core area of expertise such as technology and analytics. It is important for the lead business process owners to not only keep an open mind but also to project one to their staff members and partners. Even a few careless negative comments can guide others in the business process owner's area to follow suit by closing up and resisting new ideas and possibilities, which reduces success.

Technical Team

The technical team works together to build and scale the analytics by gathering the data, cleaning and transforming it to suit the analysis, and finally putting it into production. Without this team, no analytics happens. However, without active and engaged participation from business process owners and executive champions, no action will be taken, hence, no practical value will be realized. Therefore, it is essential that the technical team learn to work with at least one of these groups, and sometimes other groups, too. For many on the technical side, outside collaboration does not come naturally. It is therefore important for the technical teams to be cognizant of the following points as they work with others:

▪ **Develop understanding.** You cannot fix what you do not understand. I have seen many analytics professionals try to model something before taking time to fully understand what they are modeling and why. Skipping this step rarely works and usually destroys trust because the business process owners do not feel understood and lose confidence in your ability to help them. The old adage "seek first to understand" is a good motto for this group to adopt.

▪ **Cultivate partnerships.** The technical team should always work with the business process owners, executive champions, and others in the spirit of partnership with the goal of helping them do their jobs better. It is easy for some analysts to get frustrated with what they perceive as a lack of understanding of technology and analytics and/or others' resistance to change. Any signals you are there to do anything other than make their lives better will not go down well.

▪ **Improve current process.** The technical team may see ways to completely replace the current process with a new one. Sometimes it is necessary, but most of the time this approach will engender distrust, fear, and resistance, leading to a likely failure, especially before trust and partnerships are strong. Improving the current process is more likely to succeed, and with enough rounds of successful improvements, the goal of automation or replacement may be achieved naturally.

- **Become analytics translators.** Task 2: The Team introduced the idea of the analytics translator. This role is usually filled by a very senior person who is respected by executives and the technical team and is accomplished at straddling both worlds. However, Ahmer Inam advocates that as analytics matures, the organization needs to also grow its translators, which means having a certain portion of the analytics team's time allocated to building partnerships and translating analytics to those at similar levels, helping them understand what it can do. In this case, the executive-level translator continues to work with those in the executive ranks, while less senior members of the technical team take up a similar role corresponding with those at their levels within their organization.

- **Envision unintended consequences.** With nearly every change, including with analytics, there are unintended and unanticipated consequences. The technical team has a duty to try to envision and anticipate likely consequences, as will be discussed in Task 7: Responsible Analytics, and to make sure they are managed appropriately.

Other Team Members

Depending on the analytics trajectory, level of maturity, and business strategy, there are likely other stakeholders who need to be involved, including legal and ethical reviewers, project managers, customers, partners, other employees, and/or external stakeholders. Anyone likely to be affected by an analytics solution should be considered as a probable stakeholder and should be identified with a plan made for how best to manage or include them in the process.

Diverse Analytics

I have often been surprised by how a company that is doing cutting-edge, press-worthy analytics in one area can be so behind the times in other areas. Organizations are large and complex and maturity is often uneven across different units and business lines as opposed to having a monolithic maturity level. The larger and more established the organization, the more likely this is to be true, and the harder it is to change it.

Mature analytics organizations use analytics in many ways and places, and have a culture of turning to data for answers and guidance across the organization, not just in one or two areas. Yes, it is important to start somewhere and build. Often this starting point is in a few critical functions. But for long-term success, it takes expansion to other areas. Otherwise, non-data-driven areas of the organization hold back progress and threaten the stability of your growing analytics culture, which is much easier to lose than it is to build.

Craft Versus Industrial Analytics

Analytics is a useful tool for finding valuable insights in data and harvesting that value. However, there are different approaches to analytics that yield differing magnitudes of value. The first is the craft approach, which is often used in the early days of analytics adoption for one-off problems.

Craft analytics is a highly customized form of analytics in which an expert looks for a highly tailored solution to a very particular problem. Think of it like a tailor sewing a suit or dress for a particular person. It can turn out very well: a beautiful, high-quality, well-designed garment tailored to that individual's needs. However, it is also expensive, time-intensive, and difficult to scale, which limits the magnitude of value it can create.

Industrial analytics is done at an industrial scale, hence, the name. What it might lose in precision and customizability, it makes up for in volume and scale, giving large organizations the potential to increase the value from analytics by orders of magnitude.

Both approaches to analytics have their place, and innovative firms will routinely use both. Yet, the most valuable analytical models are generally those that can be deployed at an industrial scale, where mature analytics firms focus most of their energy.

Analytics Methodology

Mature analytics companies use a standardized, repeatable methodology. These methodologies were built on lessons learned from successes and failures. Using them helps you stabilize successes and avoid failures. This approach is critical to scaling analytics beyond a few heroic individuals. It helps build trust and analytics stability by reducing the randomness and variance often found in projects.

A methodology should not be confused with a method, such as building a decision tree. A methodology is instead a tried-and-true process, employing principles, techniques, procedures, and best practices at each stage of a project to effectively achieve results. Some have been designed and endorsed by professional associations, giving them more credibility. Importantly, it is a set of best practices organized coherently that helps analytics scale beyond a few individual innovators into a mature process and helps a project outlast any individual team member.

Although there are several analytics methodologies that can be used, the one I have found most useful and likely to succeed is the one endorsed by the professional organization INFORMS (Institute for Operations Research and Management Science) in its Certified Analytics Professional (CAP) designation. I recommend it for these primary reasons:

- **Business focus.** The main focus of the CAP is on solving the business problem and adding value to the organization, as opposed to other certifications that focus on model building with fewer relevant implementation safeguards.

- **Vendor neutrality.** Tools and techniques change and not all are appropriate for what you need. The INFORMS CAP focuses on the needs, not the tool, enabling you to use whatever tool best suits the task, rather than seeking a task that suits the tool.
- **Impact assessment.** This methodology includes doing an assessment of the analytics impact on the business, and documenting it along with lessons learned, helping you know how well it performed.
- **Model monitoring.** Data changes, concepts drift, and old models become less relevant. Included in the methodology's framework is a requirement to monitor the model's performance over time and review and approve it as needed.
- **Ethics.** Every CAP holder pledges to follow clear, ethical guidelines, reducing the risk of irresponsible analytics.

This vendor-neutral certification and methodology focuses on enhancing the analytics process, is not overly technical, and is geared toward ensuring analytics success. Even non-analytics professionals can learn and understand much from studying for this certification and applying its principles for analytics success.

Whichever methodology your organization chooses, it is critical that you formally adopt and consistently use one, and follow it across the organization, rather than practicing "cowboy" analytics. Anyone driving over a bridge would want the engineers who designed it to have used a tried-and-true, best practices methodology to avoid errors. They might even be held legally liable if they did not follow best practices. The same should be true of analytics professionals.

Internal Engagement

A mature analytics firm engages their organization broadly and deeply, not just the executive champions and business process owners but also those likely to be affected by analytics now and in the near future. Mature organizations engage by building better analytics products, by harmonizing their data stories, and by engaging the organization with the data directly.

Product Orientation

When organizations design products for sale, they invest heavily in time and resources to test and design them in ways that help the organization succeed. Many specialize in proven methodologies for developing winning products and bring a deep body of knowledge of best practices with their experience. Some companies, such as Apple, have even made designing great products their competitive advantage.

Well-known analytics author and professor Thomas Davenport and his coauthors make a convincing case in a *Harvard Business Review* article[2] titled "Why Your Company Needs Data Product Managers," and we should learn to apply similar principles of product design to our analytics efforts. This approach improves quality and engagement and helps to bring the desired impact and effect to the organization. Indeed, this critical principle of engagement can ensure reliable, impactful analytics at scale.

Operationalized Storytelling

Good storytelling is a powerful communication technique to connect and motivate people. In fact, our culture is largely built on and influenced by thousands of stories that create a shared bond, convey meaning, expand impact, and motivate change. It is hard to overestimate the impact of storytelling on our society as we have been guided and enriched by stories for a thousand generations. They play a critical role in mature analytics organizations as well, helping build culture and fuel change.

I recently heard Lee Feinberg, founder of DecisionViz, do a webinar for the International Institute for Analytics on operationalizing storytelling. Here are a few things I took away from it. Feinberg is an advocate of scaling and standardizing data storytelling across the organization. One-off stories are interesting, but they do not build culture or scale, similar to our prior discussion of craft versus industrial analytics. Yes, storytelling is part art, but it is also part science, and that science part can be learned, applied, and scaled across the organization.

When organizations provide guidance and a set of best practices, effectively building a storytelling culture, it magnifies the impact and resonates with other stories. This effort builds a collective culture that resonates with, rather than detracts from, similar stories in the organization, as they all effectively sing harmonically to the same tune. This harmonization of stories with a common approach guided by best practices for the firm creates a clear direction that coordinates efforts and leads to faster, more widespread adoption.

Feinberg published a research brief on this topic titled, "Operationalizing Data Storytelling,"[3] also with the International Institute for Analytics. It offers an excellent introduction to this concept and can help guide broad spectrum engagement with analytics in the format most readily digestible to people in the firm, that of empowering stories, which can lead to better adoption and use of analytics products.

Data Dabbling

Patrick Getzen, former chief data and analytics officer for Blue Cross Blue Shield of North Carolina, shared an experience in building an analytics culture. Getzen found in the early days of analytics that you often need to standardize and centralize the data to ensure quality and reliability. However, as the quality of data is established and trusted, it helps to expand the culture by opening up the data to others for self-service analytics.

There is no better way to build trust in the data and put insights into action than to have some of those insights generated, in part, by those who need to change and adapt to them. Similar to how encouraging a kid to play with LEGOS can spark their curiosity and joy in building and designing in a safe structured way, giving employees a sandbox to play with data can be a critical part of engagement.

It should be a well-designed and easy-to-use sandbox filled with high-quality and understandable data relevant to employees. It should not be overwhelming with the most advanced features and data. A carefully curated dataset, full of highly relevant, quality data for employees to dabble with, can help engagement as they generate their own powerful insights, which can be validated by professionals before action is truly a hallmark of a mature organization.

Josh Belliveau, a principal solutions engineer at Tableau, shared how powerful, intuitive tools like Tableau can be used by non-analytics professionals to generate insights and engagement with data. Belliveau was an early adopter who experienced this process in action in previous positions at other organizations before joining Tableau to spread this passion to users to find ways to engage with data. Belliveau also echoed the importance of enabling a self-serve sandbox for data exploration by those with intimate domain knowledge, regardless of their technical skill set. In Belliveau's experience, the organizations that allowed business users to explore their data were the most successful analytic organizations, whereas those that restricted self-serve exploration were often hindered.

However, there are limits to internal engagements, as Bill Franks, director of the Center for Data Science and Analytics within the School of Data Science and Analytics at Kennesaw State University, notes. Data literacy should be prioritized to those who need it the most, to those who can use it to take action. These efforts should match the level of maturity in the organization. Early on, the focus will likely be on executive champions and business process owners, then expand to others affected by analytics or those who can use analytics to do their jobs better in some way. However, as Franks notes, that does not mean that everyone needs to be data literate. It also does not mean that data literacy looks the same to everyone, but that it should match what they need to know to help the organization in the areas where they work.

External Engagement

In addition to harnessing the collective knowledge and wisdom inside your firm through engagement, you should also engage with the broader knowledge and wisdom often found outside the firm. It may not always be as deep or focused as internal engagement, but as others have wrestled with similar issues in other contexts, there is much to be learned from other creative approaches. It also affords an opportunity to give back, share experiences, and tackle complicated problems together.

Although there is a time to keep strategies and approaches internal, mature firms also know there is a time to share and collaborate. Dr. Sherrill Hayes, director of the School of Data Science and Analytics at Kennesaw State University, shared the importance of balancing the need for competition with cooperation, believing it is a key to success, not just to us individually but also to our firms, our profession, and the broader society.

There are many ways to achieve this balance between competition and cooperation, including by learning, connecting, sharing, integrating, and becoming more internationally aware, which we discuss next.

Lifelong Learning

Lifelong learning is a near universal practice advocated by nearly everyone interviewed for this book. Technology is changing rapidly, as is the environment in which we live and work. Without lifelong learning, our knowledge and skills soon become obsolete. It is unimaginable to believe we can successfully lead our organizations into the future with technical and analytical skills mired in the past.

However, it is more than that. The best analytics leaders and practitioners are inherently curious and naturally love to learn and grow. This curious mindset and commitment to learning is emblematic of the very nature of the field and defines what it takes to succeed. A learning organization is made up of learning individuals. The more learning is encouraged inside and outside of analytics, especially for new and emerging areas like technology and analytics, the more widespread and effective the adoption of analytics will be in your organization.

Mature analytics organizations create and foster a learning culture, supporting education broadly, not just for the short term, but the long term, not just for a few highly valued professionals, but for those up and down the organization. If it does indeed take a ratio of 10 non-analytics professionals for every 1 analytics professional for sustainable growth in analytics, as this research suggests, then learning, growing, and educating about analytics across the entire organization is critical.

Organizations should encourage all types of learning, from supporting such classic methods as university degrees and certifications, to professional certifications, to conference attendance, to any other way to facilitate learning and growth related to analytics. For some highly regarded lifelong learners, sabbaticals can also be an important source of engagement, enabling deeper connections and learning that can often help move the organization into new and interesting directions.

Connecting

Encouraging connections to other professionals in other organizations is an important part of maturity. These connections engender knowledge sharing, creative collaborations, and mentorship in a safer political environment where professionals can speak and explore more freely. Many creative insights are generated from seeing how others, facing similar problems in a different context, have addressed them.

These interactions enable more broad and robust analytics approaches as knowledge is transferred and practices are inspired through collaboration with others from different places, industries, and backgrounds. These interactions also can lead to promising recruiting activities and worthy tips and warnings for working with certain vendors or technologies. Seeking these interactions is how knowledge spreads and matures and is an important part of mature analytics organizations.

Part of being a professional is being part of a professional association. Organizations can encourage connections through conference attendance in one's own discipline and in others that have vital domain knowledge to share. Polly Mitchell-Guthrie shared the value of professional association membership.

Indeed, Mitchell-Guthrie has gotten a lot of value from, and has given a lot of value to, INFORMS, which we discussed previously, but she has also benefited from being cofounder of the Women in Machine Learning & Data Science chapter of North Carolina and from being a member of other associations. Regardless which association or associate type is right for you, there are many good reasons to be part of professional associations, including the following reasons Mitchell-Guthrie shared during the interview:

- **Broader network.** Very few people will spend an entire career in the same company. But you can be part of the same professional association for the span of your career, creating and broadening your network and opening opportunities to give and receive.

- **Continual learning.** In addition to conferences and seminars, many professional associations offer certifications and various other educational opportunities, including journal subscriptions. They will help keep you up-to-date with new developments, engage you in emerging topics, and provide a forum for exchanging experiences with other professionals.

- **Best practices.** We highlight INFORMS in this section (referenced in this course), because they offer additional services that can aid in your development. Best practices, such as those encoded in the INFORMS *Analytics Body of Knowledge*, offer a clear methodology for doing good analytics, as codified in their CAP credential, and provide customized assessment of analytics maturity, which can help you know where to focus your growth efforts.

- **Ethical guidance.** We live in a complex, changing world with many potential places for ethical pitfalls. One of the critical services a professional association provides is bringing the best minds in the field together to deeply think about ethics and write ethical codes and guidelines. Too often, professionals do not realize how important and relevant these guidelines are—until it is too late. Please pay attention to them.

I recommend being part of at least two types of professional associations: one for the profession in which you practice, where you can share best practices, network, and engage in continual learning related to your skills, and one associated with the industry in which you work so you can enhance your domain knowledge in that industry and make connections that can help you identify and solve relevant problems from those who know them best.

For example, when I was chief analytics officer for HiveTracks, I regularly attended, and presented at, conferences and meetings for beekeepers and bee researchers and analytics conferences for my profession. This experience was incredibly valuable in focusing our analytics efforts on what mattered most, while also getting the word out about our results.

Sharing

Not every insight can be shared immediately as some are trade secrets or a source of competitive advantage. However, if no one shares, learning is limited and we are all worse off because of it. Mature organizations share by publishing research, presenting at conferences, mentoring others, collaborating on research, and developing and supporting the advancement of the profession.

They also lead by example, becoming experts in the field and influencing others to follow, not just looking to their immediate and narrow self-interest. The International Institute for Analytics, for example, hosts data and analytics leaders and key members of their team in non-competitive cohorts for peer-to-peer exchange, along with a research and advisory network designed for one-to-one conversations between clients and practitioners. This approach enables firms to learn and grow in an objective, competitively safe environment, thus encouraging growth.

Integrating

Joshua Cazier, a senior executive at Qualtrics, and Josh Belliveau of Tableau, both strongly emphasized the importance of engaging vendor ecosystems. The best analytics products are supported by ecosystems of users and fans.

Many of you may be familiar with open source communities, but vendor communities also exist for commercial products. Engaging with and supporting these communities builds strength and resilience, improves the ecosystem, and should be encouraged and supported in many ways. Organizations should evaluate not only what tools can do, but the strengths of the ecosystem and how their organization can contribute before selecting and committing to a particular ecosystem. If your organization is not likely to be able to contribute to the ecosystem, it is also not likely to be able to receive the full benefits of belonging to it.

Internationally Aware

Most of us know our home country better than any other place or culture in the world, so much so that we sometimes forget or do not realize how much there is to learn from other people and practices from other places, or how much some of our practices may seem, well, foreign to them. David Houser, now at ReverseLogix, has spent more time abroad in more places than most, and is a strong advocate for always being mindful of the role of customs and culture generally, and with analytics specifically. This mindfulness should also include being aware of differences in legal and ethical laws, customs, and norms.

Culture of Organizational Learning

Companies with a mature analytics culture focused on organizational learning have three key characteristics: (1) they are willing, perhaps even eager, to change for the better; (2) they have the skills needed to change in a meaningful and intentional way; and (3) they execute on that change by actually learning and adapting, guided by analytics. We discuss each one here.

Willing to Change

As mentioned in Task 4: Tools, Piyanka Jain, CEO of the analytics advisory firm Aryng, emphasizes the importance of an analytics mindset being required to achieve analytics success. This idea is more important than tools and technologies and fundamentally essential to any analytics maturation. If you are not eager to change, perhaps not even willing to change, you will not, no matter how fancy your tools. If, however, you are eager to change, to make better decisions driven by data, you will find a way.

To change and become a mature organization, developing an analytics mindset, the belief that things can be done better with data and analytics, is fundamental. It cannot exist in just one or a few individuals. This belief must deeply and widely embed itself into the organization. Sure, other things matter, too, but this mindset is a prerequisite.

Here are a few key characteristics of an analytics mindset:

- **Curiosity.** An analytics mindset is one that is first and foremost fueled by curiosity, not just any idle curiosity, but one that is focused on continual improvement and experimentation to find a better way to do things. You might think of this concept as goal-orientated curiosity.
- **Data driven.** The goal-oriented curiosity of someone with an analytics mindset leads them not just to do blind experiments but also to seek evidence in theory and data to guide and verify this curiosity.
- **Cannibalistic.** With a true analytics mindset, nothing is sacred. Those with an analytics mindset practice *corporate cannibalism*, a term coined by Harvard professor Clayton Christensen in the book, *Innovator's Dilemma*. These organizations are willing to change and cannibalize short-term profits and opportunities for long-term gains and survival after careful analysis and with sufficient evidence.

These are the essential traits of an analytics organization, and they can be incorporated when building an analytics culture if they are dispersed widely and deeply enough across the organization and the ecosystem living within it.

Skills to Change

It is great to have a desire to use and support analytics, and many firms do. However, desire is not enough. In addition, a firm must also have and develop the skills needed for change. These mature organizations know how to lead and guide the process in a way that is helpful to facilitating change.

Data literacy helps, but it is not enough. Data literacy makes you aware of data and analytics, but does not necessarily give you the skills and know-how to support it. Data literacy, at best, teaches you how to read and understand relevant analytics topics. The actual skill starts with being able to write, to complete the analogy, and to guide data and analytics to finally be able to build analytics successfully.

It takes knowledge of the seven manageable tasks of analytics, as outlined in this book, and not just knowledge of what they are, but the skill to manage each and every one of them effectively. A failure in any of them will cause an overall analytics failure.

This book can be part of the beginning of your journey, but it cannot be the end. Neither can it end with the analytics team, executive team, or employees. Of the seven critical tasks, only one of them, Tools, is directly or mostly under the control of the analytics team. Every single other task depends on cooperation and support from others in the firm, who not only have an analytical mindset and data literacy but also have the skills to actively support analytics effectively with any tasks they touch.

For this reason, and others, I believe it takes a ratio of somewhere on the order of 10 analytically minded non-analytics professionals who know how to manage these seven analytics tasks to every 1 analytics professional for analytics to have a durable, lasting impact on sustainable success.

Actually Change

Skills, too, are important, but they are not enough. You have to actually change based on your analytics to realize the value. Even if you know how but do not have courage and commitment, perhaps, similar to exercise, it will not happen. As shown in the MIT BCG study discussed in Task 0: Analytics Leadership, to get value from analytics you have to "learn to change and change to learn." Change is hard, but without it, nothing is accomplished.

Analytics-Driven Adaptability

The DAD analytics framework, introduced at length in Task 1: The Problem, with its focus on decision-centric, action-centric, and data-centric analytics and their interactions and synergies, can be used to help drive analytics maturity across the organization. This is through the reciprocal to DAD, if you will, ADA or analytics-driven adaptability.

Leading cannot, should not, go one way in the organization. It is not just that we build models to help us do what we already do better. Given its importance, the DAD framework from Task 1: The Problem is shown here again in Figure 6.2.

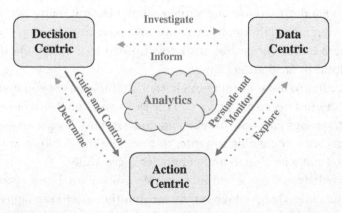

Figure 6.2 The DAD Framework

We also need to learn and evaluate what it is we should be doing in the first place, which is where data-centric analytics can help. Once a direction is decided through decision-centric or data-centric analytics, action-centric analytics can, and likely should, be used, ethically, to drive and scale those changes through the organization.

You can use analytics not just on your clients, products, or customers but also on your organization to help you do better, too, just as someone might use a smart watch to monitor and adjust their exercise intensity or sleep patterns.

For a long-term competitive advantage fueled by analytics, firms should not stop at the organizational learning that is the foundation that MIT and BCG noted as the secret to today's analytics success. Rather, firms should go to the next level, which I argue will be analytics-driven adaptability, or learning how to learn and change with analytics.

Here are the primary levers organizations can use to go to the next level, starting with the most intrusive and then progressing to more persuasive coaching methods. This progression is usually determined by the level of autonomy those trying to be influenced have, and whether it comes from a decision-centric or data-centric process, as shown in Figure 6.2.

- **Control employees and processes.** Go a step further than guiding and actually control those behaviors with analytics and automation. Exercise care with ethics if you are employing this technique.
- **Guide employees.** Guide employees to the best decisions with analytics.
- **Persuade.** Present evidence and likely outcomes in a way that encourages action. Persuasion is more focused on those with a greater degree of autonomy, mostly executives and professionals.
- **Monitor.** Create a reward and punishment approach for those with more autonomy to listen to the analytics by showing the outcomes when employees did, or did not, use the analytics. If done well, they will get quick feedback reinforcing the desired, improved behavior, similar to coaching.

This progression is a step beyond the traditional view of a learning organization, one that uses mostly traditional analog, or non-analytics, ways to drive change. Traditional methods of organizational change will always be critical, but they can also be guided by and accelerated with analytics through analytics-driven adaptability. Analytics-driven adaptability is when an organization regularly uses analytics to help (1) find and harvest new opportunities, not just make better decisions with current business models, and (2) drive and scale adaptability across the organization.

Analytics should be a gateway to reflection and continual learning, not just in the sense of learning how to do things better, but in the sense of learning how to learn. It builds in mechanisms for reflection, feedback loops that let you know if what you did worked, and tools to nudge the system to continual improvement and learning across the organization.

But let me emphasize again: analytics-driven adaptability goes beyond learning how to do what you do better. It is about changing the culture to one of continual learning through an iterative cycle of investigation, action, feedback, and reflection that will help the organization survive and thrive by remaining competitive over the long term. As described in the MIT[4] report on organizational learning cited in the very beginning of this book, it is only those who also learn from machines, not just the reverse, that reap the full benefits of analytics and are truly analytically mature.

GROWING ANALYTICS MATURITY

In this section, we return to the MIT report highlighted previously in this book, which focuses on organizational learning with AI, to explore building value with analytics. Next we look at Inam's recipe for growing analytics maturity in an organization, followed by Steve Stone's story of restoring trust in the analytics necessary for maturity after it was lost. We conclude with a discussion of how to structure the analytics inside an organization.

Steps to Organizational Learning from the MIT Report

This MIT report on organizational learning we have referenced often in this book gives some hints to the value added in terms of increasing analytics success at each stage in the maturity process. I have paraphrased their names and simplified the idea in Figure 6.3 for clarity and readability. It shows the following stages and their success rates.

- **AI team.** This stage consists of the analytics team mostly doing a few very targeted projects in a few applications. There tends to be minimal engagement across the organization.
- **Tools and strategic alignment.** This stage consists of investing in the appropriate tools and technologies aligned with an appropriate business strategy and adapting the business strategy to include AI. It needs to go both ways.

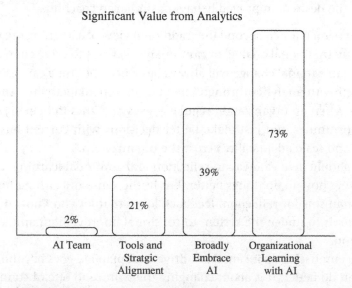

Significant Value from Analytics

Figure 6.3 Levels of Organizational Learning and Success

- **Broadly embrace AI.** In this stage, the organization deftly aligns analytics production and consumption in a way that improves adoption, while going beyond automation to be broadly used across the organization.
- **Organizational learning.** This is where learnings are shared among and between humans and AI. They both change and adapt based on needs and effectiveness. It also consists of mature interactions, relationships, and structure between people and AI.

A recent update[5] to the MIT BCG's report expands on this idea by saying that in the most successful learning organizations, these employees see AI more as a coworker rather than a threat. The report also notes that when employees feel more competent and successful in their jobs, with the help of AI, the employees and organizations are much more likely to achieve value.

Ahmer Inam's Recipe for Growing Analytics Maturity

Ahmer Inam, a senior analytics leader for the likes of Nike, PwC, Sonic, Cambia, Relanto, and others, is one of the smartest and most experienced deep analytics professionals I know. Inam shares a personal step-by-step recipe for successfully building analytics maturity, written from the perspective of a new analytics leader recently hired or promoted by the organization to develop and grow an analytics practice within it. Note that this advice is primarily for non-digital-native organizations new to analytics or struggling to scale.

Step 1: Start Small

Change is hard and analytics is still new, in practice, to many of the people in the organization who need to adopt it. Because analytics requires a change in people's behavior, a little bit of fear and trepidation by those, especially in the non-executive ranks, is natural. Going too big, too fast, will increase this panic.

You, and/or your ideas, may also be new to the organization. It will take you time to react, build trust, and understand where the most valuable and pliable opportunities exist for analytics success. Do not rush in too early, recklessly, or blindly and miss your chance to see clearly and build support.

For a chance to change, you need to have some well-accepted and well-regarded success. The first few projects are the most important and critical here, even if the dollar value is modest. More than anything else, at this stage, you are trying to build trust and acceptance. Do not overwhelm or overcomplicate. Stay focused on that goal for long-term acceptance and adoption.

You therefore need to tackle and solve a problem that is big enough to matter and small enough to be achievable. You need the project to be noticed, spark wonder, and build trust to open the doors to future projects or else analytics will likely be rejected and not take root at this time.

The project also needs to be a quick win that can build acceptance. If the organization recently hired you, or authorized and invested in a new analytics initiative, speed also matters. You will need a quick win to justify the recent and continual investments needed to build support for analytics, which provides another reason to start small with a solvable problem that will be noticed.

Step 2: Engage an Executive-Level Analytics Translator

As discussed in Task 2: The Team, analytics translators can be powerful accelerants to analytics adoption. They bring credibility, trust, and understanding to the role that analytics could play in the organization and communicate in a language executives understand. At this stage, most of the efforts of the translator are focused on building support among executives who fund and build further support for their initiatives.

As Bill Franks pointed out in Task 2: The Team, this translator must be very senior, with fluency in both business and analytics and have a reputation that will build trust. This role cannot be filled by a project manager or junior person. It must be someone the executives see as a respected and trustworthy peer who can share their vision for what could be done and give executives confidence that it will succeed.

Step 3: Assemble a Lean Team

Start with a lean team, an essential for success with early projects. Even if your team can quickly come up with valuable ideas and analysis, it will take time for adoption, especially in these early stages. Executives always look at ROI and other business metrics because this is their function. The faster your team grows, the more cost the company incurs, and the greater the analytics impact needs to be for return on their investment.

Executives will feel the need to "stop the bleeding" more urgently as costs and commitments rise, making them nervous and causing the bar to rise on their definition of success. A bigger team may be able to find insights faster. But if the firm is not *yet* ready to adopt those insights, a bigger team too early in the adoption cycle will raise the hurdle for a successful ROI by increasing the cost before the organization is ready to act on those insights, simultaneously lowering the short-term benefit.

A lean team, as Inam counsels, tailors the analytics to the level currently digestible to the organization without bloating the cost before they are ready to digest more. Although it is tempting to always try to expand and do more, especially for smart analytics professionals who see many possibilities, it is critical to match the pace of the organization's willingness to adopt. Correctly managing the pace will lead to long-term success and the ability to grow your analytics efforts in step with the organization's ability to adopt and benefit.

Step 4: Ensure Action

Value does not come from insights. Value comes only when you act on those insights, as outlined in the DAD analytics framework found in the first chapter of this book. Executive champions and business process owners should require the analytics team to focus on action to maintain a clear ROI. Even with action-centric or data-centric analytics, there should be some ultimate action that happens.

Additionally, it should be the action that the executive supporters are looking for. Once trust is built and analytics is accepted, they will listen to other ideas. However, at this stage in the process, you must dive deeply into historical problems they care about, that have not been solvable another way, and that you see a path toward solving.

This focus on their pain, and where they have failed to make progress with a chronic problem you can solve, is one of the best ways to build trust. When you take away their pain in a way they were not able to do on their own, it builds trust much more effectively and durably than solving a new problem they have not wrestled with, even if the new problem is more valuable. This is emotionally charged support, because they felt the pain and are glad for the relief. They will spread your success story far and wide, fueling broader adoptions and additional support in the future.

Step 5: Grow from Project to Process

In the early days, your analytics almost always starts as one-off projects as you help a few executive champions or business process owners succeed in analytics, building support for the idea by showing that your analytics team can deliver value. These craft analytics solutions are critical in helping start analytics adoption and better decision-making. Yet, to add real value, you must move beyond craft analytics projects to a stable, mature process eventually culminating in industrial-scale analytics.

Dr. Bill Disch, of DataRobot, expanded on this idea by sharing that not only does growing from individual products to a mature process help scale analytics but also it creates synergies that lead to new approaches and ideas. As you grow to a mature analytics process by prioritizing and scaling, you discover where the synergies are.

For example, rather than redo transformation and data cleaning for important variables, you start to do these together, making them available for similar problems. Your confidence grows when you are able to detect what will likely be important based on what worked well. You will have identified important "features" or transformations and combinations of your data that have proven to be valuable and are likely to be valuable again. You should have come to better understand the key decisions that are most helpful and workable.

All of these craft analytics projects will work together to create analytics synergies when properly prioritized as a group or stream of related analytics projects that help you scale and magnify your impact. It will take time to get there, but this is how to maximize value.

Step 6: Engage Multilevel Analytics Translators

Early adoptions efforts are largely focused on understanding executives' needs, prioritizing what can be done to have the most impact, and securing their approval and enthusiastic support. Later stages of adoption need to expand beyond the executive circle and engage other levels of the organization. Here, we engage multilevel analytics translators. By this we mean we not only engage the highest level senior translators discussed previously and aimed at executives, but the others on the analytics teams who also do analytics translator work with peers and lower management levels of the organization.

Let your analytics team become product owners so they can spend up to half of their time building support for analytics by sharing success stories. They need to be engaged directly with the business process owner teams during this time, building, supporting, and generating new ways to serve. The analytics team, and those who sponsored or benefited from other successful projects, should share their stories broadly across the organization to build momentum for more projects, while also listening for more ways to help. Inam gave me permission to use a visual adapted and simplified from an article he published about the concept,[6] which you can find in Figure 6.4.

The analytics team should especially target levels and groups in the organization where adoption would offer significant potential value. This value should be communicated in business terms, based on KPIs and other metrics important to them, not to the analyst. Do not confuse the picture with technical, mathematical, or other types of jargon, which will distract from the benefit and discourage adoption.

Step 7: Grow from Lean to Mature Analytics Team

As success stories mount and acceptance, even eager adoption, takes hold in the organization, it is time to grow and expand the analytics team to deliver the value that others are demanding. If you expand too early before delivering the value executive champions want, you will get pushback on the cost. After they see value, become allies, and benefit from the increased ROI, you will have the support you need to grow.

Here you can add different flavors of analyst, as illustrated in Task 2: The Team, depending on the organization's needs. Add new skills that can help you help more parts of the organization. Possibilities could include studying the skill sets of a cloud engineer, architect, analyst, or more engineers. Titles will change, so focus on what will add value to your firm and best serve their needs.

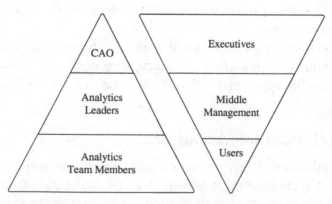

Figure 6.4 Multilevel Analytics Translators
Source: Figure inspired by Ahmer Inam.

Step 8: Build Partnerships Not Empires

It is tempting to try to use the support you built, up to now, to build an empire of analysts. Although you do need to grow, you do not need an empire. Instead you need partners. Loners fail, no matter how big their empire. You cannot change the organization alone, nor do you have the power to compel anyone to change. Instead, focus on building allies and supporting them where they are. This process might include training their staff members and enabling self-service analytics or building analytics products they love. But it must involve win-win partnerships.

The key here is to continue to expand the depth and breadth of the partnerships indefinitely, with a focus on optimizing for the firm as a whole, not just for an individual department. It is also critical to focus on supporting the organization's most important initiatives, while avoiding political land mines.

Step 9: Fire the Luddites

Inam shared that the farther along one gets in their career, the more urgent it has become to do analytics or die. In the 20th century, a company on a downward spiral might still survive another 50 years. Then we saw that survival time cut to 20, 15, or 10 years and now it has become common to see an organization struggling to succeed in analytics be wiped out in 5 or fewer years. Inam believes this will become even more common as those firms that truly succeed at competing on analytics drive more firms out of business.

I tried to illustrate Inam's thoughts in Figure 6.5, which shows a downward arrow for survival time of firms when faced with increasing competitive pressure from other firms succeeding in AI and data analytics, where they are left behind. It also shows the idea that we are facing more threats than in the recent past, as the world and technology are changing more quickly than at any time in historical memory. In these types of environments, there may no longer be time to wait for all the laggards to come along willingly.

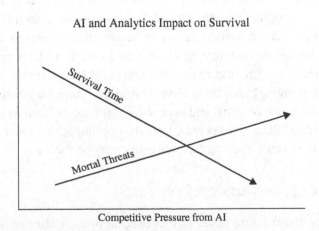

Figure 6.5 Impact of Analytics Pressure on Organization Survival

Most of the time, analytics adoption and use is held up by a few Luddites who continue to resist, using their power and influence to stall adoption, even when they sometimes appear to support it. They often stall, misdirect, and otherwise seek to undermine efforts. Many readers will recall that a Luddite was a group of individuals in England at the dawn of the industrial age, roughly 200 years ago. They were opposed to new technology, which at that time was manufacturing equipment, fearing for their jobs and livelihood. They often resorted to vandalism and sabotage due to their fear of change.

Though modern-day Luddites may not resort to physical vandalism today, they are quite real, and they can resist quite effectively. Many people are actually terrified of change and especially change that is driven by new technologies they may not understand. I recall doing a study of rural nurses who were faced with changing technologies for a project funded by the local Area Health Education Center (AHEC) in the early 2010s. We met with many nurses, during our focus groups, surveys, and other data collection.

What surprised me at the time was how many nurses swore that they were going to retire or quit before the next medical record system was installed and the number of former nurses who identified this fear of new technology as a key reason for leaving. None confessed to sabotage, and we did not ask, but their resistance was clear, and likely not futile. We wrote about it in this article,[7] but I am sure it is not just nurses that feel this way. There are those in any profession who will resist change, either by leaving or by sabotaging it. To succeed, this issue sometimes needs to be addressed a little more forcefully.

Inam shared an example of an organization many readers might recognize. There were a few powerful players at the organization who had managed to block analytics and AI adoption too long. With the company at risk, the c-suite executives called a large organizational meeting. In that meeting, they named, shamed, and publicly fired those who stood in the way of analytics adoption and use. The CEO then turned to all the remaining employees, looking them in the eye, and told them this is the direction their company was going to go, had to go, to survive and thrive. The CEO then invited anyone with any doubts to leave the company before they, too, were fired.

Inam said that the company is now moving forward at breakneck speed, making great progress in competing on analytics and there are no more doubters in the organization, or at least they are cowering in fear or becoming converts as they see the success with the roadblocks being removed. Here is the point: in today's hyper-competitive world, we no longer have the luxury of waiting around for everyone to voluntarily get on board. By then it may already be too late. Therefore, Inam's final advice is to fire the luddites so you can move forward and save the company. As hard as it is to let people go, if you do nothing, all may quickly be lost. Do not delay. You must act to save your organization today because waiting for tomorrow may be too late.

Stone's Story of Fixing Analytics Distrust

Steve Stone talks about using an action-focused approach after becoming CIO of a Fortune 100 organization. Although there had been many dashboards and attempts to use analytics earlier, they had failed to lead to meaningful adoption and use due to an inability for anyone to act on analytics models in a way that added value, which led to an environment of distrust in analytics.

Stone immediately began to refocus their analytics on action and usability. This change included turning off many of their current dashboards and reports that did *not* drive action. Stone recalls that about 80% of them were not being used, discovered after running a test by turning them all off and seeing if anyone asked for them! Based on this result, Stone and the team removed some of the clutter of "useless" analytics and freed up space for actionable ones.

Next, Stone and the team carefully studied how executives were actually making decisions, not the theory of how they should make decisions. By understanding executives' decision-making process, how they thought about it, what was important to them, and, most important, what drove their actions, Stone and the analytics team understood where they could help.

Stone and the analytics team then took this knowledge and built on their current process, rather than trying to replace it with what they thought would be best. By listening to, and building on, the current executives' and business process owners' processes, they were able to build decision tools that were actually used. This approach built trust in an environment full of distrust. In fact, Stone likes to quote the organization's long-time CEO who said, "I don't trust analytics, but I trust *your* analytics."

Once the CEO started to trust and rely on Stone's actionable analytics, other executives quickly followed. As the rest of the organization saw their leaders using and relying on analytics, they too began to adopt and rely on them. Stone is quick to emphasize that employees follow the example of their leaders, not just what they say. He strongly believes, if you want employees to use it, leaders must use and trust it, too.

Stone's remedy for bringing trust to an environment full of distrust paved the way for an organization that today is seen as a world-class leader in analytics and holds lessons for all of us.

Analytics Structure

Although there are many structures that can be used successfully for different firms at different times and in different places, there are a few principles on which these experts largely agree that are shared here:

- **Locate near power center.** Every organization has a power center, which varies based on culture, origin, and industry. For analytics to be the most successful, it should be located within that power center and be supported by that power center, which can highly influence adoption and use.
- **Centralize data.** Data should be centralized to better control quality, accessibility, and standardization and to ensure general good governance.
- **Democratize access.** Although data should be centralized, access to the use of that data should be democratized and shared across the organization to facilitate the analytics process and build a data culture.

- **Control appropriate access.** Although data should be democratized, not all data should be shared broadly. Only useful and relevant data should be shared, and less relevant or sensitive data should be guarded with appropriate access controls.
- **Align incentives.** Incentives for analytics should be aligned with their impact and results. Although it may seem obvious, some organizations have organized their analytics efforts in a way that sets up a zero-sum competition between units and analytics applications, which hampers their use and adoption.

TOOLS FOR MATURITY

Several of the experts interviewed pointed out, and my research for this book supports, that culture is king when it comes to analytics adoption and use. Without the right culture, no amount of technology or tools will get you where you need to be to succeed. Yet, good tools can facilitate a much more pleasant and productive experience with analytics, accelerating adoption. Additionally, few would attempt to do analytics manually with any degree of success, so tools are still essential, if not sufficient on their own, to success.

This section shares some insight regarding the tools needed to support analytics maturity.

Platform Versus Product: Part 1

There are so many tools available to us it can be hard to make sense of them all. Also, the rate at which they are evolving further complicates the situation. We find that categorizing them helps, but first we review a few key terms:

- **Product.** A product is a stand-alone piece of software, an individual program, that solves a specific problem. For example, SPSS focuses on statistical analysis and MySQL is a database solution for traditional datasets.
- **Platforms.** A platform connects a variety of products together in a way that enables easy hand-off of data, code, and models from one to another. In the business world, Microsoft 365 is a good example of a platform. SAS and DataRobot are also examples of analytics platforms.

Note that although there are many platforms, there are very few that have succeeded (maybe none) in creating a universal platform with best-in-class service throughout the entire analytics chain. Most platforms today are still fairly basic, combining a few products, but not coming close to a universal goal we may never reach. Thus, you will still have to connect multiple platforms in the foreseeable future.

Most products aspire to become platforms, and most platforms aspire to become universal platforms that do everything. Meanwhile, more and more platforms and products keep emerging, each generally with some advantage in some specific area. It means that the ecosystem is constantly changing as new products and platforms are born, merge, and die.

Open Versus Closed

Many products and platforms are open source, which means the software code is available to be seen and modified by anyone, and it generally comes with a license that allows the software to be used, modified, and freely distributed. Other platforms are proprietary, meaning they are the property of another organization, and the license does not allow the code to be modified, viewed, or freely distributed. Hence, they are closed source, as in the source code of the software is closed to review, limited in use and in customizeability.

Open and closed systems have their advantages and disadvantages. Many firms give away their software and make money in support and custom applications. Many firms with proprietary closed source systems sell and service their software.

Experts Favorite Tools

This section shares a few of our experts' favorite open or closed source products and platforms to give you a better idea of each category. Then we give advice about navigating between all of the options. Please note, this book does not make any recommendations for or against any particular product or platform but seeks to illustrate a few of the popular tools in the categories of products and platforms and open and closed source.

- **Alteryx.** Alteryx started as a product to store and process data efficiently and rapidly, making it an important input platform for fast data access that is expanding in other analytics areas.
- **Anaconda.** Anaconda is a common open source version of R and Python that hosts various packages for math, science, and analytics.
- **Columnar Data Storage.** Columnar Data Storage is a database focused on storing data in columns rather than rows. It offers some speed and efficiency for certain applications. Standard SQL works on traditional and columnar data storage solutions. Amazon Redshift is a popular Columnar Data Storage solution.
- **DataRobot.** DataRobot started as a product and has grown into a small platform with focused analytics solutions. It is closed source and focuses on automating the machine learning process, either making AI more accessible to those with less training or increasing productivity of data scientists.
- **Domo.** Domo is a company focused on closed source processing of data for business intelligence and data visualizations.
- **IBM Watson.** IBM Watson is a natural language processing product focused on question-and-answer solutions that integrates into IBM's platform. You may recall in 2013 when Watson won *Jeopardy*.
- **JMP.** JMP is a stand-alone statistical software product acquired by SAS that is focused on quality control, engineering, and experimentation.
- **Jupyter Notebooks.** Jupyter Notebooks is an online open source notebook and computing interface for writing and executing open source data and analytics languages, including Python and R.

- **Microsoft Azure.** Microsoft Azure is a closed source, cloud-based platform for hosting and managing very large datasets as a service. Amazon, Google, and a few others have similar cloud-based ecosystem solutions that integrate multiple tools and tool types.
- **Python.** Python is an open source program language that is very common for many analytics solutions today. What makes it so useful is the community-support libraries that provide many prepackaged data science solutions. Anaconda is a common distribution of Python that also hosts Jupyter Notebooks, a computing interface for writing and executing open source data and analytics languages, including Python and R. Scikit-learn is a free software, machine learning library for the Python programming language.
- **Qualtrics.** Qualtrics is a software product focused on gathering and integrating experiential data into an application. It has several partners and features that are helping it grow into a platform.
- **R.** R is an open source, functional programming language. It originated as a domain-specific language for statistical computing, but it has developed functionality in a broad range of applications, such as visualization, machine learning, automated reporting, and web app creation, through a robust selection of open source packages.
- **SAS.** Similar to SPSS, SAS was originally a closed source, statistical solution that has grown into an expansive, self-contained platform that offers complete analytics solutions and integrates with a few partners such as Teradata. It is beginning to offer limited integration with open source tools such as R and Python, and offers full SQL integration.
- **SPSS.** SPSS was originally focused on statistics (Process) as a closed source solution for social science research. It has since been acquired by IBM and integrated into their broader platform with a focus on statistics, business intelligence, and multivariate analysis, with some data management capabilities.
- **SQL.** Structured query language (SQL) is a standard open language for data manipulation that is incorporated into most databases and data management systems. It has been the dominant data manipulation language for relational databases since the 1970s. About three-quarters of the world's data is still stored in relational databases best accessed with SQL.
- **Tableau.** Tableau started as an easy-to-use business intelligence tool offering high-quality, real-time visualizations of data. It has evolved into a platform known as Einstein Discovery, which offers greater integration with other tools and additional services.
- **Teradata**. Teradata is a closed source data platform focused on storing and processing very large datasets by building data warehousing and cloud-based solutions.

Tool Trade-Offs

The open versus closed source tools debate is one that will not be settled by this book. Many argue passionately on both sides and both have good points. Here are some things to think about with open versus closed source products:

- **Security.** In some ways, open source tools can be more secure because an entire community is looking at them and keeping them more up-to-date. However, it also means that anyone can look at the code directly and, if they are skilled enough, find undetected flaws. Alternatively, I have heard stories of companies switching away from closed source systems because of vulnerabilities, particularly if a product or platform was integrated with commercial software and it was expensive to keep the integration code up-to-date. Companies thus have an incentive to reduce cost by not keeping them up-to-date for economic reasons, exposing users to known vulnerabilities.

- **Ecosystem.** Both closed and open source software can have robust ecosystems to support them, including development partners and experts. For example, Qualtrics and Tableau are best in class for robust ecosystems supporting their commercial products. However, many open source communities like R and Python also have robust support. It is important to evaluate not just the product or platform but also the support available in the ecosystem and how it can fit to your needs.

- **Total cost of ownership.** Many people assume that because something is open source it is automatically cheaper, but this is a false assumption. Do not focus on the tool's initial sticker price. Instead, consider the total cost of ownership. This includes maintenance, time and effort, licensing fees, integration work, quality impact, training, and opportunity costs. To make better business decisions, you need to focus on the true cost of ownership, not just the sticker price.

Platform Versus Product: Part 2

Platforms offer seamless solutions that can work together in harmony, facilitating adoption by making these solutions easier to use and especially easier for sharing data and deploying models. I have observed that platforms like SAS and DataRobot have the ability to share data and deploy models quickly and efficiently, and I can clearly see the advantages to a platform that offers quick scalability and deployments.

Even though long-history platforms like SAS have very good tools for many data science applications, no one platform has ever achieved best in class for all tools. I would be quite surprised if any platform ever manages and sustains such an achievement. This means that organizations need to balance the need for best-in-class tools with the benefits of strong platforms that facilitate use, scalability, adoption, and, important, deployment.

Here are a few things to consider when making those difficult trade-off decisions:

- **Learning curve.** Standardizing on an interoperable platform can accelerate your learning curve because many products that live on that platform will have a common look and feel and analysts will have a clear direction to go when enhancing their skill sets, as will HR managers when hiring talent. However, it can be harder to adapt if your platform fails to keep up with market trends, tools, and techniques or does not innovate well, leaving you to trail in the market with outdated talent.

- **Scalability.** Having a unified platform allows for quicker scalability with a known partner who likely offers many add-on services. However, if you are locked into a particular platform, that scalability might be very costly and hard to change.

- **Switching cost.** If you do need to change platforms, due to a change in strategy or cost or because your platform is lagging behind others, it can be very costly, not just in dollars, but in the pain incurred to switch.

Integration

I was fortunate enough to recently hear a top researcher present a preview of the results of a forthcoming peer-reviewed journal article in one of the field's most recognized publication outlets. The topic was the adoption of hospital information systems. The researchers did an analysis over the last few decades in which systems had been adopted nationally. At the beginning of the analysis period in the 1990s, most hospitals had chosen a best-in-class strategy in which they looked for the best products in each class, then purchased them. However, today, these researchers showed that hospitals had switched to a very strong platform strategy in which integration was one of the most important factors they were looking for. There were several reasons for this change, including changing health care laws, mergers and acquisitions, and insurance needs.

One of the primary reasons, however, was the flow of data and the value that could be achieved by streamlining and improving that flow. Hospital systems were required under the Obamacare rules to switch to electronic health records. However, they were not required to make them interchangeable. Different platforms were generally not compatible, creating data silos and making it very difficult to do analytics on any data, among other issues. Therefore, the only way for them to take advantage of the data was to move to a uniform platform and away from the best-in-class platform to get that value.

Hospitals are perhaps an extreme case, but also are a relevant one. When it comes to tools to enable analytics maturity, I believe, as do many of our experts, that the single most important factor is the ability to integrate platforms and products seamlessly across the organization. Successful implementation of the right integrated infrastructure helps you scale and move to industrial analytics. Without it, you are stuck with custom craft analytics that will always be limited in scope and value.

This step to analytics maturity is so important that I am going to pause here to share a couple of stories of integration that shed a little more light on this critical factor.

Yse's Innovative Approach to Predicting Crop Failure

Diego Lopez Yse, now a VP of operations at Moody's leading data science teams in Latin America, shared a story about leading a remarkably innovative and successful data science project with Bayer. Yse's task was to go beyond general forecasts of crop failures to predicting which crops would likely fail. This was important to Bayer, with its major agricultural division.

Lopez Yse saw an opportunity to move from traditional general forecasts of overall crop failure to predicting which crops were most at risk of failure, and was able to pull in a variety of records from many different sources, with a focus on Lopez Yse's home location of Argentina. Sources included granular weather data, satellite images, historical records, and crop modeling data, such as a feature called *growing degree days*.

Lopez Yse was then able to integrate all of this data into a comprehensive model that proved remarkably successful, surpassing Lopez Yse's and the sponsor's expectations to the point that it was expanded to more crops and a broader territory the next season. Yse explained that what was most surprising was how this data integration worked in South America where data is generally more sparse and harder to come by than in some more-developed countries. Nevertheless, even in a sparse data environment, it is sometimes more about finding and using the right relevant data in innovative ways to add value, as Lopez Yse has shown.

Of course, the key was Lopez Yse's ability to integrate all of this data from different sources. Most of it started as craft analytics to prove the concept but, once it was integrated, it allowed for far greater value.

Dr. Bill Disch Leads Integration

Dr. Bill Disch shared a story about the challenges of integrating various platforms and products to seamlessly work together while serving as the chief analytics officer for a mid-size firm. They initially had a patchwork of many different systems that were not integrated. When Disch started, everything was a manual process built on a patchwork of products and platforms not designed to integrate and work together well.

The challenge arose largely due to a lack of executive oversight, discipline, and participation in the tool selection process. Analysts were each left to choose their own tool, without thought to how it fit with everyone else's tools. Although the analyst certainly should have some say in the appropriate tools, executives must make sure their entire organizational impact is also considered.

One of the key problems Disch faced is there was no integration. When someone did one type of analytics on the platform of their choice, there was no easy way for the data, model, or other feature stores to be easily shared and used. It had a detrimental effect on analytics success by reducing the ability to get from one station to the next, let alone from out of the lab into production. Disch was wise enough to know that for analytics to succeed, they had to break down the silos and make all the tools communicate with each other seamlessly, which included discontinuing some tools to increase standardization and interoperability.

This became one of Disch's main focus areas. As they prioritized the job that the tools needed to do, they were able to shed products that did not play nicely with others and settled on a few best-in-class platforms. Once they had those priorities, Disch had programmers and data engineers automate and stitch together all of the remaining tools to increase the knowledge flow rate between all the systems.

It took Disch and the team, with full support from executives, three years to complete the integration. But they did it and their analytics maturity and use soared, as did the value they received from their analytics efforts.

Tool Maturity Advice

Tools are critical, but sometimes what matters more is what goes into them, so do not forget the data. Here are points to remember when thinking about tools to aid your analytics maturity:

- **Data diversity.** More data, especially more diverse data, is key to building durable, robust models. You cannot model data you do not have and more of the same data offers only incremental improvements. To really improve your model, think about all the things that might affect your problem and then look for data to test it. Adding experiential and third-party data, along with data from more diverse sources, even if it is outside your firm, will often make a bigger difference than the choice of a particular tool.

- **Data preparation.** Better quality data that has been cleaned, transformed, and enriched makes a big difference. It also takes a lot of time and effort! Respect and support this process. If you put garbage in your model, you will get garbage out.

- **Data structure.** It is not just the data quality that matters. The structure of the data and how it is stored, even for identical data, is critical.

- **Robust platform.** Analytics is a rapidly evolving industry, and your analytics team needs to have room to test ideas and keep their skills sharp. Although this may look like play, keeping them engaged and trying new things is essential to analytics success. Investing in a robust data ecosystem, with the appropriate integrated tools and technologies, helps you grow and retain your team while providing better solutions.

- **Investment in ecosystem.** Your analytics ecosystem, whether open or closed source, is a potential source of competitive advantage or liability. Whatever system you choose, do not just evaluate it. Invest in it, make it better, and help everyone in your ecosystem. In today's world, it is not just companies competing against other companies, but also sometimes ecosystems competing against other ecosystems.

- **Team trust.** Members of your analytics team are likely quite intelligent and well trained in their craft. They may not know everything about your business, but when it comes to their area of expertise it is best to listen to and support them, while keeping them focused on solving your most pressing business problems.
- **Problem solved.** Every tool needs to solve a relevant business problem, and preferably several. If it does not solve your problem, why do you want it?
- **Shelf life.** Technology ages quickly. That shiny new platform or product will likely be out-of-date tomorrow. Carefully consider the shelf life of your tools.

CHAPTER SUMMARY AND EXERCISES

Task 6: Summary

The first five manageable tasks focus on succeeding in a given analytics project. Task 6 is about building a mature analytics process and pipeline and developing a culture that adopts and learns from analytics, one that is willing to embrace change to succeed and compete on analytics. This is an organization that does analytics at an industrial scale and practices many types of analytics in many places across the entire organization.

Part of being a mature analytics organization is following a proven analytics methodology, such as the one outlined by INFORMS. It involves creating partnerships inside and outside the organization, while engaging the broader analytics ecosystem. It requires the adoption of platforms and products that are integrated across the organization to allow data and insights to flow freely across the organization, enabling action to be taken on them. Most of all, it involves an analytical mindset spread across the organization, one that embodies an eagerness to embrace change and do things better based on data and its wise analysis.

Task 6: Exercises

1. Describe the role of *each* member of Pleines's minimal viable team and their supporters in building analytics maturity, and why it takes all of them to succeed.
2. Describe the importance of following a proven analytics methodology, like the one espoused by INFORMS, to develop an analytically mature organization.
3. Discuss the role of external engagement in building analytics maturity, what it is, why it matters, and five ways you can do this more effectively across the organization.
4. Discuss the difference between platforms and products and the critical role of integration between them. Then list and describe two of your favorite products or platforms and share why you love them.
5. List and describe each of the nine steps for building analytics maturity in non-digital-native organizations, as described by Ahmer Inam. Give an example of how you might use or adapt this process to build analytics maturity and acceptance at an organization you care about.

NOTES

1. Thomas G. Cech, Trent J. Spaulding, and Joseph A. Cazier, "Data Competence Maturity: Developing Data-Driven Decision Making," *Journal of Research in Innovative Teaching & Learning* 11, no. 2 (2018): 139–158. https://doi.org/10.1108/JRIT-03–2018–0007.

2. Thomas H. Davenport, Randy Bean, and Shail Jain, "Why Your Company Needs Data-Product Managers," *Harvard Business Review* (October 13, 2022).

3. Lee Feinberg, "Operationalizing Data Storytelling," International Institute for Analytics, March 2023.

4. Sam Ransbotham, Shervin Khodabandeh, David Kiron, François Candelon, Michael Chu, and Burt LaFountain, "Expanding AI's Impact with Organizational Learning," *MIT Sloan Management Review* (October 2020).

5. Sam Ransbotham, David Kiron, François Candelon, Shervin Khodabandeh, and Michael Chu, "Achieving—and Organizational—Value with AI," *MIT Sloan Management Review* (October 31, 2022).

6. https://towardsdatascience.com/how-to-be-a-successful-chief-data-officer-e34b6ae56443

7. M. J. Dotson, D. S. Dave, J. A. Cazier, and T. J. Spaulding, "An Empirical Analysis of Nurse Retention: What Keeps RNs in Nursing?" *The Journal of Nursing Administration* 44, no. 2 (2014): 111–116.

Responsible Analytics

OUR ANALYTICS RESPONSIBILITY

Analytics is a wonderful tool for understanding the world. As illustrated with the DAD (decision-centric, action-centric, and data-centric) analytics framework throughout this book, it can help you make better decisions, explore new possibilities, and drive action. All of these benefits can be incredibly useful to organizations and our society. They have been shown to lead to a competitive advantage, rapidly change entire industries, and improve positive behaviors such as with health and well-being.

However, it can also lead people astray, to be fooled or tricked by randomness without the proper safeguards, and deceived by those who use biased numbers masquerading as analytics, to essentially lie with numbers for political or monetary gain. Even with good intentions, it is easy to be led astray by micro-focusing on things that do not matter much, missing other more important tasks and opportunities inside and outside of analytics.

It is easy to be fooled by someone or some algorithm with fancy numbers, graphs, charts, and predictions. As long as it has been around, statistics has been used to lie and mislead by those with their own agendas who see it as nothing more than a tool to get what they want, rather than a philosophy of discovery, one that can lead to truth and better outcomes for us, those we care about, and the world.

It is also just as easy to be fooled by randomness, finding something that is not true, even when we follow best practices, strive to discover the best answer to our question, explore the best path, or drive the best actions. Even so, the data universe sometimes has other plans and you can find random patterns in mountains of data that just do not hold up over time—even when you do everything "right."

Analytics is and can be the answer to many problems, but it is not the answer to every problem or challenge. Some problems have better solutions or approaches from other domains. Sometimes the analytics is too complicated or time-consuming to give a cost- and time-effective answer when it is needed. Sometimes the data is too sparse or does not apply because it is not relevant enough to the situation. Other times it does apply, but the environment is not right for it to be done, accepted, or used in a way that adds value.

Although analytics can and has been used for great good, it has been and is being used in ways that cause great harm, too. The last task is to do responsible analytics, that is, analytics that is done in the right way, at the right time, with the right purpose, making our organizations and society better. To do analytics that avoids legal and ethical backlashes from poorly thought out or purely self-serving analytics. To do responsible analytics you can trust and rely on. To do analytics for good. To be a wise and discerning creator or user of analytics.

All of these aims are important for analytics longevity and success. This chapter is designed to help by presenting and reviewing a few key points about analytics discernment and the principles of first, do no harm and seek to do good. It concludes with some final parting words of wisdom from a few of our expert contributors.

ANALYTICS DISCERNMENT

As we saw in Task 1: The Problem, not all problems are amenable to analytics solutions. Leaders should first investigate whether a particular problem they want to solve is a good candidate for being solved by analytics, that it, is amenable to it, as outlined in that chapter. But even more, leaders need to use judgment and discernment, even when, or perhaps especially when, analytics is applied to solve a problem.

Limits to Gain

Right now we seem to be in an ascending hype cycle around analytics, where expectations for it and what can be done outpace the reality of what it can do. Maybe someday the reality of what can be done will exceed current expectations, but that day is not today. Leaders should be mindful of what analytics can do and what it cannot yet do.

Yet, even when analytics can do something, that still does not mean that it is the right solution for you. Analytics has a cost and usually an expensive one. Most often that cost is in dollars, sometimes it is in operational impact or risks from being misled by bad analytics. Even when the analytics is good, often the cost and investment is more than the benefit, in which case good projects are perceived to be failures because they did not deliver the expected value even when they worked flawlessly.

Executives are often misled, according to Bill Franks, director of the Center for Data Science and Analytics within the School of Data Science and Analytics at Kennesaw State University, and hence often have unrealistic expectations. No one wants to give bad news to the CEO, and often by the time that news makes it up to the senior ranks, it has been either intentionally or unintentionally sanitized in many ways to seem less bad, which is human nature. On the flip side, many vendors and others spread myths to sell their products and services, according to Aryng CEO Piyanka Jain, to garner attention or sometimes for other reasons.

You should not believe everything you see and hear. Analytics judgment and the ability to discern what is really essential and useful and what is not is a critical skill for success. Over-trusting and under-trusting analytics are problems that can cause you to either get lost in every costly wave of hype by trusting too much or miss out on the needed improvements and benefits by trusting too little.

One of my favorite articles in the *Harvard Business Review*[1] provides more insight on having the right balance. Their research broke organizational decision-makers into the following three groups:

- **Visceral decision-makers.** Making up about 20% of the population studied, this group is filled with distrust for any type of analysis and generally makes decisions unilaterally based on their gut, ignoring most input by others.

- **Unquestioning empiricist.** Making up a little more than 40% of their population, this group trusts analysis more than their judgment, leaning on it. They value consensus to the point they are often paralyzed by it and fail to effectively move forward.
- **Informed skeptics.** Making up just under 40% of their population, this group applies judgment to analysis, effectively blending the two while listening to others and being willing to still dissent when the situation requires it.

Informed skeptics are balanced decision-makers blending the best and avoiding the worst of the two approaches. If we are wise, this type of decision-maker is who we should aspire to be and encourage others to become. Beyond just being the right approach, their results showed that these informed skeptics performed an average of 24% better than the other groups on a variety of performance metrics.

For anyone leading or working with analytics, this mindset is essential. As good as AI and analytics can be, there is no silver bullet that can do it all. It is important to be discerning and match expectations to reality.

Knowledge-Based Certifications

Being an informed skeptic can help you determine when and when not to rely on analytics. Yet, when it is time to rely on analytics, it is even more important to make sure it is done right. In Task 6: Analytics Maturity, I introduced the importance of following a proven analytics maturity, which is critical to doing good analytics.

Given how important it is to do quality and responsible analytics, I recommend that organizations either hire people trained in proper, responsible analytics or insist so soon after hiring their analytics professional employees. Polly Mitchell-Guthrie, VP of industry outreach and thought leadership at Kinaxis and past chair of the Analytics Certification Board, explained there are three different types of certifications.

- **Skill-based.** Focused on a specific skill, algorithm, or method
- **Tool-based.** Focused on using a specific tool, usually sponsored by a vendor
- **Knowledge-based.** Focused on overall knowledge of a process and what needs to be done

Skill-based and tool-based certifications are helpful in verifying someone knows a part of the analytics, but it is not enough to show they understand the entire process. Skill-based and tool-based certifications are good for those early in their careers or for those working to stay current as technology and practices evolve because this training permits people to immediately become useful to the organization with many low-level tasks. But especially for leaders with a responsibility for quality and impact, a knowledge-based certification focused on ensuring quality, relevance, and responsibility throughout the process on these high-level leadership tasks should be preferred and sought by hiring managers and supported by supervisors.

Here are a few good certifications to consider:

- **Certified Analytics Professional (CAP).** Offered by the Institute for Operations Research and the Management Sciences (INFORMS), this certification validates the knowledge and skills of analytics professionals in various domains, including data management, modeling, and deployment.

- **IBM Data Science Professional Certificate.** Offered through Coursera, this certification includes a series of courses that cover key data science concepts, tools, and techniques, such as data visualization, machine learning, and statistical analysis.

- **SAS Certified Data Scientist.** Offered by SAS, this certification validates the knowledge and skills of data scientists in data preparation, machine learning, and predictive modeling. I watched the launch and have been quite impressed with its quality.

The IBM and SAS Certifications are also tool based, but I recommend them because their focus is on good data science principles. They use proven analytics methodologies throughout their certification programs, which can help ensure more responsible analytics. In addition to providing a good analytics methodology, the CAP is also a vendor-neutral, knowledge-based certification. It ensures the analytics professional is knowledgeable about the entire process, including working with stakeholders, which increases the likelihood of implementation and eventual value. Although all of these certifications are good, here are a few reasons why the CAP is my favorite:

- **Problem-focused.** A hallmark of the INFORMS process is making sure you are solving a valuable problem and addressing it by converting it into an appropriate analytics problem you can solve. Thinking about this process up front, as CAPs are trained to do, rather than jumping right into analysis, is a key to doing the right analytics.

- **Quality process.** Once the right analytics has been developed, CAPs are trained to follow a careful methodology to make sure the analytics is done right, that it is reliable and trustworthy.

- **Implementation and monitoring.** CAPs are taught to think about implementation and business impact from day one, and to involve stakeholders in the process throughout, both of which help improve success. CAPs are also trained to monitor results afterwards to ensure they have the desired effect and to catch concept drift when data or its relevance changes.

- **Vendor neutrality.** Not being tied to a particular product or platform enables CAPs to avoid conflicts of interest that can cloud judgment and keeps the focus on solving the real problem, regardless of the tool.

- **Continual learning.** As part of maintaining their certification, CAPs are required to engage in continual learning, staying up-to-date in their field, and documenting that training annually to be reviewed by INFORMS.

- **Ethics.** INFORMS CAPs pledge to follow ethical guides and a code of ethics as part of the certification process.

I believe INFORMS is a great organization, and that CAP is a valuable and useful certification. Still, there are several very good organizations to choose from, all of which have their unique and complementary value to offer, including certification. Here are a few other professional associations to consider:

- **International Institute of Business Analysis (IIBA).** This nonprofit professional association focuses on the advancement of business analysis and offers various certifications and resources for business analysts.

- **The Society for Industrial and Applied Mathematics (SIAM).** This professional society focuses on the application of mathematics to industry and other areas of science.

- **The International Association for Statistical Computing (IASC).** This professional society promotes the use of statistical computing and related methods.

- **The Decision Sciences Institute (DSI).** This professional society focuses on the application of quantitative methods to solve business and organizational problems.

- **The Association for Computing Machinery (ACM).** This professional society promotes the study and application of computing and information technology.

Having employees and partners who are affiliated with responsible professional associations and who hold a knowledge-based certification focused on the process of doing quality and responsible analytics is an important safeguard against negligent and irresponsible analytics. In today's fast-changing world, timeless, ethical principles that define responsible analytics are important for knowing whether you are doing responsible analytics and for guiding you on how to do analytics better, which is covered in the next section.

INFORMS ETHICAL GUIDELINES

Regulations, unfortunately, often lag decades behind innovations and are focused on cleaning up messes more than preventing them. Even more, different states and countries often disagree on approaches and end up passing conflicting regulations. I wish our political leaders were knowledgeable and forward thinking enough to give clear rules and guidelines about the future before it arrives, but that has seldom been the case. Therefore, it is often left to others to lead.

Fortunately, my favorite association for analytical professionals, INFORMS, is taking a leadership role in ethical practices in analytics. For example, they recently asked me and my friend Dr. Terry Rawls to help build and organize a course on ethics in analytics. INFORMS arranged for us to interview some of the smartest and most knowledgeable leaders in the field of AI and analytics ethics and analytics, which we synthesized into a short course designed to help those becoming CAPs or associate CAPs to understand not only what their ethical duties are but also how to follow them when under pressure.

Although many similar associations also champion ethics and are well worth it, please forgive me for saying that being asked to coordinate and host the development of that course was an honor I will remember forever and a highlight of my career. It was such a pleasure to meet and learn from these experts and digest their knowledge to share with CAPs and INFORMS members. INFORMS was kind enough to give me permission to share here a few highlights and key takeaways from the course.

Why Ethics Matters

As opposed to other professions, someone new to analytics might wonder why ethical considerations and the commitment to follow established guidelines are so important. I believe ethics matters everywhere, but it is especially relevant to analytics for some of the reasons that emerged from the experts interviewed during course development:

- **Impact.** The models we build and the decisions made based on them affect real people in very real ways.
- **Unintended effects.** Many of our models have unintended consequences and/ or are used in ways in which they were not designed. It is important to think through likely outcomes and uses early in the process to avoid doing harm.
- **Speed of innovation.** Our tools and technologies are advancing faster than our laws and regulations. We need ethics to guide us through these uncharted territories.
- **Reputation.** Your reputation should be important to you, just as your organization's reputation is important to their bottom line. Following ethical guidelines helps preserve everyone's reputation.
- **Right thing to do.** Integrating ethics into all of our processes is simply the right thing to do to avoid harm and maximize benefit.

It is not only important to behave ethically, it is also important to manage public perception and any possible backlash from ethical lapses. Bill Franks recounted the story of the retailer Target, written about in *Forbes*[2] among other places, as an excellent example. The article reports on Target using predictive analytics, based on store purchases, to determine when someone was pregnant so Target could better target market pregnancy-related products.

This practice is perfectly legal in most jurisdictions and is very similar to other practices in which businesses would engage. Many would argue it is also likely ethical, as you might be helping these women find products and services they desire.

However, as the story goes, an irate father found out about his 16-year-old's pregnancy because of Target's algorithms, and a public backlash ensued due to the "creepiness" of the predictions. Franks uses the story to emphasize the importance of considering ramification beyond just the legal and ethical, and to also consider public perceptions.

Principle of No Harm

The first principle of the INFORMS Ethical Guidelines can be summarized by a phrase common to the medical field: first, do no harm. This principle is especially important, as INFORMS notes, for vulnerable populations who cannot adequately protect themselves. With analytics, this is actually much harder than it sounds. As with any field that is inherently complex in its formations and interactions with a dynamic changing environment, there are many unintended consequences that can and do occur.

Even when the best intentions are at play from the beginning, this situation can be problematic. It is even more so for those with bad or even just self-serving intentions with little or no thought or care to those who are affected. This situation is especially concerning as many of the incentives of analytics are to get you to look at or do something, regardless whether it is true or helpful, which leads to false or misleading information being circulated as the algorithms optimize for engagement, not for accuracy or a better society.

Even more so is the problem of dual use of analytics. Often we develop a useful algorithm for one purpose, which may be ethically sound and perhaps even a positive benefit for society. However, others may later decide to use that same algorithm, analytics, data, or technology for another use, without notice or permission, that does violate ethical principles, even though the original use was carefully vetted. This secondary or dual use is much more likely to be opportunistic and not vetted or done anyway because of some political or economic gain.

Johann Vaz, who has decades of experience as a CIO/CTO for a variety of multimillion-dollar organizations in the technology, pharmaceutical, and finance industries, shared an example of doing no harm. The pharmaceutical company Vaz was working with at the time had developed a new promising drug. This drug had many benefits, and they were exploring the best way to keep and store the data. As part of their formal ethical review, they realized that although this particular biotherapy had many benefits, in the wrong hands it could also be abused and weaponized to do great harm. This discovery guided them to radically change their approach to safeguarding this data to make sure no harm could be done because of it.

Our Ethical Duties

Fortunately, INFORMS[3] gives us a little more detail on where we should look and what we should consider when building and deploying our analytics. They start by enumerating our duties to society, our organizations, and the analytics profession. I will share a short introduction to each duty by paraphrasing the words of Dr. Julie Swann, president-elect of INFORMS, and then highlighting a few best practices from the experts interviewed for the INFORMS ethics course.

Duty to Society

Our work directly affects the society in which we live and work. By being accountable, forthcoming, honest, objective, respectful, and responsible to society with all of our work, we help ensure our interactions are positive and beneficial for all, build trust, and avoid negative, unintended consequences to society from the analytics we build and decisions we make on them.

- **Think about could versus should.** Just because you can do something does not automatically mean you should. Take time to think about whether it is something you should do, guided by the principle to first, do no harm and second, to do good if you can.

- **Conduct a formal ethical review.** Make sure you have a formal ethical review process, one that makes you stop and think at every step of the process about what you are doing and how it could be used in the wrong hands, to ensure you are currently and continually on the right track. Make sure you document it to create rigor and make sure it gets the attention it needs.

- **Think beyond ethics.** You must be ethical. Yet, even ethical projects can be, shall we say, creepy. These projects, even if considered ethical, can elicit a very negative reaction from the public. Do not stop with ethics. Consider the appearance of the project as well in your review process.

Duty to Our Organizations

It is our responsibility to help our organizations make better decisions and help them succeed. Being informed about best practices, alert for possible problems, and questioning and realistic in our assumptions help us be more accurate and realistic in our work. This approach increases the value of what we do for our organizations and builds trust in the profession.

- **Solve the right problem.** Nothing is less efficient than solving the wrong problem. When people come to you, they often report symptoms and pain points of concern. It is up to you to dig deep enough to solve the real problem and guide it to one that should be solved not only for its benefit to the organization but also because it is ethical.

- **Undertake trustworthy analytics.** Think it through and make sure your analytics, methods, and experiments are well designed, rigorous, and trustworthy. This approach helps ensure your recommendation will work and address the organization's problem while building trust over time.

- **Engage subject matter experts (SMES).** Most of us are trained in technology, math, and data. Very few of us also have deep domain knowledge on the business side of the data, such as how it was collected and how the organization uses it. This information is critical for building and implementing models that are efficient, would solve the problem, and are likely to be adopted.

- **Manage bias.** There are biases everywhere. Historical data often captures biases from the past we do not want to perpetuate. We have many cognitive biases in how we, as a species, think and act. There are also biases in certain methods, processes, and even ways data may have been collected. Know and control your biases, even study them, so you can do well.

- **Assess legal risk.** Be alert for potential legal risks, now and in the future, for any projects in which you are associated and the possible monetary or reputational damage that could come from them. Be sure to include and alert the appropriate organizational officials and document any potential risks. Many in the legal department may not understand what you do and the risk associated with it. It is your duty to help them understand when risks they may not be aware of are present.

Duty to the Profession

By working together, being inclusive and tolerant of others, and cooperating with each other, we all do better. We all have different backgrounds, training, and skills. That diversity is our biggest strength as we learn from each other and grow together. Being impartial, truthful, and vigilant in all we do will build trust that enables us to more effectively work together.

- **Compete versus cooperate.** There is a time to compete and a time to cooperate. We need to find the balance for the time and place we are in while remembering we are all professionals in the same field and it is a small world. When in doubt, cooperate.

- **Be open minded.** As analytics professionals, it is our duty to seek the truth. To do that, we need to be open minded, willing to consider every side of an issue, and willing to change our minds as new information and perspective come to light. If we want our organizations to change and grow based on data and analysis, we should be willing to do the same.

- **Engage diversity.** Including and understanding diverse viewpoints, knowledge, experiences, and perspectives is not only the right thing to do but also this openness has been shown to help us avoid many pitfalls and improve outcomes. Every type of diversity matters, including equity and inclusion, neurodiversity, and educational/training diversity. Sam Volstad, data analytics service manager at the national accounting and advisory firm GHJ, observed that diversity also creates a much better bias detector because it is difficult for any one person to imagine how a model might be inequitable to a group whose lived experience is nearly completely removed from their own.

- **Leverage professional associations.** Ethics is hard! Engaging with professional associations, like INFORMS, help us stay up-to-date, share best practices, find friends and mentors outside our organization, and come together for the common good. Do not be a loner. Engage with others before you need them and make sure you give back, too.

Managing Ethical Dilemmas

Being part of a profession with valuable skills at the forefront of innovation means facing ethical dilemmas. Sometimes we will face pressure from well-meaning colleagues who may not understand the ethical implications of what they are asking. How could they if it is not their specialty? Occasionally, some selfish or unethical people may knowingly and intentionally pressure someone to violate ethical standards for political or monetary gain.

We always face the danger of unintended consequences resulting from our work. It is part of being at the forefront of a dynamic, ever-changing, innovative discipline. The first step in successfully dealing with ethical dilemmas is knowing they will happen and deciding today, before they do, who you are and how you will manage them.

The next step, according to Bill Franks, is to be sure of this fact even before you start working for an organization. Make sure, even in the interview, that the organization has a formal process for ethics review and that systems are in place when you are faced with a dilemma. Think deeply before joining an organization that does not take ethics seriously enough to have a formal process to manage it.

Dr. Julie Swann shared some advice on how to manage ethical dilemmas if they arise:

- **Delay.** See if you can postpone giving an answer or agreeing to a given approach. This delay gives you time to think and explore options.
- **Mentor.** Avoid going it alone! Seek out a competent mentor for advice, one who is removed from the emotion and politics of the situation. Check whether you both see the situation the same way and listen for alternative perspectives and ideas for managing the dilemma effectively.
- **Identify the real problem.** Try to identify the real problem and suggest ways to solve it. Well-meaning leaders will be open to exploration. They do not want to violate ethical principles. They just need a problem solved. Use your skills to suggest ways to ethically meet their needs and sidestep the dilemma.
- **Escalate.** Escalate to those above you for help, if necessary. If there is a formal process for ethical review, now is the time you need it most.
- **Think long term.** Avoid sacrificing your values or who you are for short-term gain. Focus on the long-term, know why you are here and who you want to be. This attitude will give you the strength you need to see you through the dilemma to the other side.

In addition to following these best practices, I highly recommend reading Bill Franks's book *97 Things About Ethics Everyone in Data Science Should Know*[4] before you find yourself in an ethical dilemma.

Ethical Issues in Action-Centric Analytics

In Task 1: The Problem, we introduced the DAD analytics framework with a focus and discussion on action-centric analytics. I believe action-centric analytics has the potential to do amazing good, as my former assistant Jennifer Kass-Green and I wrote about in this article[5] entitled, "Life Coach: Using Big Data and Analytics to Facilitate the Attainment of Life Goals." It describes how to use analytics to help attain our own goals by nudging ourselves to action to achieve our dreams.

My friend Olu Ogunlela, founder and CEO of Liferithms, independently decided to use action-centric analytics to do something similar with users on this company's platform. In our book interview, Ogunlela shared how they would first listen to and document the user's goals, not the company's goals. Then the user would share their data with the system either through direct data entry and/or linking it to smart devices such as a smartphone or watch that would share data.

The system would then analyze the data, looking at how good it is, leading users toward the goals they set for themselves. Next, the system would develop a prescription, updated regularly based on data, nudging their behavior at effective times to encourage action toward their goals. Liferithms would also plan to use modeling and feedback data to see what type of nudging worked better for different customers, all with the objective of helping users meet their goals. Figure 7.1 shows a screenshot of the current version of the Liferithms application.

Figure 7.1 Liferithms Life Coaching Application
Source: Screenshots courtesy of Olu Ogunlela.

The goal is a level beyond what companies such as Fitbit and Apple are doing now, and also more holistic in nature. For example, Apple does let you set a fitness goal, like how many calories to burn a day. This goal is based generally on best practice guidelines or average movements and it does nudge you to move more. I personally rely on my watch every day. What is different between these companies and the life coach algorithm Liferithms is developing is the focus on the users' intermediate and end goals, balanced between many good goals they have for their whole life and prioritized by them. They then use these prioritized goals with customized nudging to help users reach the balance they are seeking. None of us can achieve every good goal for our life at the same time. Sorting out priorities is key, and that is where guidance comes in. Not everyone has the same goals, and goals often change over the times and seasons of people's lives.

Goals have trade-offs, too, and pushing to maximize all of them at the same time misses the priorities of the individual goals. Liferithms hopes to customize models to generate individually tailored goals, versus an overly generic goal prescribed to everyone, and gives customers custom coaching toward their own personalized definition of success. The key is that guidance is used to help direct someone to the actions they need to more effectively meet their objectives, with data, models, and feedback to support them to achieve those goals and objectives.

There are, however, many uses of this type of control-focused analytics that could also be considered morally questionable. Consider a story in the *Financial Times*[6] that showed how Amazon was using this type of action analytics to control nearly every detail of their employees' lives and how that affected their happiness and job satisfaction.

A later national news reports in *Time*[7] magazine shared similar stories of Amazon warehouse employees claiming they felt like they were feeling dehumanized and managed like robots. The goals here seemed similar to having robots do the task. It is not just Amazon. Many firms are using control mechanisms implemented with analytics in similar ways. Even Google falls in this category with their so-called ghost workers who work to manually improve search results. The ghost workers are fighting for rights, including more autonomy and equal pay, according to a recent NPR report.[8] Also consider Uber drivers who are campaigning for better working conditions and pay.

Obviously the issues are complex and not likely to be solved in a few short paragraphs here. Still, leaders should be aware of the potential benefits for appropriate uses such as the life coach example, and the risks like those posed in recent news reports. The issues of how, where, and when to use control analytics should be considered very carefully and care should be taken to avoid the dangers of a society as outlined by George Orwell in the book *1984*.[9] Eventually, most types of tasks these analytics control are likely to be taken over by machines, which could be a mixed blessing depending on how jobs and economic wealth distributions are handled in the future.

Security

Part of doing no harm is taking actions to protect others from harm. Even if you do not do that negative action yourself, you can still be held liable if negligent in your duty to protect others through quality information security practices. A deep dive into information security is beyond the scope of this book, but here are a few thoughts from our experts to get your started:

- **Keep leaders engaged.** Steve Stone, who led the transformation of Lowes into a data-driven firm with rapidly accelerating growth as their CIO, reminds us how closely people follow their leaders, which is also very true when it comes to information security. If leaders do not take it seriously, no one else will either. Chris Pitts, an information security manager for TIAA, points out that members of the board of directors should understand and embrace security principles to exercise their duties to protect the organization.

- **Manage cloud storage risk.** Storing data in the cloud has many advantages. Most of them are well known by business leaders. But for certain types of data, there can also be risks. Take care before posting your most proprietary and sensitive data anywhere outside of your control.

- **Access control.** Although the data should be available to people in places that can support the business, it does not mean all data should be available at all times to everyone. Take care to ensure the right data is available to the right people at the right time and place.

- **Aggregate data identification.** Even after taking great steps to de-identify data from unique attributes, when more data is combined with additional information, it is often possible for that data to become uniquely identifiable. There are a few well-known stories about data anonymized and released by big tech companies such as AOL, Netflix, and others. People found themselves in a lot of trouble over it because cyber sleuths were able to piece together enough de-identified data to uniquely identify individuals. Exercise great care in protecting and reasoning even when data has been anonymized.

- **Ensure proper data classification.** Albert Owusu, graduate of the Federal Chief Information Officers' Competencies Program, stressed the importance of properly classifying data to prioritize the proper security measures. Without classification, it is hard to know the most efficient and effective way to deploy your security assets using the most appropriate data security practices and resources matched to the needs.

- **Consider synthetic data.** Sometimes your models can benefit from synthetic data. This approach is generally not used to replace secondary data. Rather, it is used to enhance the quality of your current data by filling in the under-represented portion of what you are trying to model with substantially similar data to produce more accurate models with partially synthetic data. This approach can improve model accuracy and robustness and reduce bias by giving a full range of what is being modeled, even rare events. Fully synthetic data can also be used to model legally sensitive or ethically sensitive data while protecting privacy. Bill Franks talks about synthetic data in a blog post for IIA,[10] which I found quite insightful.

- **Upgrade to AI.** Chris Pitts shared how security is not just about compliance anymore. It is also about using analytics and AI to actively protect and monitor data security. Attacks happen faster than humans can possibly respond in today's digital world. If you are not using AI tools to help guard your data, you are out-of-date and vulnerable.

AI, quantum computing, and analytics are evolving very rapidly and are likely to accelerate in that growth. As I finish the last few edits to this book, many concerns regarding ethical and employment changes related to tools such as ChatGPT have captured public attention. I am actually preparing to do a TED-style talk on this topic for regional executives next week to help them prepare. I am also reading articles about how quantum computing can pose a serious threat to traditional security measures in the near future, such as the article[11] by the respected consulting firm Oliver Wyman. I wish I knew the answer to these likely threats, but I do know it is important to be mindful of them and prepare for their likely impacts.

ANALYTICS FOR GOOD

There are many inspiring experts profiled in this book whom I have personally seen do good business, but who also walk away from opportunities that were not a win for both the other side and society because they also consider society as a whole, focusing on win-win-wins for their firm, their business partners, and society. Max Rünzel, Libor Cech, Polly Mitchell-Guthrie, Dr. Terry Rawls, Dr. Dan Cohen-Vogel, and Patrick Getzen stand out as inspiring examples to me in this regard. No doubt I missed many others who deserve to be here. The point is, you can and should not only run a good business for you and your clients/customers but also for the planet and society as a whole.

There is a difference between deploying self-serving analytics, regardless of morality and ethics, and doing analytics for good. Everywhere we look today we see both, but those who have succeeded in scaling faster globally generally appear to be more on the self-serving side, unfortunately. Of course there must be benefits to the organization. Even Steven Covey, author of *7 Habits for Highly Effective People*, is fond of saying "no margin, no mission." It must be profitable to deploy.

What concerns me is not that organizations are making a profit with analytics. I am actually grateful they are as it advances the field. What does concern me is that too many of the algorithms I see deployed at scale across the globe today are making a profit at the expense of society or the planet. A few may be that way intentionally. But I truly believe most were done carelessly, without really thinking about the impact, or, more troubling, once the negative impact was realized or observed, leaving or putting it in place because they love the profits more, even knowing the damage it is doing to society.

Dr. Bill Disch, of DataRobot, said it best: "You can make money without hurting people." This statement embodies the philosophy of do no harm embedded in the INFORMS Ethical Guidelines discussed previously, and is the minimal responsibility of every analyst and organization. I know Disch lives by this principle and am grateful for it. I also know Disch would say, and has said, that it is not enough. It is just the minimum we need to do.

The next principle of ethics is to "seek to do good." To create the society we would all want to live in, and not destroy the one we live in now, we must not only avoid the harm, but actively engage the good. I dream of seeing AI and data analytics deployed mindfully to not only help the organization but also to improve society in meaningful and scalable ways, while also making a profit.

This aim must be true for analytics if we want it to last. We are already starting to see a societal backlash from consumers and governments tired of the abuses of analytics and their impact on society. Whether they were initially done intentionally, the impact is real. Couple that with the often perceived uneven distribution of its benefits and the widespread negative impact of its many shortcomings, which are quickly amplified by the press. The public is naturally in turmoil on this issue. I fear that if we do not take steps to actively embrace the good while policing the bad, we will soon find ourselves in a very dark place.

Lindsay Marshall, data scientist and director of data and analytics at Gilbane Building Company, expressed concern for a firm's longevity if they engage in unethical practices. We have already seen a few high-profile analytics organizations, such as Cambridge Analytica, rightly forced into bankruptcy when their patently unethical, self-serving analytics practices were revealed. A few have even called for a moratorium of advances in AI and data analytics research and development. For the longevity of not only our organizations but perhaps even the profession, we must avoid doing harm and, even better, embrace the good by using analytics responsibly.

In addition to some of the harm being done, there is the sheer waste of talent of some of the most brilliant minds of our age working on trivial, but well-paid, tasks. Instead, society should steer these brilliant minds to focus on tasks that really matter and can improve society, more than optimizing ad clicks. Patrick Getzen, who recently retired as the founding chief data and analytics officer for Blue Cross Blue Shield of North Carolina, reminds us that we all have limited time and we should do something useful with it. Sure we can make money. But if that is the only benefit, what will we really have accomplished in the end? To do more, we should think carefully about the incentives we have in place for our organizations and analytics, and make sure they are aligned in a way that creates and supports the type of society we want to live in.

I wish I knew all the answers, but I do not. Yet, I do know this: I have spent decades studying the concept of value congruence, which is what happens when the values of those in society do or do not align with the organizations in which they interact. When those values align, trust is created and people share more information and pay even more for products and services. When values do not, trust is destroyed, people guard their data more closely, and they avoid or minimize commercial entanglements.[12]

I am sure it can explain at least part of the mechanism and cause for the longevity issue raised at the start of this section, one that if not addressed will likely get worse.

I also know, as my colleague at Arizona State University, Matt Sopha, wisely reminded everyone in a recent department meeting that all of us, working together, are smarter than any of us working alone.

I believe if we apply the principles of doing mindful AI, as outlined here by Ahmer Inam, currently chief data and artificial intelligence officer at Relanto, following protocols for responsible data science developed by Grant Fleming, a senior data scientist from Elder Research, and inspired by the case studies of people doing their best to do analytics for good, we can begin to make progress on this important issue. I also know if all of us work together to practice responsible and ethical analytics, we can leverage the part of us that is smarter than any one of us to make a difference in and with analytics.

Mindful AI

Ahmer Inam offered some advice on designing our analytics mindfully and being aware of our analytics, what is going on in them, and how they affect the world. Inam defines mindfulness as "the mindset of being aware and purposeful of the intentions and emotions we hope to evoke through an artificially intelligent experience that augments human potential." This mindfulness rests on three pillars:[13]

- **Being human-centered.** Having end-to-end, human-in-the-loop integration in the AI solution development life cycle, from concept, discovery, data collection, model testing, and training to scaling for lovable experiences and products with measurable outcomes
- **Being trustworthy.** Being transparent and explainable in how the AI model is trained, how it works, and why the analytics team recommends the outcome
- **Being responsible.** Ensuring that AI systems are free of bias and are grounded in ethics and being mindful of how, why, and where data is created and the ethical impact on downstream AI systems

I believe these three principles of mindful analytics, outlined by Inam, can go a long way in helping us pay more attention to our analytics' impact on the world. Having humans in the development loop who understand the entire process and love the results can help identify and repair potential issues. Having a trustworthy, transparent process with explainable models we can understand and verify will increase trust. Having a transparent, responsible process to ensure our systems are free of bias and grounded in ethics is the right thing to do, which is where we turn to next.

Responsible Data Science

I recently had the pleasure of meeting Grant Fleming at a recent INFORMS conference. Fleming gave what I found to be a very thoughtful presentation on how to do responsible data science and is coauthor of a book[14] by the same name. Fleming was kind enough to share the slides with me and review my summary of the framework for responsible data science that Fleming helped develop. Here are the key points of Fleming's presentation:

- **Current AI development process is flawed.** AI approaches are very useful but flawed. They fail in unexpected ways and propagate bias by design.
- **Unintentional harm results.** Our default best practices for building AI models are not enough to avoid causing unintentional harms to others and to ourselves.
- **We can do better.** We can make specific organizational, procedural, and technical changes to mitigate some (but not all) of this risk of harm.
- **Responsible AI improves performance.** These changes oftentimes directly support the business/analysis objective and are useful regardless of whether the application is high risk. Doing responsibly equals doing better.
- **There are new challenges ahead.** Large language models (LLMs), such as ChatGPT and other generative AI approaches, have high potential and high risk of harm.

Fleming identifies three main causes of bias in our analytical models, followed by the harms that can come from them, all of which leaders should know to ensure the causes and harms are addressed by the analytics team.

Causes of Bias

- **Pre-existing data and views.** If models are built on data or views we have acquired from the world we live in, they will perpetuate and amplify the benign and harmful biases of that world. Synthetic data, discussed previously, may provide a partial mitigation strategy.
- **Statistical bias.** Some statistical models may miss important relationships in the data or be off target in a consistent direction. This situation should be carefully tested by the analytics team.
- **Differential performance.** Models may perform differently on different pockets of data representing different groups, and not give similar results across different groups represented in the data. This occurrence can sometimes be attributed to sparse data in those categories, bias in data collection, or other hopefully unintentional causes. It is important for executives and business process owners to be aware that overall performance is not necessarily the same as performance in a class or group within the sample. Testing should look for differential performance bias on important groups.

Harms of Bias

- **Intentional harm.** This type of bias occurs when models are built with the intention of causing harm, including for war, hacking, political, or commercial purposes. This is a sad reality for the analytics profession. An example is when Epic Games was fined $520 million for abuses of children's data for monetary gains.[15]

- **Allocative harm.** This type of bias occurs when an individual or group is harmed due to biased decision-making, such as from one of the causes. An example is when people of color receive different medical recommendations for the same symptoms.

- **Representational harm.** This type of bias refers to the negative impact of stereotypes being coded in the data or analytics process, which the algorithm perpetuates. An example is when women, particularly Asian women, have been overly sexualized in imagery made by generative AI.

- **Privacy harm.** This type of bias refers to the negative impacts on people and groups that can be caused by the unauthorized or inappropriate collection, use, or sharing of data. An example is someone being flagged in a facial recognition system for data that should not have been collected.

Fleming went on to share a process for the analytics team to follow when developing analytics models, believing it reduces bias and harm. It takes the core model most of us use in going from Data → Model → Prediction, and expands it by including ethical social factors that should be considered on the front and back ends. This process focuses on reducing or mitigating the causes of bias in the data and then reducing harm that could result from prediction before the model goes into implementation. Figure 7.2 illustrates Fleming's model.

Although I do not believe executives and business process owners need to understand the process and technology to fix these biases and harms, I do believe they need to be aware of them and mindful in their analytics approach to ensure that biases and harms are adequately addressed by their technical team members and that the approaches have been tested and validated to mitigate them in analytics. Fleming's framework for responsible data science seems like a good place to start. Failing to address bias and harm, even if imperfect, is the wrong way to manage these risks.

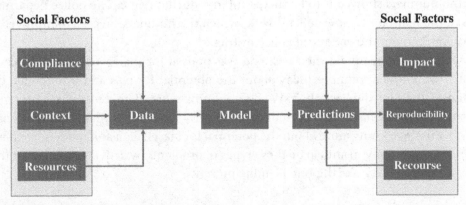

Figure 7.2 Responsible Analytics Development Framework
Source: Illustration courtesy of Grant Fleming.

In addition to Fleming's model, I want to add a couple thoughts of my own:

- **Explainability.** It is much easier to verify models that are explainable are doing the right thing. When possible, I advise using models that are explainable and interpretable.

- **Good inside hypothesis.** Many, but not all, of the problems with bias stem from imperfect data collected in an imperfect world full of historical biases and imperfections. Any model built on imperfect data will likely have bias in it. To the extent possible, all Pleines's minimal viable team members and their supporters should try to collect and develop data that represents the fair and just world we want to live in. This goal could be achieved by supplementing or augmenting an organization's data with synthetic or other data. Though not perfect, the more the data reflects our desired future, meaning the data is "good inside," the easier it is to build a model compatible with that future.

- **Testing.** Testing for biases, as Fleming recommends, often reveals it, which is the first step to fixing it. Sam Volstad shared the following example from his experience testing for bias in our banking system. Banks use fair-lending models to check for disparate impact of protected classes. So predictive models are built using protected classes as dummy variables (i.e., yes or no membership marker for a given class) and if they show up as significant, then there is said to be a disparate impact and the bank can be considered noncompliant.

Doing good analytics to make a positive impact on the world does not happen by accident. It takes mindfulness and dedication to get it right. Hopefully, the principles in this chapter will help. Even when you set out to do good in the world, it may not always turn out that way.

For example, Albert Owusu discussed a project from many years ago with this goal: to improve policing by predicting where crime was most likely to happen and when, and then deploying officers to that area to prevent crimes before they happen. Owusu said the numbers showed it to be successful in reducing crime. The police department praised the team for their excellent work, which the numbers suggested improved the safety for many in the enhanced police district.

Although the team did their best and was praised for their work and a successful project, we know a lot more today about the potential for bias and unintended consequences than we did back then. We do not know what, if any, biases or unintended consequences may have been present in those early models, however unintentionally. But now that we know more about the potential for biased data and models, we have a greater responsibility to anticipate these types of problems by actively looking for them using a methodology like the one Fleming presents.

Analytics for Good Case Studies

My little brother, Joshua Cazier, a senior executive at Qualtrics who is quoted many times in this book, likes to say that we should actively take risks to improve the world to make it a better place. Some have said if we are not helping make other people's lives better, we are wasting our own, and that working to improve the world is just the right thing to do. Many others have echoed this sentiment: we should seek to do good in the world with the life we have and help those who need it most with the time and talents we have.

We already shared several stories of people taking risks to improve the world to help others, including Max Rünzel with HiveTracks, Olu Ogunlela with Liferithms, and Libor Cech in sustainable lumber. Here are a couple of short stories I saved for the end.

Dr. Dan Cohen-Vogel: Financial Aid

Dr. Dan Cohen-Vogel, principal at DataWorks Partners, shared an inspiring story of how his team used analytics to collect student data, tax data, and student data from other sources. By integrating these many diverse datasets, they were able to identify thousands of students who were eligible for, and entitled to, financial aid they were not receiving. The students were then able to get the financial aid that had been made available to them by law. This project helped students succeed in their studies while making their lives a little easier.

I wanted to share this story first because Cohen-Vogel stresses that all the uses were very simple analytics. No machine learning algorithms or generative AI were needed for this service. The point is, you can do good, or bad, with whatever tools you have now. It is not about fancy math, but commitment and mindfulness to ensure you make a positive impact, as Cohen-Vogel did on this and many other instances I have witnessed.

Sam Volstad: Breast Cancer

Sam Volstad works for a national advisory and accounting firm now. But once upon a time, Volstad worked for me and, along with a few other researchers passionate about this topic, led the analysis. Volstad helped analyze data scraped from the web for stories of women writing about their breast cancer ordeal. We used a relatively new, mixed-methods methodology, including clustering and sentiment analysis, to provide insights into the breast cancer experience, coming from women's own voices, and capture the meaning behind these health narratives. Because breast cancer has controllable and uncontrollable elements, the results suggest ways to improve both kinds of support. Significantly, better understanding of these difficult health experiences greatly improves interactions and outcomes for patients and their families. We were able to publish the results in a peer-reviewed journal[16] to help get the word out about what we learned.

David Houser: Reverse Logistics

David Houser, chief revenue officer for ReverseLogix, shared efforts to help make the world more sustainable by using analytics and supply chain management for reverse logistics, which is what happens to returns and products when the buyers no longer want them. According to Houser, this is a $2 trillion challenge with close to 30% of online purchases being returned. This type of analytics, which fuels third-party logistics, not only helps returns but also can track carbon emissions and facilitate a second life for products (re-commerce and parts harvesting as examples to help with improving our focus on circular economy trends), improving sustainability, remanufactured electronics, and design for reuse from the start based on observed trends.

Jabari Myles: Traffic

Jabari Myles, now a senior data scientist at MetLife, shared a story about being part of an analytics project focused on improving traffic safety, when in a previous position. They used GIS mapping, traffic accident data, and shape algorithms to identify and prioritize the most hazardous intersections across the state, helping its department of transportation find and fix issues before people were hurt in accidents. I think we would find driving a little easier if all states did more of this type of work.

Chris Pitts: Security

Chris Pitts is a proven information systems security leader with a true service heart from time spent in the military, a heart focused on protecting others. Pitts did not start out in analytics, but shared with me the type and number of algorithms they deploy and use daily to protect us all from those who wish to steal from us, take our data, or harm our country.

BEING RESPONSIBLE FOR OUR ANALYTICS FUTURE

As much as I love all aspects of predictive analytics, when it comes to something as important as our future, our children's and grandchildren's future, I do not want to predict it. I hope we will go a step beyond prediction to building a prescriptive future, a future where we mindfully create the world we want instead of waiting passively to see what happens. Our future is too important for a wait-and-see approach. Indeed, inaction will be harder to reverse. It is our responsibility to guide our future in the right direction.

Here are a few ideas I think we, as a society, should do to make the world a better place and what we should monitor to make sure we, as a society, are moving in a desirable direction and take corrective action if needed.

Collect Data for Good

We have an abundance of data, mostly commercial, some government, some relevant and useful, most not. I wish that we, together, would put more thought into what is collected and used, and what is not collected, with a focus on using highly relevant data, not just for our businesses but to make the world a better place. Let us collect data, not just to make what we are already doing better but to do new things, things we have never done before, more effectively. Let highly relevant data become the foundation for the future we desire.

We can never analyze data we do not have. Without data, decisions are made based on people's politics, personal agendas, and opinions. These decisions tend to preserve the existing power structures, perhaps some we need but others that are harming us or at least not helping in the way they should or could be. It is difficult to know the best path into the future. It is difficult to know if what we are doing now is even effective or the best approach. Yet, if we do not collect and analyze the data about how our actions or inactions are affecting the world, we will never truly know if our actions are working as intended or needed.

A few years ago I worked with a few friends, Max Rünzel, whom you met in this book, and Dr. James Wilkes, the original founder of HiveTracks. Wilkes and I flew to Rome for a conference at the UN Food and Agriculture Organization (FAO). We gave several presentations on collecting, analyzing, and processing data regarding bees and pollinators, which are crucial to securing our food supply and supporting biodiversity.

By this time, I had been leading the International Working Group on Bee Data Standardization for a while, and knew the importance of collecting and harmonizing the world's data for these pollinators. In fact, I had recently presented and testified to its importance to the European Parliament in Brussels and subsequently published this magazine article.[17] Momentum was starting to build for a concerted effort to support collecting and standardizing this data.

That week in Rome, Wilkes and I had the idea to develop what became the world bee count, an effort to take a global census of bees, bats, butterflies, and all pollinators, and the flowers they visit. We saw this data as crucial for establishing a baseline of pollinator and biodiversity data for our natural world. We shared the idea with Max Rünzel, who was working for the UN FAO in Rome at the time, and who agreed to co-lead the project. The excitement was real and growing. We knew the importance of this data and believed it would generate momentum. Many partners agreed to support and fund the project and wanted to partner with us to use and build on the data.

Wilkes led the public service application development, friends at the analytics firm SAS led the mapping and public visualization functions that were displayed globally, and others sponsored and supported the project in a thousand ways. This collaborative effort helped us meet the short timeline to design, build, and do a global launch in just a few short months in time for World Bee Day.

Rünzel and I had the honor of giving a keynote address as part of the UN celebrations of World Bee Day to kick off the six-week data collection window. With additional supporters such as Apimondia, Flow Hive, HiveTracks, The World Bee Project, and SAS, we were able to quickly get the word out and collected more than 20,000 pollinator images from all over the globe, quadrupling our goal. We hope to do another world bee count again to track changes in our pollinators and environment over time and share the results and learnings with the world.

This project was a great proof of concept that showed the readiness, maybe even the eagerness of the general population to participate in the task to crowdsource the collection of data that has a social or environmental purpose. Even more broadly, I believe it shows people recognize the need for data that can be used for good to be collected, analyzed, and freely shared, and they are willing to help.

The fact that so many citizen scientists are willing to help gather and share valuable data for good is really gratifying to me, because I believe and know with every part of who I am, that there is relevant data we do not have that could be used to make the world a much better place if collected and made available for analysis. We are not just missing data about bees and pollinators, but data about many relevant and important things. I will share just a few examples here:

- **Mountain water.** In many parts of the world, people live in drought-stricken areas and some have too much water and worry about flooding. Companies such as Airborne Snow Observatories[18] are using planes and lasers to get a more accurate estimate of the water in the mountain snowpack, helping us better manage our water resources and flooding risk as well as monitoring changing climate trends.

- **Global health.** The World Health Organization just released a dataset called the Health Inequality Data Repository,[19] with the goal of measuring health outcomes and their inequalities around the world so we can more clearly see how to prioritize and focus our efforts to help those most in need.

- **Gene bank.** I was recently asked to advise and consult on a project led by the global, nonprofit agricultural research organization CGIAR. The project was for the development and deployment of a global gene bank for agriculture crops that stores not only the seeds but also the genetic profile of the world's most important crops. This data will be helpful in improving and securing our food supply, especially in the face of geopolitical risks and climate change.

- **UN Sustainable Development Goals.** The 17 United Nations Sustainable Development Goals[20] are the world's most agreed-on goals for making the world a better place. Perhaps they do not include everything that is relevant or prioritize the goals the way some of us may prefer, but they are the best road map we have today to guide us to the data we need to build the future most of us desire. Any data that helps us more efficiently get there is likely relevant and useful to collect.

There is a famous quote attributed to the great management guru Peter Drucker that says, "You can't manage what you can't measure." Most people in businesses or governments would agree with this sentiment, and it matches my experience, too. One would hope and think that governments and organizations worldwide would be laser-focused on collecting this type of data and using that data to improve our planet.

Some are, and I am grateful to them. However, there are also many others who do not want this data collected, who block efforts to collect this type of data, who do not want things to be managed better, who are entrenched in the current power structure. Some do not want to leave their comfort zone and relinquish their biases. Others do not want the truth known because it may damage their wealth, power, or prestige. Unfortunately, I have seen firsthand when leaders conveniently turn blind eyes, preferring not to know or call attention to humanity's problems, and even some that intentionally hide truth with misinformation and misdirection.

I see and read about how lawmakers and regulators, pushed by lobbyists, have even outlawed collecting data on such important issues as gun safety, climate change or risk, diversity, or inequalities in an effort to avoid change and responsible management, preferring to keep the knowledge hidden to preserve the status quo where they and their supporters have what they want and prefer to avoid responsibility and accountability for their actions and inactions. We can and should have healthy debates on all of these issues. But if we do not collect real, relevant, unbiased data about these important issues, there will be debates based on opinions and personal benefits, instead of debates with facts. This is how we will fail to build a better, more sustainable future.

To manage our world better, we need to follow Drucker's axiom and measure it. These measurements need to be focused on fair, accurate, and unbiased data and analysis done with skill and integrity, but they must be collected, shared, and opened for analysis by all. We should collect and freely share this data for the most important issues of today and tomorrow.

For this reason, a few friends and I have started a peer-reviewed journal, *Data and Analytics for Good*,[21] focused on collecting relevant, high-quality data that can make the world a better place, and sharing it freely with anyone who wishes to use or analyze it, whatever their politics or preexisting opinions. The goal is to change the debate in our society to one of fact and quality analytics, to help us use our judgment, as a society, to chart the best, most promising path forward, wherever that takes us. We are still getting started, and need data, people, and support. You can engage here: http://dataforgoodjournal.org/.

Use Data for Good

As important as it is to collect data for good, it is also important to see that it is used for good and abuse is avoided. Here are a few ideas to think about related to using data for good:

- **Data sharing.** Most companies have an incentive to keep most of their data private, as they should. However, some data, especially data that can be used for societal good, should be shared. Governments, nonprofits, non-government organizations, academics, and others have even more reasons to share. By pooling, aggregating, and enriching this type of data, a lot of global good could be achieved.
- **Interoperability.** Even when organizations such as hospitals have valuable data that could be used to improve society, it cannot be aggregated and shared effectively because it is not standardized or interoperable, meaning it cannot be

easily moved to a new system in a way that preserves its meaning and value. If we better identified this relevant data, and then standardized it on formats and systems, it could be shared and used much more effectively.

■ **Data privacy.** As important as it is to collect and use relevant data for the public good, it is also important to protect the public from data abuses and abusers. There should be more privacy controls and protections for our data, especially for data collected on children and the most vulnerable populations among us. Some of the data I see companies secretly collecting and selling about us is very troubling. Even some of the data our own government offices sell about us can be concerning.

■ **Data ownership.** I am not sure I believe, as a few have advocated, that we should own all the data about us and have full control over it. But I do believe that we should have a say in some of it and how it is used, that we should be protected from abuses, and that if there is a benefit from someone using our data we should share in that benefit.

■ **Data forgetting.** Some data should be forgotten. Data that does not build a better future or that perpetuates biases from the past should be gradually and thoughtfully replaced with data that can build the future we, as a society, desire, instead of perpetuating yesterday's problems.

■ **Data design.** I believe we should actively design and curate good data, data that can improve our planet. Much of it real, some of it synthetic or simulated, but all of it should be thoughtfully created, curated, and made available for analytics.

■ **Data derivatives.** Generative AI can now create works of art or music with ease, based on the data of works created by the original artists, often collected without permission and with no shared benefit. These data derivatives sometimes harm the original creators by cannibalizing their market or destroying reputations. I believe when these derivative works are clearly in the style of the original artist that some of the value derived from them should be shared with the artists who created the original work.

■ **Data benefits.** Many benefits are derived from using analytics, and more are to come. There are also risks. The question is, how should the benefits be divided and the risks shared? Today, it seems, most of the benefits go to very few and many of the risks get transferred to society. Unfair sharing of risks and rewards will lead to greater destabilization of our society and the world in which we all live. We should think clearly about what is best and seek to move in that direction in a way that is fair for all.

I wish I had more answers to these issues, but I do not. I do know that there are many today who practice and scale unethical data and analytics for their own self-serving reasons at society's expense. Some may be well meaning and unintentional, but there are serial abusers, too, who only care about themselves.

Just because data may be useful to them does not make it relevant to building the society most want. Relevance should be symbiotic and help all parties, not one at the expense of others. There is a proverb I think about often that says "if you never think about yourself, who will? If you only think about yourself, what are you?" Of course organizations should think about their own needs, but that should not be the only thing they think about if we are to protect and build a better society, which is the first duty in our INFORMS ethical guidelines.

These issues and more can be addressed only if we, collectively, are more data literate and transparent in our practices. It is not just that the executives and business process owners are literate, which we need for organizations to succeed with analytics, but that the majority of the public is literate about these issues and can intelligently contribute to the discussion and make informed decisions about these issues. To create a better community living in harmony and benefiting from analytics, this more broadly defined notion of data literacy must eventually exist.

I actually have great hope for this possibility as many of those I see and work with regularly on campus in this younger, digitally native generation seem to be more aware and mindful of these issues than those of us who grew up without the widespread use of these technologies. Perhaps they will be able to help us find the right balance and set up a society that is more responsible with analytics and technology than we have today. I sincerely hope that is the case.

Data Minimalism

Task 3: The Data introduced the idea of data minimalism as a way to improve focus, data quality, and relevance, which improves the realized value from your data. Data minimalism can also help us do more responsible analytics by avoiding unethical and risky data collection and use practices. If you do not collect, store, or use inappropriate or risky data, it cannot be abused or irresponsibly exploited.

For example, Dr. Sherrill Hayes, director of the School of Data Science and Analytics at Kennesaw State University, likes to talk about the "science" of phrenology and has trinkets on a desk and bookshelf reminding people of the time when phrenology was very popular as a science-like discipline. Hayes even wrote a chapter about it in Bill Franks's book about data science ethics,[22] which I highly recommend. Hayes gave me permission to share an example and some of the lessons from this book.

You may recall that phrenology is the study of how the structure of the skull could be measured to then explain or predict a person's various attributes, including the potential for criminal behavior, just from these measurements. These phrenologists were very disciplined about collecting all kinds of measurement data of skulls and predicting the behavior, personality, intelligence, and success of people with those shapes. It very much appeared to be a scientific-like activity based on the collection of high-quality data and the application of scientific methods. Figure 7.3 shows a rendering of the different parts of the head and how they were believed to be related to various behaviors.

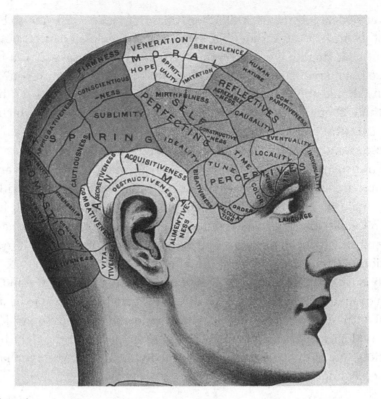

Figure 7.3 Phrenology
Source: https://www.britannica.com/topic/phrenology.

However, it was almost all a lie. Perhaps not an intentional one, as I am sure many scientists were well meaning and sincere in their efforts, if not in the outcomes that often fueled racial stereotypes and oppression. The reality is that the data they were collecting on skull shape and size was completely irrelevant to the intelligence and behaviors they were trying to explain, even though it masqueraded as a science. Even more, the whole idea behind the collection of that data was harmful to society, with some of it being very clearly racially motivated.

When anyone shares data with me that has confidential or protected information in it, or even data that could be abused, it immediately raises my anxiety and reduces my productivity as I shift resources to protect that data instead of focusing on analyzing it. Most of the time, the protected or sensitive data is not even relevant or necessary for the goal of the project, and I would have much preferred to have never been given access to that data. Even if it were relevant, such as by improving predictions, it may be data that is illegal or unethical to use and perpetuate the worst of society's biases, such as in using racial data or its derivatives to predict crime or loan repayments. This is true even though this data may sometimes improve those predictions. Those committed to doing responsible analytics will seek to avoid even the potential for this type of abuse by carefully deciding what data is relevant and appropriate to collect and use before it is ever collected, stored, or analyzed.

In addition to the potential for inappropriate use within the organization, there are also the increased security risks associated with even having data, especially data not relevant to your goals and purpose. If you do not have the data, it cannot be hacked, stolen, or leaked. Apple Computer has been quite forward thinking in this regard by implementing end-to-end encryption for sensitive customer data that not even Apple can decipher.[23] Creating more trust in their practices has encouraged many customers to be more loyal to Apple and their products.

In an age where many organizations covertly collect every piece of data they possibly can and use it for ethically questionable purposes, I believe there is more value than ever in focusing on data relevance and practicing data minimalism, along with everything else.

Prepare for Emerging Technology

The world is changing faster than many could have imagined and seems to be accelerating in this change, driven in part by advances in technology. We do not know what impact these emerging technologies will have on the field of analytics or our society, but we do know they will have an impact and likely a very big one. It is too early to know how to effectively manage these changes, but we should watch them and measure their impact as they develop and are positioned to further affect both analytics and society.

There are many science fiction–type advances that many talk about, such as people and machines merging, AI taking over the universe in a singularity, when AI becomes smarter and more powerful than its creators, or other end-of-civilization scenarios. Although they make good movies and are interesting to contemplate, I choose to focus on emerging analytics technologies that are here, are proven, and we know can be used today for global impact, even if they have not yet been scaled. There are a few I have seen with my own eyes I believe will, in fact, change the world, and I hope for the better.

Citizen Data Science

Citizen data science is well on the way to reality. Dr. Wayne Thompson, retired chief data science officer for SAS, was an early pioneer in the development of self-service analytics for citizen data scientists. Thompson spent many years developing easier-to-use analytics tools at SAS, including a product named Aristotle, which would guide users through the analytics process and automate many tasks for them. Though Aristotle never made it to market, it was integrated into SAS Visual Analytics, which is a powerful business intelligence tool for data visualizations similar to Tableau. Tableau and Qualtrics are also well known for enabling self-service analytics, as does DataRobot.

The goal of these types of tools is to provide business analysts easy access to data visualizations, predictive modeling, and other advanced analytics techniques. These types of tools make data scientists more productive and analytics more accessible to citizen data scientists who have an analytics mindset without having advanced training in coding. With the right tools, they can help spread the analytics movement across the organization by harvesting much of the low-hanging fruit. This trend is beyond early stages and nearing maturity. This trend of engaging more citizen data scientists is likely to continue into the future, enabling analytics to be done at scale and more easily across organizations, if they have the right mindset and skills in knowing where and how to apply it.

Blockchain Technology

The world is already familiar, maybe even too familiar, with blockchain technology, what it is and how it has sometimes been abused. Setting these immature uses of the technology aside, it actually has the power to transform much of our society. Cecil John, an enterprise architect, is a visionary who believes in and writes about the power of blockchain to transform our world, making many positive changes. I strongly agree with him, if we use it the right way and avoid the abuses, that it can have a dramatically positive impact. Money and currency is only the tip of the iceberg to what this technology can do, especially when combined with analytics, creating synergies that can expand trust across industries and societies.

For example, a few friends and I, including Max Rünzel, showed that by combining analytics and blockchain together, we could create trust using a new method. By combining both analytics and blockchain technology, you can move beyond just the traditional immutability of blockchain technology to include analytical verification throughout the entire history of a product or service. Immutability is just one feature in this process.

We named this new method for creating trust *intrinsically verifiable trust* (IVT) in a recent peer-reviewed journal article[24] where we showed how the interplay between blockchain and analytics could do this to create a traceable honey supply chain. It included a pollen verification system with machine learning algorithms, geo-coded images of the hives, and weather and flower bloom monitoring, all from the very beginning of the season to verify the authenticity of the honey from the bee yard to the store shelf. As part of the pollen verification process, consumers could even check a sample of the honey with a smartphone and an inexpensive microscope attached to the phone.

Using analytics and blockchain technology together, we showed that trust could be created more robustly and durably than with either technology working alone. The idea is you can record information and transactions in a way that can prove they were real and represent events accurately, at least from the data and time it was recorded. This means that the classic methods of creating trust, through processes, institutions, and personal characteristics, are no longer the only way we have for creating trust. We can also do it at scale, in real time, and in a way that is intrinsically verifiable, indisputable, and provable beyond any reasonable doubt, as illustrated in Figure 7.4.

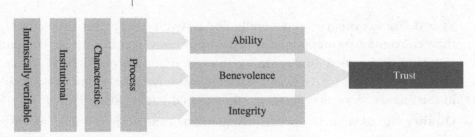

Figure 7.4 Extended Model for Trust Creation
Source: Graphic courtesy of Max Rünzel.

Already we have shown how this type of technology can be applied and used to increase the livelihoods of and empower marginalized groups by writing about it in this peer-reviewed journal article[25] that won the top research award for social impact at my last university. It showed how IVT, combined with analytics and relevant data collection, could work together to create trust and traceability in fraudulent markets.

Even so, there are many other applications we and others have only begun to think about. What if we lived in a world with near perfect trust and data? What would that mean for governments, record keeping, voting, identification, property records, auditing, sustainable supply chains, and traceability? What would it mean for developing a society based in harmony with our values?

I think we are only beginning to see what is possible. We are also likely blind to many of the risks. However, it is clear blockchain technology could change many things and should be watched with interest and steered toward a positive direction.

Quantum Technology

Although I have used and studied blockchain technology, and hold a Certified Blockchain Expert designation, I am newer to quantum technology. Still, I have observed others use it and seen its power. Therefore I interviewed Alexandra Koszegi, of the D-Wave Quantum Computing Company, to make sure I understood and correctly reported on this technology and what it could and could not do today. I also asked Koszegi to peer review this section of the book for quality control.

D-Wave is a clear leader in the field of quantum computing, with more than 20 years of testing and development of quantum computing technologies. It claims to be the largest and most well-known provider of off-the-shelf, commercially viable quantum computing solutions today that offers a hybrid approach by blending quantum and classic computer environments.

Because this book is intended for a broad audience and I promised in the introduction there would be no math, we will spare ourselves from diving into the mysterious world of quantum entanglements and abstract math and focus instead on what it can do and what problems it has proven it can solve today. The following highlights some of the main advantages of quantum or quantum hybrid computing compared to purely classic computing systems:

- **Speed.** These systems can generally find answers to complex problems faster than conventional computing for certain problems, if conventional computing can even find a good answer. In some cases, quantum can unlock previously intractable problems.[26] An example shared was solving an optimization problem in the finance sector that decreased time to solution by 90%.[27]

- **Quality.** In addition to speed, the quantum computers are able to cover a greater "solution space," which means looking in more places for optimal solutions to increase the likelihood of finding better quality answers that deliver better results than conventional systems.

- **Diversity.** Beyond speed and quality, the quantum environment provides a more diverse set of answers, instead of just one, giving you resilience and choice in picking how to best go forward.

- **Sustainability.** Quantum computing environments use significantly less energy than classic systems for the same problem. That is, they use about one-tenth the energy for equivalent FLOPS (floating point operations per second) of classic computing.

Next are a few actual use cases where quantum computing has already been effectively deployed to help us better visualize the possibilities:

- **Waste logistics.** D-Wave worked with Groovenauts and Mitsubishi to optimize truck routes for waste collection and CO_2 emissions, resulting in greater operational efficiencies while reducing environmental impact, creating better living conditions in cities.

- **Fraud detection.** Deloitte tested the quantum-hybrid approach for feature selection and ensemble learning compared to classic approaches in fraud detection. Quantum produced solutions that were comparable to or better than current state-of-the-art techniques. Additionally, their ensembles were more explainable, understandable, and traceable than traditional, deep-learning techniques.

- **Drug discovery.** The pharmaceutical industry has already used quantum computing for better protein sequences, a precursor to drug discovery, and quantum methods such as annealing, which are ideally suited for this type of work in life sciences.

These are a few of the use cases I reviewed. I am sure many more applications will be discovered and shared as the technology matures. Note that this technology is most useful with prescriptive analytics, where traditional computing environments struggle and quantum shines. Hopefully, as our organizations reach a higher level of analytics maturity, these technologies will be ready and viable to help us move to the next level at scale.

Anticipating Future Impacts

Before we conclude this chapter, it is worth taking a few moments to consider the impact of all of these and other technological advances on our society, and particularly those, like us, living in it now and in the future. I frequently get asked something along the lines of what does our future look like. My first answer is that no one really knows.

However, just like we use data from the past to predict the future in analytics, insights from lessons learned from the past could be the best guide to our future, with the caveat that they will be so only to the extent that the future looks like our past, just like we say with our data. Disclaimers aside, I do think it is interesting and important to understand that past, even if the future may be different. Because we do not have data from the future, the past is the only data we have, and we might as well use it, while understanding its limitations, to prepare as best as we can.

I prepared this graphic in Figure 7.5 in response to give a TED-style presentation at a regional chamber of commerce event focused on how ChatGPT and similar technologies will change business and labor practices, and thought it might be relevant to include here. I am not an economist, so this graphic is conceptual only and is not meant to be precise in exact monetary terms or timing. It is just used to communicate important macro-level trends in a way that a large audience can understand the future implications of these trends in a few minutes without time for deep discussion, digestion, distractions, or questions.

If we go back to the Middle Ages, we see that there was a very large wage gap between skilled and unskilled labor, much of it from skill level, some of it from political or other forces such as guilds, but regardless it was real. To be more relevant, I will leave out impacts from nobility and inherited wealth common at the time. The point is there was a significant gap between those who had desirable and marketable skills, such as the various tradespeople, carpenters, and craftspeople, and those who did not.

When we entered the Industrial Age, much of the knowledge of these skilled craftspeople was embedded into various manufacturing processes and scaled with machines that could do it thousands of times faster with less-skilled labor. Certainly there were

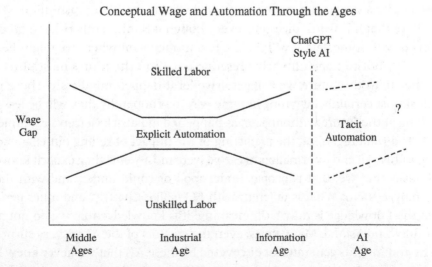

Figure 7.5 Wage and Automation Through the Ages

lapses in quality, but nonetheless products were good enough to be purchased at scale across the globe at more affordable prices.

This led to a drop in relative wealth and income for many highly skilled workers and shop owners, and an increase in income and wealth, over time, for unskilled and semiskilled workers and the greatest expansion of the middle class in world history. Yes, the relative wealth of the most-skilled workers dropped, in part because their chokehold on production by the guild was lessened, but mostly because the bottom level was able to rise up so far, reducing the wealth gap. It was a long, painful, process, but it did create a more equal society.

This expansion was based in part on the automation and scaling of explicit knowledge, that is, knowledge that could be explained, written down, or communicated, which was "programmed" or built into machines or tools that could then run it at an industrial scale. This movement from craft production to industrial-level manufacturing was only possible with this explicit automation, which enabled the transferring of skills to machines that automated and scaled many craft processes.

If you fast-forward to the Information Age, the age when data, not just explicit knowledge or skills, could be used more effectively since the 1970s or so, we see that there has again been a widening division in the wage gap between the lowest and highest skilled workers. Again, like before, some of this division is driven by political reasons, but most of it is for productivity increases in the most skilled. Namely, it enabled those skilled in working with information and knowledge to become incredibly more productive than before, increasing their knowledge. However, much of the decline for unskilled labor was from the automation and outsourcing of low skill while also enabling high-skilled employees to become incredibly more productive at processing and learning from information, further satisfying society.

As of today, there is a lot of discussion about large language models (LLMs) such as ChatGPT, which recently captured much of the world's attention. Although LLMs have been around for a while in many custom applications, the growth and utility of them has caused quite a stir among much of the public and many of our institutions. There is enough there that it is worth digesting, even though it is inherently risky to predict the future, even with some data. I will share a few thoughts on where we might be going, not to predict, but to hopefully help prescribe a path to the future most of us would want, rather than the future we will get if we let it happen mindlessly. These predictions will almost certainly be wrong in some way, but hopefully they will be less wrong than looking at the future without data, as happened in Patrick Getzen's example given in Task 3: The Data regarding the predicting of the impact of rolling out Obamacare.

In the Industrial and Information Ages, we were mostly encoding explicit knowledge. We took tasks that we, that is people, understood or could understand with the right tools to analyze them. What is different with LLMs like ChatGPT and other generative AI is that the knowledge is now tacit, meaning, it is knowledge that we do not already know or fully understand. Many times, even the creators of the AI are very surprised by the results and insights generated or discovered by these AIs that we never knew before. They enable us to move from replicating knowledge to creating or generating it in a way we could never do before at scale. Knowledge creation is very different from knowledge replication, and although the effect will likely be at least as broad and as impactful as it was for the Industrial and Information Ages, it is also harder to predict.

Here is what we know about how generative AI might affect our productivity and value added. In a not-yet peer-reviewed working paper, Noy and Zhang of MIT[28] report on one of the first controlled experiments of an earlier version of LLMs being used as a productivity tool for mid-level professional writing tasks, in which they found the impact of this knowledge generation was to uplift the low-skilled workers, making them nearly as productive as their more-skilled counterparts. It did not seem to affect the skill level of those who were *already* experts, which I believe is temporary, because more data from other experts and situations will undoubtedly help these workers improve, too, but maybe not by quite as much early on.

This increase in productive capacity affects value created in two clear ways. First, by making unskilled workers more productive faster it enables them to contribute almost immediately, just like the factories of the Industrial Age. Second, it makes the current experts more valuable, even if they themselves do not initially improve, because the generative AI needs them to build the intelligence to help the low-skilled workers. Therefore, both groups are able to add more value, low-skilled workers directly and high-skilled workers indirectly, to the organization.

Eventually, the experts may become less necessary, once the AI captures all that is known. Perhaps the low-skilled workers will also be automated away. Or maybe, just maybe, these increases in wealth can help us rebuild the middle class, as hoped for in this recent NPR news story,[29] and help us all live in a more equal and sustainable society, one where everyone is able to effectively contribute in their own unique way.

The ability to create knowledge has always been a factor in creating wealth at a massive scale across broad sections of our society. I am nearly certain there will be incredible wealth generated from AI that will affect us in profound and enduring ways, just like every age before. But there were also winners and losers in every age before, which means that if we want it to go in a responsible direction, for society, we should start now in deciding what should be done with the wealth that is generated. What happens next and how that wealth is shared is up to us and should not be left to chance or mindless allocation.

CHAPTER SUMMARY AND EXERCISES

Task 7: Summary

Doing analytics responsibly is a solemn duty we take on when we become analytics professionals. Our role as analytics professionals and even consumers is to help people make better decisions with data and analytics. If we want people to listen to us, to trust us, we must be worthy of that trust. It means at all times behaving ethically and with integrity in all we do. Even more, we have a duty not just to the organizations that hire us but also to our society and to the analytics profession.

From time to time, we may see an individual or organization use analytics irresponsibly. We often also see them suffer the consequences a short time later. To survive and thrive over the long term we need to be responsible in how we do analytics. This endeavor includes following our ethical duties, doing quality analytics, learning how to evaluate and respond to potential dilemmas, and going beyond the principle of do no harm by actively seeking to do good.

Additionally, we can make sure we are actively seeking to do good by using a mindful and responsible approach to AI and analytics, using methodologies designed to catch and mitigate bias, as espoused by Grant Fleming. We can collect and share data that can help guide us to solutions for many of humanity's ills. We can practice data minimalism to avoid risks associated with causing harm and distracted analytics. Finally, we can prepare for the future, not only to keep our skills up-to-date but also to think about how to use new and emerging technologies responsibly and ethically, to do good in society and the world we live in.

Task 7: Exercises

1. Describe the concept of being or becoming an informed skeptic and why it is important for all of us to be one.

2. Describe each of our duties to society, our organization, and the analytics profession. Share why you believe these ethical guidelines are important and how you intend to live by them.

3. Even if you do everything right, you will face ethical dilemmas. There are too many unknowns, unintended consequences, and self-serving individuals and organizations out there to avoid ethical dilemmas forever. The important thing is to watch and be mindful of them, avoid them where possible, and manage them when not. Share what you can and will do to manage ethical dilemmas as they arise across your career.

4. Discuss why it is important to not just avoid doing harm, but to actively seek to do good.

5. Discuss why and how we can and should effectively prepare for emerging technologies.

NOTES

1. Shvetank Shah, Andrew Horne, and Jaime Capellá, "Good Data Won't Guarantee Good Decisions," *Harvard Business Review* (April 2012).
2. Kashmir Hill, "How Target Figured Out a Teen Girl Was Pregnant Before Her Father Did," *Forbes* (February 16, 2012).
3. https://www.informs.org/About-INFORMS/Governance/INFORMS-Ethics-Guidelines
4. https://bill-franks.com/97-things-about-ethics-everyone-in-data-science-should-know.html
5. J. A. Cazier and J. A. Green, "Life Coach: Using Big Data and Analytics to Facilitate the Attainment of Life Goals," Hawaii International Conference on System Sciences HICSS-49, Grand Hyatt, Kauai, Hawaii (January 5–8, 2016).

6. Sarah O'Connor "Amazon Unpacked," *Financial Times* (February 8, 2013).

7. Emily Guendelsperger, "I Worked at an Amazon Fulfillment Center; They Treat Workers Like Robots," *Time* (July 18, 2019).

8. Dara Kerr, "Google's 'Ghost Workers' Are Demanding to Be Seen by the Tech Giant," NPR (March 31, 2023).

9. George Orwell, G. *Nineteen Eighty-Four* (New York: Penguin Classics, 2021).

10. Bill Franks, "Why Synthetic Data Is a Next Big Thing," *Analytics Matters* (December 12, 2022).

11. Paul Mee and Hany Mesha, "The Quantum Computing Threat Is Just a Matter of Time," Oliver Wyman (2023).

12. J. A. Cazier, B.B.M. Shao, and R. D. St. Louis, "Value Congruence, Trust, and Their Effects on Purchase Intention and Reservation Price," *Association for Computing Machinery: Transactions on Management Information Systems* 8, no. 4 (August 2017): Article 13.

13. Ahmer Inam, "Accelerating Drug Discovery with Mindful AI," *Forbes* (August 4, 2021).

14. Peter C. Bruce and Grant Fleming, *Responsible Data Science* (Hoboken: John Wiley & Sons, 2021).

15. Amanda Silberling, "FTC Fines Fortnite Maker Epic Games $520M over Children's Privacy and Item Shop Charges," *TechCrunch* (December 19, 2022).

16. Jennifer B. Gray, Wendy Lee Winn, Joseph A. Cazier, and Sam Volstad, "Stories of Breast Cancer: Using Textual Analysis and Analytics to Understand Better the Illness Experience," *International Journal of Multiple Research Approaches* 12, no. 2 (August 2020): 202–215. http://dx.doi.org/10.29034/ijmra.v12n2a3.

17. Joseph A. Cazier, "Bee Week in Brussels: Why Americans Should Care," *Bee Culture* (September 2018): 26–29.

18. https://www.npr.org/2023/04/20/1171133635/lasers-can-measure-mountain-snowpack-important-data-for-drought-stricken-areas

19. Nurith Aizenman, "How Do You Get Equal Health Care for All? A Huge New Database Holds Clues" NPR (April 21, 2023).

20. https://sdgs.un.org/goals

21. https://data-for-good.pubpub.org/

22. Bill Franks, *97 Things About Ethics Everyone in Data Science Should Know: Collective Wisdom from the Experts* (Beijing: O'Reilly).

23. Kyle Wiggers, "Apple Launches End-to-End Encryption for iCloud Data," *Tech Crunch* (December 7, 2022).

24. Max A. S. Rünzel, Edgar Hassler, Brandy Hadley, Aaron Ratcliffe, James T. Wilkes, and Joseph A. Cazier, "Harvesting Intrinsically Verifiable Trust: Building a Honey Traceability System for Sustainable Development," *Journal of Information Systems Applied Research* 15, no. 1 (March 2022): 24–34. https://jisar.org/2022-15/n1/JISARv15n1p24.html.

25. Max Rünzel, Edgar Hassler, Richard Rogers, Giovanni Formato, and Joseph Cazier, "Designing a Smart Honey Supply Chain for Sustainable Development," *IEEE Consumer Electronics Magazine* (2021), doi:10.1109/MCE.2021.3059955.

26. A. D. King, J. Raymond, T. Lanting, et al., "Scaling Advantage over Path-Integral Monte Carlo in Quantum Simulation of Geometrically Frustrated Magnets," *Nature Communications* 12 (2021): Article 1113. https://doi.org/10.1038/s41467-021-20901-5.

27. D-Wave, "CaixaBank Group, D-Wave Collaborate on Innovative New Quantum Applications for Finance Industry," *D-Wave* (March 3, 2022).

28. Shakked Noy and Whitney Zhang, "Experimental Evidence on the Productivity Effects of Generative Artificial Intelligence," Non-peer-reviewed working paper released by MIT (March 2, 2023).

29. https://www.npr.org/sections/money/2023/05/09/1174933574/what-if-ai-could-rebuild-the-middle-class

Conclusion: Crossing the Last Mile

WE *MUST* CROSS IT TOGETHER

The goal of this book is to help you overcome the nearly 90% analytics failure rate and add value by sharing best practices from those who know how to succeed so you can reach that last mile of analytics traveling from failure to success. This is a path that cannot be traveled alone. No matter how smart you are, how great your skills, success will only happen with collaboration and support from Pleines's minimal viable team. It requires the executive champions who can help identify where that change needs to be, the business process owners who can guide how to change in a way that can be adopted, the analytics team determining what the change needs to be, and the technical team integrating the change into business processes.

Sometimes other stakeholders are also needed, and are always helpful. But without united support, collaboration, and commitment to organizational learning, coupled with the skills to do it well, we will continue to have a far too high failure rate in analytics. This failure rate is a tremendous and painful waste of both resources and opportunities for organizations that strive to better serve society. We can, and must, do better. I sincerely believe the principles and best practices shared by the more than three dozen experts associated with these seven critical tasks are the most important ones for us to master in the age of Big Data. They may not address every problem of failure, but I am satisfied they address the key ones and signal where we should prioritize our efforts to improve the rate of analytics success.

Here is a short review of a few key points associated with each of these seven tasks. I hope you remember and apply across your organization, industry, and society.

Task 0: Analytics Leadership

Without analytics leadership from executive champions, business process owners, and the analytic team working and coordinating together, most analytics projects will continue to fail. A commitment to leading in and with analytics is a prerequisite for all of the other tasks needed for analytics success. This leadership is required to guide analytics to where it is needed, what needs to change, and how it can be made better. Leadership is also needed to drive and encourage change and see that the fruits of these analytics efforts and insights are actually harvested to create value.

Task 1: The Problem

Not all problems can be solved by analytics, and not all problems that *can* be solved are worth solving. Finding the best analytics opportunities among all approaches to analytics, including decision-centric, action-centric, and data-centric, is the first step to solving a valuable problem. Next comes ensuring it is amenable to an analytics solution, followed by prioritizing it to assess the impact of the solution, the likelihood of finding it, and a commitment to make sure action is taken on the results. Going through the process through the lens of the DAD framework helps ensure action is taken and value is created.

Task 2: The Team

It takes a broad team, working together, for analytics to succeed and be adopted across the organization. Although there are many titles to team members, most can be simplified and better understood by executives looking at a few key functions they perform. Because members of the analytics team have different natural orientations for why they use analytics, executives must understand their motivations and inherent strengths and weaknesses to manage them more effectively. Effective management techniques and leadership skills tailored to the analytics process increase success.

Task 3: The Data

Understanding the nature of data and the attributes that bring it value is important to managing and putting a price on that value. The five big Vs of analytics—volume, variety, velocity, veracity, and value—can be a useful framework for managing the value of the data and a few other smaller Vs used to enhance that value. Most of all, a focus on data relevance over volume for volume's sake and building in quality at the source lays a firm foundation for analytics success.

Task 4: The Tools

The most important tool in analytics is the right mindset. After that, there are many useful platforms and products in the analytics process. One of the most important factors for moving from craft analytics to industrial scale analytics is a seamless integration of the various tools used within the organization and among their partners. Different tool classes, including descriptive, diagnostic, predictive and prescriptive analytics, should be used together synergistically to create and harvest value effectively, while recognizing there will always be some *limits* to what analytics can accomplish.

Task 5: Execution

Good executions mean ensuring action is taken, which is how the DAD framework was designed to help. Managing the analytics process and people doing the analytics and anticipating and addressing problems along the way with an eye toward action are essential to good execution. Using good leadership and managing principles, as presented here, will improve analytics success. Instilling hope and trust in the process is the key to generating participation and excitement, and explainability, simplicity, ease-of-use, and usefulness are key to adoption, use, and ultimately to lasting organizational learning and change.

Task 6: Analytics Maturity

Analytics maturity is not about maximizing every analytics tool, technique, or approach simultaneously. Analytics maturity is about using judgment to understand and use the appropriate tools in the appropriate way that best support the organizational mission, goals, and capabilities, with an eye to growth. Mature organizations have and nourish a culture that embraces change, relying on data and focusing on continual improvement based on the best evidence as opposed to opinion or politics-based decision-making.

Task 7: Responsible Analytics

Analytics is a tool, one that comes with a duty and responsibility to see that it is used well. Knowledgeable professional associations are essential in exploring, shaping, and sharing how to use it responsibly, because regulations will come too late. Knowledge-based certification and training focused on the entire analytics process, with a commitment to quality and ethical use, can help accelerate the responsible use of analytics. Collecting and sharing data that can be used to do good in the world will help our society. Minimizing the collection and avoiding the abuse of data that could be used to harm others are essential responsibilities for all of us to do mindfully.

Cross Pollination Between Tasks and Organizations

As Dr. Kempf observed, a failure in even one of these tasks is likely to mean an overall failure. I like to visualize them as the petals of a flower, inextricably linked to each other and tied to success, fed and given life by the stem of analytics maturity, which in turn is rooted in responsible analytics that nourishes and sustains the whole. Our analytics translators, similar to the experts who contributed to this book, are like the honeybees I love that go from flower to flower sharing best practices and spreading the sweet taste of success, as shown in Figure 8.1.

Just as loners fail inside of organizations, so organizations that try to go it alone also fail. It takes a diverse team, inside and outside the organization, to form an ecosystem strong enough to sustain us all, as shown in Figure 8.1. Please practice and share these tasks and the best practices associated with them wherever possible so that more of us can travel the last mile needed to succeed in analytics, together.

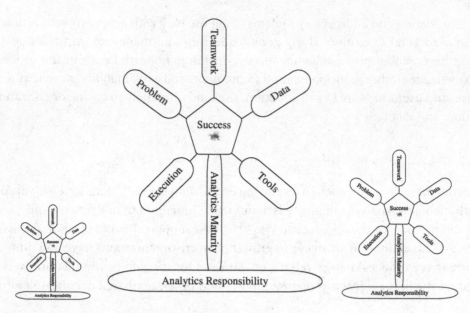

Figure 8.1 Cross Pollination of Tasks and Organizations

ADDITIONAL LEARNING OPPORTUNITIES

Here are a few more opportunities to advance your knowledge and the knowledge and skills of others in your organization:

- **Developing analytics leadership.** If you would like to learn more about how to travel that last mile to analytics success, consider the eight-week online live hybrid course offered by the Professional Development Academy and certified by INFORMS. More information is available at www.leadinginanaltyics.com and pdaleadership.com.

- **Engaging with a research and advisory network.** If you want to engage with a high-quality research and advisory network of professionals focused on practical success in analytics, especially for traditional businesses, I highly recommend my friends at the International Institute for Analytics (IIA). Many of the experts interviewed for this book are affiliated with IIA in some way. More information is at https://iianalytics.com/.

- **Supporting mindful analytics.** If you want to support research and development into the mindful application of analytics and its impact on society, consider supporting the Center for Artificial Intelligence and Data Analytics (AIDA) at Arizona State University, where I currently serve as associate director.

- **Gathering data for good.** If you want to support our work to gather and freely share high-quality, relevant datasets for good, please visit http://dataforgoodjournal.org/.

- **Improving presentation skills.** If you are a technical team member desiring to learn how to more efficiently communicate with executives, I highly recommend Bill Franks's book *Winning the Room* as a solid primer, available at https://bill-franks.com/winning-the-room.html.

- **Increasing ethical understanding.** If you want to dive deeper into ethics, I also recommend Bill Franks's book *97 Things About Ethics Everyone in Data Science Should Know*, available at https://bill-franks.com/97-things-about-ethics-everyone-in-data-science-should-know.html.

LASTING PRINCIPLES FOR SUCCESS

The more things change, the more important it is to pay attention to the things that do not. In this book, I have focused more on principles than technologies, principles that I hope will withstand the test of time, or at least form the seeds for clearer, more expansive, and better principles. Hopefully they will help guide you in times of change. If you like this book, please pass it on so others can succeed, too, or send them to the Leading in Analytics course offered by the Professional Development Academy so they can learn more about these principles directly from the experts interviewed for this book.

Afterword: Dr. Karl Kempf's Legacy

Karl Kempf inspired this book by writing about and sharing his concept of the five manageable tasks that analytics professionals, executive champions, and business process owners can focus on to improve project success. This, to me, underscores the importance of sharing our knowledge and wisdom, as you never truly know how many will be touched by it and maybe even try to build on it. I have tried to do this in my own small way, and I hope this book, and the collective wisdom of those interviewed for this book—those who, like Kempf, have also taught me through the process and whose knowledge I have tried to faithfully share—benefits you in some meaningful way.

I was fortunate enough to be able to interview and get to know Kempf a little better through writing this book and understand just a taste of how he thinks and approaches the world. I must say, yes, again, that Kempf is one of my favorite analytics heroes, whom I look up to as an example of what we all can do if we manage our analytics process more successfully, using the seven tasks outlined here.

As we conclude this journey, I thought you might want to know just a little bit more about the hero who inspired this book. Here is Kempf's legacy, in Kempf's own words, with minor edits for length and clarity. Just to note how humble Kempf is. Kempf strongly emphasized that every achievement was a *team* effort. This reinforces the idea that none of us, not even heroic giants like Kempf, can do it all alone, which is the core thesis for this book: we must travel the last analytics mile together.

PIONEERING ANALYTICS WITH FORMULA ONE RACING

My first full-time analytics job was with Goodyear, who supplied the tires for the Formula One (F1) racing teams. My small team was the first to mount a telemetry system for collecting remote data on a race car. Our team's focus was on collecting data we could use to set the cars up for qualifying and racing and redesigning the cars to do better by focusing on optimizing the interplay between suspension and tires. Much of my time was spent with Ferrari at their racing factory in Italy taking care of Niki Lauda, an interaction that yielded three world championships. Most of the rest of my time was spent with Tyrrell at their facility in England where we initially developed "active suspension" using applied analytics and control. Pioneering these analytics, not to mention traveling to all the races around the world, was incredibly fun, rewarding, and enjoyable all at the same time, especially with the incredible world-championship results from the efforts. See Figures 9.1, 9.2, 9.3, and 9.4 for a few pictures of me from my early days of pioneering race car analytics.

Figure 9.1 Kempf Building Remote Data Collection Systems for Race Cars

Figure 9.2 Karl Kempf Collecting Race Car Data

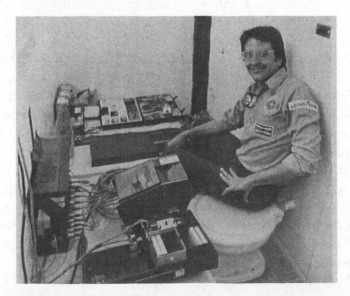

Figure 9.3 Karl Kempf Running Analytical Models

Figure 9.4 Karl Kempf Doing Race Car Math

TEACHING SUPERMAN TO FLY

My second analytics job was on one of the cinematic, special effects teams at Pinewood Studios. We used a seven-degree-of-freedom, dual robotic system to help Christopher Reeve appear to fly in the first three Superman movies from 1978 to 1983. We won an Oscar for the special effects in the first movie using these applied mathematics and control systems. Making movies and hanging out with stars such as Chris Reeve, Marlon Brando, Gene Hackman, and others was an incredible experience I greatly enjoyed.

AUTOMATING AEROSPACE MANUFACTURING

My third analytics job was with McDonnell Douglas in their AI/Robotics Group, where we automated their fighter plane factory in St. Louis, the passenger plane factory in Long Beach, and the initial Space Station in Huntington Beach. I had viewed the race car, the flying rig, and the factory and space station as "robots or mechanisms with brains," but subsequently got more and more interested in the brain and eventually decision science and less and less interested in the mechanism, which led to my next career.

MAKING BETTER DECISIONS AT INTEL

My focus at Intel has been in building decision support systems across nearly all parts of the company, from product design through manufacturing to supply chain. When we have a successful project, we get a "divisional recognition award" stating the economic value of the resulting decision support system, such as either a cost savings, a revenue improvement, or both. So far, our total benefit from all of our projects to Intel is a little over $55 billion through applied analytics from these deployed, decision support systems.

AUTHOR'S TRIBUTE

There is tremendous value in making better decisions, and Kempf's team at Intel has been recognized as only one of two in the history of analytics where the same team from the same company has won all three of the top industry-wide prizes for analytics impact. These include the INFORMS Prize for effective integration of advanced analytics in an organization, the Daniel H. Wagner Prize for excellence in the practice of advanced analytics, and the Franz Edelman Award for achievement in advanced analytics. More than this, Karl, you have proven the practical, applied value that using data to make better decisions can bring to the world. Thank you, Karl, for your inspiration and for sharing your wisdom throughout this book.

About the Author

Joseph Cazier, PhD and CAP (Certified Analytics Professional), is the associate director of the Center for AI and Data Analytics and a clinical full professor at Arizona State University. He coaches students and business leaders on how to succeed in making better decisions with data. Cazier previously served as the Dean's Club Professor, associate dean, and the founding executive director of the Center for Analytics Research and Education at Appalachian State University, where he designed and directed analytics programs and worked with industry and governments in finding ways to make better decisions with data. Additionally, Cazier was selected for the prestigious role of the first Faculty Fellow for the University of North Carolina System Office, where he led projects related to technology, analytics, and innovation. Cazier also cofounded the International Working Group for Bee Data Standardization, the World Bee Count, and served as the chief analytics officer for HiveTracks.com. Cazier has been an invited speaker for groups such as the United Nations, the American Public Power Association, and the European Parliament, and he currently serves as an analytics consultant for the global research organization CGIAR. He has published more than 100 peer-reviewed and popular articles, books, and chapters related to better use of technology and data, and holds a patent for the application of analytics for medical devices.

Why Read *Leading in Analytics*

A step-by-step guide for business leaders who need to manage successful Big Data projects

Nearly 90% of analytics projects fail to deliver significant financial benefits. Yet, the primary causes of failure are known and can largely be managed, influenced, and controlled by executives. Indeed, they must be managed by executives, as only they have the power to effectively manage most of the roots of analytics failure. *Leading in Analytics: The Seven Critical Tasks for Executives to Master in the Age of Big Data* takes you through the entire process of guiding an analytics initiative from inception to execution. You will learn which aspects of the project to pay attention to, the right questions to ask, and how to keep the project team focused on its mission to produce relevant and valuable projects that succeed. Then you will learn how to grow beyond successful projects to build a mature analytics organization with a scalable, repeatable process that incorporates the analytics wisdom to succeed over the long term. As an executive, you cannot control every aspect of the process. But if you focus on seven high-impact factors that you can control, you can ensure an effective outcome. This book describes those seven factors and offers practical insight on how to get them right.

Drawn from best-practice research in the field of analytics, the seven manageable tasks described in this book are specific to the goal of implementing Big Data tools at an enterprise level. A dream team of analytics and business experts have contributed their knowledge to show you how to choose the right business problem to address, put together the right team, gather the right data, select the right tools, and execute your strategic plan to produce an actionable result. Become an analytics-savvy executive with this valuable book.

- Ensure the success of analytics initiatives, maximize ROI, and draw value from Big Data.
- Learn how to define success and failure in analytics and Big Data projects.
- Set your organization up for analytics success by identifying problems that have Big Data solutions.
- Bring together the people, tools, and strategies that are right for the job.

By learning to pay attention to critical tasks in every analytics project, nontechnical executives and strategic planners can guide their organizations to measurable results.

Author Index

Page numbers followed by *f* and *t* refer to figures and tables, respectively.

Subject Index

Page numbers followed by *f* and *t* refer to figures and tables, respectively.